The Book of Unknowing

The Book of Unknowing

A Poet's Response to the Gospel of John

DAVID HERRSTROM

WIPF & STOCK · Eugene, Oregon

THE BOOK OF UNKNOWING
A Poet's Response to the Gospel of John

Copyright © 2012 David Herrstrom. All rights reserved. Except for brief quotations in critical publications or reviews, no part of this book may be reproduced in any manner without prior written permission from the publisher. Write: Permissions, Wipf and Stock Publishers, 199 W. 8th Ave., Suite 3, Eugene, OR 97401.

Wipf & Stock
An Imprint of Wipf and Stock Publishers
199 W. 8th Ave., Suite 3
Eugene, OR 97401
www.wipfandstock.com

ISBN 13: 978-1-61097-188-1

Manufactured in the U.S.A.

All scripture quotations, unless otherwise indicated, are taken from the The Holy Bible Containing the Old and New Testaments. Authorized King James Version. New York: Oxford U.P., Copyright © Used by permission of Oxford University Press.

Illustration permissions:

William Blake, 1757–1827
Repository title: *Jerusalem, Plate 78, "Jerusalem, C 4 . . . ."*
Collective title: *Jerusalem The Emanation of The Giant Albion, Bentley Copy E*
1804 to 1820
Relief etching printed in orange with pen and black ink and watercolor
Sheet: 13 1/2 x 10 3/8 inches (34.3 x 26.4 cm)
Plate: 8 1/4 x 6 3/8 inches (21 x 16.2 cm)
Yale Center for British Art, Paul Mellon Collection
B1992.8.1(78)

Leonard Baskin: *Man with Rooster.* 1994. © The Estate of Leonard Baskin; Courtesy Galerie St. Etienne, New York.

Jacob Landau: *Eagles.* 1961. Woodcut (392 x 302 centimeters). The Jacob Landau Institute. Art © Jacob Landau Institute/Licensed by VAGA, New York, NY

Takako Araki: *Ceramic Bible.* 1981. © Fukuko Kohda.

for
Constance Joy Harmon Herrstrom
who accepts the premise and rejects the promise

and

the Rev. David J. Harmon (1944–2001)
who accepts the promise and rejects the premise

To Nicodemus

Nico the scholar loved the night
its small hours moving across his forehead like the bowing of a cello.

Some nights, bent over ancient texts,
          Nico felt a stone in his right hand
  and in his left its heft,
                knew his mind to be a leaf in a wind.

He sat inside and outside himself like laughter.

He kept a lump of amber on his desk, wanting the moon within reach.
          (Nico, great insomniac
              let me walk with you for I too
  am kept awake by curiosity.)

Interpreter Nico loved the rich inexhaustible ink of night.

Contents

Beforehand ix
Acknowledgments xv

Hands 1
The Trembling Woman 3
The Scarlet Experiment 5
Body 8
The Lamb 11
Bread & 16
Voices 24
Wind 31
Nicodemus 33
The Nicodemus Letters to John 42
Light 45
Jesus 49
One Big Word 71
Signs 74
John 85
You 102
House of the Interpreters 110
The Book of Water 123
The Mother and the Mary's 135
Symmetry 145
The Book of Unknowing 157
Silence 173

My Unnamed Sources Here Named 187
Notes 193
Bibliography 201
Scripture Index 205
Subject/Name Index 211

Beforehand

WE'VE JUST FINISHED EATING dinner, and my father reads our daily chapter from the Bible. "In the beginning was the Word." His voice gives the King James English a burr inherited from the "old country," the Sweden of his youth. It seems as if every word is given its own knurl, the rough pattern of ridges that he puts on the knobs of the machine tools he spends his days making. Each word is accorded reverence and love. And at nine years old I knew this was how God himself pronounced them.

Compelled by some inchoate need as an adult to reacquaint myself, I revisited The Gospel According to John and gave a brief lecture for my colleagues where I was teaching English at the time. My talk wrestled with the beautiful shape and impossible demands of John's Gospel. Circling it, awed and intimidated by his power, I finally saw an opening and got a hold. At last, I thought I had come to terms with his book. But like William Blake's *The Marriage of Heaven and Hell*, it was too closely woven into the fabric of my life to let me rest.

So an encounter some thirty years later at the invitation of my brother-in-law, a minister, took me down, and I became obsessed with the book, reading and rereading. Nicodemus came by night in a dream. John sat beside me, conversing writer-to-writer in my daydreams. I avoided my colleagues at lunch, sneaking away to jot notes on the continual flow of my reader-reading thought.

∽

My first encounter with John's book as an adult was epitomized by the familiar medieval image of John the Apostle as an eagle, majestically soaring above us, distant, beautiful, essential. The eagle was the emblem of my awe. But my later encounter, which resulted in the present essay, is captured by the image of John as the rooster that haunts Peter.

As a boy I loved this engaging and intimidating scene of Peter's denial. I identified with Peter, knowing in my heart of hearts that I too would have failed under the same circumstances. Still John loves him, treating him with a tenderness that even a boy could understand; and still Jesus loves him. Unspeakably comforting to a skinny kid filled with self doubt. And as an adult, encountering this scene almost thirty years ago and again recently, I still love Peter. But now I also love the interplay of John and Jesus, Peter and the girl and the soldiers around the fire, and the cock who crows. This time around it's clear to me that John the writer, like the rooster in the scene, hovers just outside the action and, as the light of understanding dawns, sings for all he's worth.

But we don't have to choose between the eagle and the rooster. In John's pushing the envelope of hope, he soars with the eagle; in testing the limits of the body, he crows with the cock. Swept away by a sublime life, lifted on currents of ineffable ecstasy, he views his hero from the heights like an eagle.

At the same time, he must contemplate the life. Eye witness or not, he observes Jesus closely in order to write his book. It is necessary to select and arrange events, include and cut speeches, comment on his hero's words and actions. In short, telling the story of Jesus, as *writer* rather than follower, requires the distance that irony provides. In the close-up of wonder, every detail glows with equal importance. But to see clearly, the writer also needs perspective, the panning-shot of judgment that irony allows. Without it books cannot be made out of lives. So John's Gospel, like the rooster's song within it commenting on Peter's actions, includes an ironic perspective.

Throughout his book, then, John the follower and biographer of Jesus maintains a double vision. As a follower he desires to be Jesus; as a writer he seeks the distance that allows him to size Jesus up. His encounter with Jesus demands that he live in the center and observe from the periphery. Likewise, he invites us to give ourselves to certainty and embrace uncertainty, a recipe for the melancholy shared by all artists. On the title page to the triumphant last chapter of his epic poem *Jerusalem*, Blake portrayed just this conflicted, powerful creator-genius John, aptly drawing his head as both an eagle's and a rooster's. Here is the perfect emblem of John who is both the ecstatic follower and ironic writer.

Whether you come to John's Gospel believing or suspending disbelief, his book has the power to transport. Whatever your conclusions about his hero, whether you are the follower worshipping him as God or the writer admiring him as an incandescent figure of inclusion and forgiveness, exclusion and judgment, John's words sink to the depths of the soul. The awe-inspiring raptor and the mocking rooster haunt us all.

Because I have come to identify with John the writer struggling to make a book, I emphasize writer over follower in *The Book of Unknowing*. It is as writer that John struggles to turn into a gospel his encounter with the extraordinary person of Jesus, which he comes to experience as follower. Ultimately, however, one cannot be separated from the other, no more than how John makes his book—its sound and shape—can be separated from what his book is about. After all, a gospel is the "good news" that stays news not only because of the hero it celebrates but because of the way it is told.

In the telling, John does not proceed the way we'd expect from one who desires to tell the story of a life. Clearly, he cares more about eruptions of feeling and moments of revelation than about cause and consequence, the concerns of biographer or novelist. He gives us gestures that become emblematic, like Mary the sister of Lazarus pouring out the perfume and Jesus washing the disciples' feet. He also gives us emotionally charged, natural objects that become symbolically revelatory, like bread and water. In this John is a poet. And I am caught up in the energy transferred across the divide of two millennia by these gestures and natural symbols. John's anxieties and contrary emotional curves of certainty and uncertainty, the ways of metamorphosing his experience of Jesus into a lasting book of ecstasy and irony unsettle and exhilarate me.

I'm shaken by John's yearning, disoriented by his pathos in face of losing what he most loves. Above all, I'm troubled and comforted by the book's strangeness, which Sunday School and countless sermons cheated me of as a child. John's mind, contrary to the soothing and smoothing teaching on Sunday morning, really does have rough, even intractable edges. It moves differently than ours, seizing on unlikely characters like Nicodemus, capturing a bewildering variety of moods in the voices of Jesus, or commenting on these from odd angles.

Beyond Sunday School, even sophisticated teaching has often cheated us of the peculiar orneriness and fragrance of John's book. Much of the theological or devotional commentary on his Gospel simply translates it into another, more familiar language. Instead of looking the concrete, uncomfortable particulars in the eye, it turns away and takes refuge in abstract doctrinal or moral statements. But it's the strange particulars that grab us by the throat and call our own lives into question. It is these very details I give myself to. Along the way, I answer basic questions that have nagged me for years: How does his book affect me? Why does it matter to me? On the other hand, I don't mind raising questions which tend not to edification. Because I want not so much to convince as to create an appetite for John's book.

∽

Neither Biblical scholarship nor theological commentary, *The Book of Unknowing* is simply the personal record of one man's reading some 2000 years later of John's Gospel. A poetic talk on a poetic subject—John's account of his encounter with Jesus—my book ranges the landscape of John's language. This is a beautiful but often rocky country of sharp light, wild sounds, and sodden earthy smells.

And though it encompasses disparate places, from wedding hall to hillside, temple to shore; as well as people, from moneychangers to the woman taken in adultery, this country is one. It strikes us as the product of a unified if not single imagination. So we amble and clamber the book that has been received as a whole, rather than a layered composition, and whose impact has been felt as a whole by generations of worshippers. Although chapters 8 and 21, for example, were added at different times in the book's making and almost certainly by different hands, the work received by English poets and believers as a unity is the locus of our exploration. And for this reason, I use mainly the Authorized Version, virtually the only gospel known up through the nineteenth century, and the one preferred by most writers into the last.

As a poet's talk or lyrical "loose sally of the mind," as Dr. Johnson defines "essay" (quoting Bacon), *The Book of Unknowing* attempts to be faithful to what John wrote while, at the same time, celebrating his words. I approach them receptively but also playfully. This is the way of Midrash, the revered body of Jewish interpretation, and the spirit of John himself as he interprets the ladder reaching to heaven in Jacob's dream or of Jesus as he interprets the manna given to the Israelites in the desert. John not only invites interpretation by his own and his hero's practice but by the gift to us of his doppelganger, a fellow interpreter who like all scholars loves the night hours.

And I accept this gift of Rabbi Nicodemus who appears in the beginning, middle, and end of the Gospel, a character through whose eyes John invites us to view his book. A Nicodemean reading is disinterested—respectful, curious, evaluative, observant—not dogmatic or subservient. Yet it is also empathetic and take's John's lead, following his own obsessions—image (light), symbol (water), sign (water to wine), shapeliness (symmetry), loves (Peter, the Mary's), and above all words (the Word, the body, and the house of interpretation itself). Like all writers, John necessarily begins and ends in silence, but we see him in the middle distance probing the body—his own and Jesus'—deeper and deeper until he comes to its limit in the complexity of experience, which I call "unknowing."

Like the Midrashim, I want to nurture his words so they will "enter and spread through the whole body," as the words of the Torah were reputed to do. In this, too, I take John's lead who wanted such experience for his readers, though he believed the outcome to be belief. Whatever relationship results, association is more important than ratiocination in this endeavor, so my book leaps more than it walks. It takes the furtive goat's approach to John's mountains rather than the methodical rock climber's. I want to spark associations rather than argue a thesis (though the importance to John of the body and paradox is implicit), to be suggestive rather than exhaustive.

I ask more questions, following Nicodemus, than I answer. But the root of all my questions is this one: What would it be to write the book that John wrote? I read his book in this spirit, projecting his moves as a writer and after stumbling upon the steps he takes, asking about the ladder of argument or arc of associations that prompted them. Along the way, to help me with the how and why of John's strategies, I call on other poets, such as William Blake and Emily Dickinson.

Not surprisingly, the result is a poet's, rather than a preacher's or theologian's or scholar's reading (though I'm grateful for Raymond E. Brown's edition of John's Gospel). I celebrate John the poet, pay homage to the look and feel of his book's terrain, its snags and beautiful forms, rather than attempt to extract some pure, eternal ore that lies beneath. "Objections, digressions, gay mistrust, the delight in mockery are signs of health: everything unconditional belongs to pathology," says one of

Nietzsche's aphorisms. The poet John agrees in his obsessions and artistic moves. And in the end I cannot separate artistic from spiritual power.

∼

Ranging the country of John's book, then, I describe the waves of language that spill over me and try to catch the ear-surprises of unknown tongues, measuring the pitch of these voices, which disturb and alienate even as they promise more life, like a seventeenth-century Mexican painting I recall. At once gruesome and tender, it depicted a grape vine growing from the wound in the side of Jesus, who is squeezing the juice from one of its luscious clusters into a chalice held by a kneeling priest. The worshipper looks heavenward into the face of Jesus with ecstatic adoration as he kneels awkwardly on the earth.

We remember that John is both eagle and rooster with his penetrating and mocking mind, his combination of beyond-the-world tragic sense and in-the-world comic tenderness. The scream of the eagle and the laughter of the cock resound throughout the country of John's Gospel. He remains the complex, elusive poet, proceeding slantwise in telling the truth of his experience. At bottom, because he is both follower and writer, John's vision is paradoxical. His encounter with Jesus transports him into an ecstatic realm and, at the same time, throws him to the ground in an ironic world that demands he find words for the Word.

Acknowledgments

I AM ESPECIALLY GRATEFUL to Dr. Andrew D. Scrimgeour whose unswerving belief in this book made it a reality. It is an immense pleasure at last to thank publicly my oldest friend for being the reader over my shoulder on those cold dawn mornings and in those deep still nights where I labored in solitude to give this lyrical foray life. And for his patient reading after the book was finished, I am in Andy's debt as well, his considering my words carefully and inspiring me not to waiver in developing fully the Nicodemus chapter and in joining whole-heartedly Jesus' fraught father-son dance. A dance we both know well. Beyond his continual spiritual aid, I also thank him from the bottom of my heart for his unstinting physical effort in championing my slim book. For without such sacrifice it would not have found its publisher.

And a wonderful privilege it is to have this opportunity after so many years to acknowledge my continuing intellectual and spiritual debt to Dr. Virginia Ramey Mollenkott. I owe her many revelations, not the least being *Tristram Shandy*, which introduced me to the "True Shandeism" that "opens the heart and lungs." A spirit, I trust, informing my own book. In the classroom her presence alone was a revelation. From her purposeful entrance, each measured step resounding with the conviction of John Milton, to her deliberate commandeering of the lectern and weighing of each word to us undergraduates with the seriousness of Ezekiel, I was granted a vision of the mind burning with a hard gemlike flame. For her passion and example I am exceedingly grateful.

And I thank Rebecca Mebert for her enthusiastic response to my writings over the years. Her encouragement has meant more than she will ever know. I also want to convey my thanks to Emily Nguyen for her attentive reading and generosity.

I'm grateful to the following magazines where my poems included in this book first appeared, though in different versions:

"Letters of Nicodemus (I)." *Mars Hill Review* (No. 19).

"The Nicodemus Glyph." *New River: Journal of Digital Writing and Art* (Fall 2006). Online: http://www.cddc.vt.edu/journals/newriver/herrstrom/nicodemusintroduction.html

In the deepest convictions reaching into the very depths of our being, we deserve to live forever. We experience our transitoriness and mortality as an act of violence perpetrated against us.

— Czeslaw Milosz

I believe in the immortal origin of this yearning for immortality, which is the very substance of my soul.

— Miguel de Unamuno

We are narcissists, we want to live forever.

— Jacob Landau

Hands

JOHN WANTS TO FEEL a hand brush his cheek, a hand lie on his forehead. He wants to be lifted up in the strong hand of Jesus. "The Father loves the Son, and has given all things into his hand" (John 3:35). Jesus' words are John's words uttered from the depths of his being. We hear in them the universal human desire for comfort and security. John would give himself wholly into Jesus' hands, having never lost the child's desire to place a small hand in the father's.

But the yearning for Jesus, a hero with power and wisdom beyond ours who will keep us in his hand is more than this. It is the aching desire for more life, the fullness of life, real life itself (10:28–29). Proffering immortality, the hand is a refuge for eternity (13:3).

Though master of the symbolic, John never lets go the physical hand. Its symbolic palm offers comfort and, as it did for Ezra, interpreter and scribe like the writer John himself, wisdom (Ezra 7:21). Yet its physical backside threatens—the hand raised throughout John's book until it finally strikes Jesus (19:3).

Alone among the writers of Jesus' life, John insists on hands becoming the object of our attention. The last glimpse we get of a favorite character, Peter, is Jesus' prediction that old and dependent, he will "stretch forth" his hands (21:18). As John's book ends, we're left with the image of hands stretched out in need.

This simple, physical gesture crystallizes the desire that drives John's book and its strangeness. We come to share his idiosyncratic gaze, and in it we find the writer John. "In the beginning was the Word," but it becomes truth only in the flesh and ultimately in the art of John's words. The details that he singles out take on a strangeness; by his power as a writer, they become new.

Art and life, John knows, dwell in the particulars of experience: the severed "right ear" of Malchus (18:10); the charcoal fire in the courtyard (18:18) and on the beach (21:9). Or when Jesus insists on washing the disciples' feet, Peter blurts out like a child: "not my feet only, but also my hands" (13:9). These details arrest us in John's book because of their very singularity. An eagle soaring in lyrical heights, John does not miss the smallest movement far below of a hand.

∽

Jesus stoops down, as a hostile crowd becomes eerily silent, stretches out his hand and with his finger writes on the ground. At Jesus' invitation Thomas stretches out his hand, while the disciples look on dumbly, and puts his finger into the bloody hole in Jesus' hand.

These marks in dust and blood are John's most singular. They go beyond language in a book babbling with talk and argument and interpretation, and pass into the realm of pure presence. No appeal here to anything greater or higher than the gesture itself. It does not require elaboration or explanation. For it is its own authority, and we can only witness.

With the woman taken in adultery, Jesus refuses a test; in the exchange with Thomas, Jesus accepts a test. In the former scene, refusal is rooted in faith, a complete and unfounded act of compassion. While in the latter, acceptance is rooted in doubt. Neither love nor faith can be established by tests; they can only be revealed in acts of compassion and commitment.

Simple acts of extending the hand, but both are outrageous. They are silent, for one thing, their power derived not from the word but from the infinite space before and after. They threaten to be more powerful than the book which contains them. Mere gestures, both acts shake the walls of John's book and like Jesus walk right through without opening the door.

For another and more unnerving reason, they are intractable. Both the hand of Jesus in the story of the woman taken and of the man, Thomas, are as difficult to expel from our experience as grit in the eye. Two different but complementary perspectives: the one threatening public order, the body politic; and the other threatening private order, the body itself.

The Trembling Woman

In contrast to the encounter with Thomas, where we look on with a combination of horror and fascination, we are drawn unreservedly into the scene with the unfortunate woman caught "in the very act." Almost too easily. We are awed by the courage of Jesus and moved by the compassion and sheer power of his gesture.

At the same time, as easily as we inhabit the scene, we are struck by its strangeness. Jesus the talker asked directly to speak and refusing to answer. Meeting act with act, he initiates us in a ritual event. And John intensifies this by depicting Jesus stooping down and rising up twice, and the hostile crowd at the end leaving "one by one" in the most orderly fashion, from the eldest to the youngest (8:9). All playing out in the teeth of violence.

Here is the hostility and self-righteousness of a lynch mob combined with the rightness of the Law carried out by duly constituted judges. And into this charged atmosphere falls the radical gesture. Silence against clamor, as private ritual confronts public order. Individual authority challenges social authority. Outrageous. For in contemporary terms this would be like discovering that a neighbor is a drug dealer, and when we want to run him out of town, Jesus asks us, "He that is without sin among you, let him first cast a stone" (8:7).

The magnitude of the gesture is unavoidable. In this simple act of forgiveness Jesus holds a knife to the throat of the body politic. We are shaken and exhilarated not only by this challenge to the order of society but by the spectacle of the word "law," imbued with a long tradition of common-sense meaning, utterly emptied by a single gesture. The thing named "law" now unnamed.

Jesus' finger writing on the ground, William Blake the English poet and painter was correct in supposing, dares to erase the finger of God inscribing the Law on the tablet. No wonder Blake imagines that the "trembling Woman" can hear Jesus breathing as he stoops down, the very breath of God carrying her back to Eden before "Good & Evil." Beyond the Law, beyond Good & Evil, Jesus' act explodes meaning itself.

It's as if the voluble preacher had come to the end of language, come to pure sign. Jesus is not speechless but pushes beyond speech. His act is radical both in returning us to an Eden before the split between good and evil, names and the things named, and in asserting human individuality now and for the future.

"Where are those thine accusers?" Jesus asks at the end of the scene (8:10). "Hath no man condemned thee?" These rhetorical questions reinforce our sense of emptiness, as if meaning were drained from the scene leaving only the compassionate act itself. Just the two of them left with the writing on the ground between them, which John cannily does not reveal to us, words being superceded, the body of accusers having been broken, each wandering off one by one lost in his individual conscience.

The Scarlet Experiment

THE FINGER OF JESUS touched the dust from which we were created, affirming our common humanity. Just so Thomas' finger touches the blood of a specific individual, questioning the human. The hand of Jesus inscribes the ground, while Thomas' inscribes the body itself. Jesus' finger is a stylus making the word public; Thomas' is a knife intruding into the private recesses of the Word. To question, Thomas must violate the body. He must, in Emily Dickinson's brilliant image, "Split the Lark."

His bloody act is intractable. It is as alien to the imagination as some dark custom of an ancient and distant culture. The conquered, missionized Aztecs were right in seeing behind St. Thomas their god Quetzalcoatl. His priests thrust their hand into a victim's chest, which had been sliced opened with an obsidian knife, and wrenched out the still-beating heart. After the ritual killing the body was dismembered and eaten. No surprise that the Aztecs embraced the Mass, the ritual eating, at his own invitation, of Jesus' body (6:53). Our mind cannot assimilate this thrust of a hand into the wound and red-drenched withdrawal, whether by an Aztec priest or Thomas himself.

Yet Thomas insists that he put his "finger right into the place of the nails" and his hand into Jesus' side. Obligingly, Jesus invites him: "Reach out your finger and examine my hands; reach out your hand and put it into my side" (20:25, 27; trans., R. E. Brown). Thomas accepts. Did he seek the warmth of that wound? Did he seek assurance of the body's sticky fleshiness? What exactly did he seek that his eyes and ears could not discover? In any case, we can't help but imagine the consequences as he inevitably reopens Jesus' wounds. His act would, of course, "Loose the Flood" in Dickinson's words, "Gush after Gush." Again, John asks us to accept the outrageous.

We resist. Where we are drawn into the trembling woman's scene with Jesus, we are repelled by Thomas' literalism and intimacy. Contrary to what we would expect, all of us being somewhat skeptical by nature, we are made uneasy by Thomas' challenge and Jesus' acceptance. Ostensibly this is a test, what Dickinson calls his "Scarlet Experiment." But we realize in the end that it does not prove anything. Faith like compassion is beyond testing.

Yet his experiment succeeds in one respect. Thomas confirms the bodily presence of Jesus. From Jesus' perspective the experiment was to be a test deciding belief or unbelief in an idea of life, "eternal" life. From Thomas' point of view it was to determine identity, a test deciding belief or unbelief in the reappearance of the material body, living flesh and blood. So Thomas' bloody experiment either falls short of or presses beyond belief and unbelief, just as Jesus' writing in the dust pushed beyond good and evil.

~

We are left with an act, then, as intimate as sex. John forces on us a Thomas and a Jesus who insist on this extreme of the personal. John makes us feel like voyeurs. And we can't take our eyes off them, though we cannot fully comprehend or assimilate such gory intimacy. We are in a melodrama, though moved by Jesus' gentle acquiescence in such a bizarre request. At the same time, we find ourselves in an S&M nightmare.

This violation of the body is as hard to swallow as that of the body politic earlier, the dissolution of the Law. John pulls no punches. He throws the profoundly radical scene in our face. He says, in effect, "If you cannot accept this heart of the Jesus story, then you cannot accept the story's Jesus." With Thomas, John insists on the physicality of this scene. He wants our belief just as Jesus wants Thomas', but willfully puts up barriers to our assimilating this radical core of his book.

John sets us up by having Jesus walk through the wall of the room where the disciples are gathered (20:26) just before he invites Thomas to make his experiment. John relishes here the wonderful irony of an apparently immaterial Jesus walking through immaterial walls and then asking that Thomas thrust his material hand into Jesus' material body. This is no spirit body. The visage and voice apparently not being persuasive, John insists on the actual hand in an actual wound.

A macabre scene, we want to laugh and flee at the same time. It would truly be comic if not for the earnestness of Thomas. Yet we find its straightforward physical actuality painful to visualize. Consequently, the scene is a risky move on John's part. It works, however, because the scene very effectively maintains tension by not resolving our contradictory impulses of disgust and laughter. A dilemma the medieval painters felt in its fullest force. They were clearly uncomfortable in depicting this scene, pulling back from it—Thomas' finger only touching the wound, almost daintily, not thrusting into it—or gazing voyeuristically into the scene—rendering it grotesque by details that leave us teetering on the edge of hilarity.

John refuses to allow us an escape from his scene's tension, being a resolutely honest writer. Thomas' request could understandably be taken as metaphoric, but John has Jesus accept it without hesitation as literal, as do the disciples. John is not content to build this surreal scene on realistic detail, but revels in the starkly literal. To escape this, we want in some recess of ourselves to preserve the figurative, Jesus as the Lamb shedding metaphoric blood. Yet here is emphatically not the Word of the opening of John's book but the word made actual flesh. His collapsing the metaphoric into the literal is compelling by its very strangeness.

The scene calls the utility of language into question, then, exploding our tacit agreement about what is literal and what figurative. Witnessing Thomas' encounter with Jesus, we are repelled and fascinated not only by its insistent physicality but by language bent beyond its breaking point. Thomas' act at Jesus' invitation goes beyond belief and disbelief, beyond language itself. For in the end is the body.

Body

1. Perhaps Thomas is an extremist of the senses. Certainly his experiment is radical. Yet Jesus invites it.

2. Even reeling from the scene, we can't avoid the conviction that Thomas' act supports Jesus' larger program perfectly. Not one given to theological abstraction here but centered in the physical body. Jesus declares boldly and unequivocally: "He that eats my flesh, and drinks my blood, dwells in me, and I in him" (6:56).

3. No punches pulled. Jesus insists on the literal, however much we squirm and want to retreat into the metaphoric.

4. Just as he invited Thomas to touch him, to sink his finger in a bloody wound, he invites us to eat. A radical but not surprising request, for eating is the extreme of touch.

5. What space is to us, the body is to John. The wide open spaces of America have always been the dwelling place of hope and freedom. For John their dwelling place must be the body. Everlasting life raises the stakes.

6. John wants not merely freedom for the body but freedom of the body. Not a body transformed by a place, but a transformed body subject no longer to the locus of mortality.

7. And this new body born from a new kind of womb is the center of John's book. His real subject is the body not belief. Only in the body is freedom from death, the hope of immortality.

8. First and last this is the body of Jesus. Thomas' experiment is pivotal because he acts out John's desire to put on this new body.

9. John ultimately dispels the anxiety of death by exchanging his old mortal body for the new one that Jesus offers. And within this arena of transformation, John's book unfolds.

10. John's Jesus is obsessed with living abundantly, living beyond the life assumed to be our common lot. So great is his certainty that he is willing to sacrifice his present body for a promised body.

11. Thus John orchestrates a radical redefinition of the body. He begins with flesh.

12. John probes the double nature of flesh as sacrifice and sustenance, the lamb as well as bread, redefining them both. The body is also breath, and John redefines the wind that blows through our body carrying its chorus of voices.

13. He must effect a radical change in our accustomed vocabulary. The whole of John's book is dedicated to precisely this change. From the outset he renames the essentials of everyday life—bread and water.

14. As Jesus gives them a new context and resonance, they gradually become for his listeners new things in the world. It is a brilliant strategy because as we come to use his new names, we internalize Jesus' claims for "Eternal life." Jesus' dying into a living life, that is, exemplified in the transformation of his own body.

15. Material becomes immaterial becomes both and neither, an everlasting body that passes through solid walls but acquiesces to the touch of a human hand. Thus by the life he portrays, John redefines the body as immortal.

16. Jesus is not simply the model of this body, but is in himself the body shared, inviting his followers to partake of it (6:53). In the act of eating is achieved total identity with Jesus. By this John does not merely put on the body of Jesus, like Thomas, but becomes the body of Jesus.

17. Mortal/immortal, all is contained in this new body. In Jesus is identified the real. "The Word was made flesh" (1:14), encompassing the cosmos as well as all the words of John's book.

18. Thus in the body of Jesus exists the entire world—animal (lamb), vegetable (bread), and mineral (temple). Jesus declares himself to be each of these. Self-generated and generating, he comprises all the elements of the world, including language itself, outside of whom nothing can be known.

19. All words are one word, and that one word is new. John's book is the dictionary of these words that are the one Word.

20. The Jews assumed that "sacrifice" was their own word, but by becoming the sacrificial lamb Jesus makes it his own. The disciples and the people assumed that they understood the word "bread," and the Samaritan woman the word "water," but they all discover differently. Nicodemus knew the word "wind," but Jesus renames it for him.

21. Going against the grain, Jesus' stark invitation to eat his bread-flesh remains. John forces a redefinition that effects transformation. And thereby accomplishes his ultimate aim that the "you" in his fervent wish "that you might believe," his listeners and readers, be transformed.

The Lamb

Painfully aware that his body is death in life, John desires a life-in-death body. This exalted conviction that one can possess life greater than life—"eternal life"—is the wellspring of his book. An encounter with Jesus is the source of this conviction, his book its lyrical expression. So powerful is his experience that he wants to inhabit the body of the man Jesus, the sacrificial lamb, who is alive to the degree that death is a presence.

Jesus is called the Lamb at the beginning of John's book, but becomes a shepherd by the end (10:11). How can Jesus be both the shepherd and the sheep? Though he never refers to himself directly as the lamb, Jesus' understanding of himself as a sacrificial lamb pervades John's book. And he reinforces his role as shepherd at the end of the book by his injunction to Peter, "Feed my sheep."

Jesus as sacrificial lamb is one of the book's great ironies. His life given to the proclamation of eternal life is bent on death. To be obsessed with life is to be obsessed with death because Jesus' life is incomplete without death. John sets this up in the beginning by having John the Baptist hail Jesus twice as the "Lamb" (1:29, 36). Clearly, John wants us to identify his body with the sacrificial lamb, haunting us throughout the book with Jesus' words about his "hour" of death "not yet come." To this end John deftly arranges events, counter to the other accounts of Jesus' life, so that his sacrifice on the cross coincides with the Passover sacrifice of lambs in the Temple.

The metaphoric lamb at the beginning foreshadows this literal sacrifice on the cross. We are not in the end allowed the comfort of metaphor. Jesus becomes the real lamb slain. Always John insists on the reality of the body sacrificed, a stubborn insistence designed to make us uncomfortable.

Because Jesus' life can be completed only when his body is given to death, he provokes all around him in an effort to achieve death. At one point or another, every group he speaks to wants to stone him, and he must go by another path or into another country to escape. Even his brothers and disciples cannot dissuade him from inciting the powers that be to murder. Jesus has a knack for offending everyone.

More than Socrates even, Jesus is bent on death. His entire life in John's account carries within it death, while Socrates in Plato's account provokes one jury in a single climactic incident. Jesus is the master of extended provocation. We understand W. H. Auden's visceral reaction: the difference between Jesus and Socrates or Buddha or Confucius or Mohammed is that "None of the other arouse all sides of my being to cry 'Crucify Him.'"

Jesus the provocateur is hard to take. But by this he teaches a new language of sacrifice that allows both his disciples and enemies to reconcile within life his stubborn insistence on the body of death, which is at the heart of Jesus' character.

We can't get around this, and John shows us the way through. He presents Jesus as systematically carrying out a program to inculcate a new vocabulary of sacrifice, subverting the traditional term. His aim is to bring the Jews into a new understanding, and so become new people—believers. At the same time, Jesus wishes to bring his followers into a new understanding of the body. He must convince them that his body can be eaten but not consumed. The new body of the believer can be sustained by the one Jesus, not as a substitute but as the very body itself. In short, the believer can eat the body of Jesus and have it too.

John accomplishes this by expanding Jesus' sacrificial role to include the scapegoat of Jewish tradition (Lev 16:8). The scapegoat is an appropriately ambiguous figure, for he disappears, dying to the community, yet lives in exile. Moreover, John employs the clever strategy of having the high priest Caiaphas introduce the notion of the scapegoat. He says to the Jews, "You know nothing at all, nor consider that it is expedient for us, that one man should die for the people, and that the whole nation perish not" (11:49–50). We savor the irony that the Jews themselves make Jesus' identity as sacrifice explicit, articulating what Jesus' disciples failed to see, who continue their efforts to prevent Jesus from being stoned. Nonetheless, Jesus' purpose and the Jews' intent finally converge on the trajectory of death (11:53).

The Jews and his disciples may not all have accepted Jesus' new vocabulary, assimilating his redefinition of sacrifice, but Jesus manages to get them to support him with action. We can only marvel at his powers of manipulation, just as we admire John the writer's powers in leading us to accept the new terms of sacrifice.

As scapegoat Jesus can have it both ways, being sacrifice and survivor, lamb and shepherd. At the beginning Jesus is the powerless lamb; in the end it is his listeners who become helpless sheep as he becomes the shepherd. They accept, that is, his language and concomitant power. Calling his followers "sheep" (10:11) emphasizes his authoritative role. But, paradoxically, this is why they come to accept him as a lamb, a new kind of sacrifice, a literal self-sacrifice. The sacrifice of the lamb is no longer the promise of an action as in Passover (Exod 12:13) but the act itself.

As shepherd Jesus is both a political subject within the community and not. He is both the quick (to the new community) and the dead (to a past community). John is no doubt familiar with the long tradition of the Greek phrase "shepherd of the people," which appears in the Iliad as the title for a king or feudal lord. Yet Jesus' self-understanding, of course, goes beyond the political. Jesus can say with Fernando Pessoa, the great Portuguese poet, "I never kept sheep," but "My soul is like a shepherd." More important, Jesus' language makes this private conviction publicly compelling.

∽

Jesus in his parable of the sheepfold (10:1–4) continues his redefinition of sacrifice, wresting it from the purely traditional Jewish context. He knows the power of figurative language, which he admits to using (16:25), including puns (e.g., "wind," 3:8) and parables, to create new language from old. John's abrupt transition from urban to pastoral with this move to the parable of the shepherd is a shock, a way of calling our attention to the project of redefinition. And he is keenly aware of his role in this, self-consciously interpreting (2:21) and selecting (20:30). The shock of the change in imagery reinforces the shock in change of vocabulary, the redefining and reinterpreting that is so important to Jesus.

Yet this doesn't wholly explain our uneasiness. The strangeness of Jesus' shepherd/sheep imagery goes beyond John's shift here to the metaphoric, where he had been resolutely literal with the lamb. The lamb begins as a figure of speech and ends as the literal, slaughtered body.

Jesus invites us at first in his parable to see literal sheep but ultimately turns them into metaphor. Shepherd and sheep lie uneasily in John's book. Mainly taking place in the city, the book does not readily admit them. Because of this his imagery seems almost nostalgic. True to his bent, he transforms the innocence of the lamb into the experience of blood. But the sheep restore some of their innocence, associations of a past place and future time. They retain their aura of innocence by remaining a figure of speech.

In the countryside Jesus is the shepherd. In the city he is the lamb destined for slaughter. The pastoral seems to call the urban into question. Jesus' journeying to the country or retreating to a mountain is movement toward life. Throughout the book Jesus oscillates between the country and the city, between the periphery and the center. John exploits this tension by subtly informing us that in the center, in the city is death. When Jesus retreats to the periphery, he is holding death off. The closer to the city, the closer to a celebration and feast, the closer Jesus is to becoming himself the feast.

John expands the pastoral arena of sacrifice, however, deepening its significance. Jesus' metaphor of the seed dramatically shifts our new vocabulary of sacrifice from the animal to the vegetable world, as if ultimately rooting it in the rich tradition of fertility religions, which the prophets like Isaiah abhorred (Isa. 17:8–11). More important, the parable intensifies while completing Jesus' program of redefining sacrifice: "And Jesus answered them, saying, the hour is come, that the Son of man should be glorified. Verily, Verily, I say unto you, unless a corn of wheat fall into the ground and die, it abides alone: but if it die, it brings forth much fruit. He that loves his life shall lose it; and he that hates his life in this world shall keep it unto life eternal" (12:23–25).

The central paradox—lose one's life in order to save it—is impossible. This new vocabulary of sacrifice is frighteningly literal. We instinctively turn away.

But John insists. He puts these words at the center of his book, just as they are at the center of Jesus' life. Their great aphoristic force resounds down through the centuries. Yet they're also repellent with overtones of hatred for the world. Do they allow room for Jesus' love of wine at Cana? The sensuous caress of Mary's hair brushing his feet? Friendship for Martha and Lazarus that moves him to tears? Or the spirited even joyous dialog with friends like Peter, and Zen exchange with strangers like Nicodemus? Jesus loves the world one moment and despises it the next. We are returned to the paradox of the slaughtered lamb.

The notion of sacrifice now extends beyond the Jews. Jesus subverts their religious understanding of sacrifice and expands it to a grain of wheat, encompassing the whole living world. This constitutes a new vocabulary. It is no longer limited to a specific religious context, nor can we take refuge in the lamb or the seed as metaphor. And uneasiness with the pastoral as a protective space accompanies this, dispelling any whiff of nostalgia. The program of redefinition is radical. John keeps returning us to the literal, sacrificial body. And he moves relentlessly forward, increasing the pressure on his audience's old understanding of life, as he redefines bread.

Bread &

*Our desire is appeased only by feeding on Thee,
bread of immortality.*

—Miguel de Unamuno

The seed in Jesus' metaphor, sacrificed to the mill and ground up, is transformed into bread. The fruit of the vine, crushed, becomes wine. Bread and wine presume sacrifice, but more than this they come into being by metamorphosis. The vegetable is literally transformed to animal.

Bread & wine were married long before John wrote his book. They are a perfect symmetry, an ancient expression for eating and drinking. Ever since, as in the verses of Omar Kayyam's *Rubaiyat* or in the space of Picasso's still lifes, their marriage has been reaffirmed. Bread & wine have become part of the furniture of our mind. John, however, breaks this symmetry.

He is explicit in more than one place about the flesh of Jesus being bread. Yet despite Jesus' radical invitation to eat his flesh and drink his blood (6:56), nowhere does John explicitly equate blood with wine. His readers fill in. Having experienced the magic of the marriage at Cana where Jesus turned water into wine, they complete the implied equation. John, however, refuses to make the obvious move. While he lets the marriage at Cana revolve in our minds without interpretation, he quotes Jesus at length in two increasingly demanding interpretive discourses on the miracle of feeding 5000 people with "five barley loaves" and "two small fishes."

By not allowing us the complement of bread-equals-flesh, refusing to complete the wine-equals equation, John carves out space for a redefinition of bread. And, as we would expect, his anxiety fills this space. Because he is obsessed with the body as a destined sacrifice to mortality, he desires nothing short of an "everlasting life," immortality, as do we all in health and prosperity. Bread by being flesh brings life. John desires above all to possess a transformed body, one that will be a true sacrifice and "live forever" (6:58).

THE LANGUAGE OF BREAD

Bread redefined fulfills this promise. Simply stated, if you eat this new kind of bread, you will "not die," possessing what Jesus calls "eternal life" (6:50, 54). This is the most difficult redefinition that any of Jesus' hearers and John's readers will be asked to accept. For it demands a radical reassessment of where we've come from, where we are now, and where we're going. Our accustomed vocabulary crumbles. Patterned on Elisha the prophet's feeding the multitude with 20 loaves of barley and some ears of corn (2 Kgs 42), John uses the simplest of stories. Jesus' feeding the 5000 has very much the feel of a folktale in its attention to two of these and five of those, yet it is the fulcrum for his onslaught of redefinition on that simplest of commodities—bread.

"Now there was much grass in the place" (6:10), John tells us at the beginning of his story. A curious and charming detail, but we're puzzled, not knowing why he would include such a seemingly irrelevant, even trivial fact. Not until the end of the story when Jesus is about to lay out his radical redefinition of bread, does John satisfy our curiosity. He sets "grass" in opposition to "desert."

Grass, we discover, is the scene of Jesus' new vocabulary of bread, while the "desert" is the scene of the conventional language of bread. The miraculous bread of the past, the manna that saved the wandering Israelites in the desert, is not the bread he's interested in. The people themselves make the point that Jesus' miracle of the loaves has precedent in the miracle of the manna in the wilderness. This gives Jesus an opportunity to interpret his own act. John frames Jesus' double discourses with references to manna (6:31, 58), exploding within this space the people's conventional understanding of bread.

First, bread is political. Second, bread is literal, always and insistently literal. The people satisfied their hunger with barley loaves, not figurative but fragrant bread with texture and color. Barley, moreover, is the bread of the poor who cannot afford wheat. Just as literally, and these two meanings of bread are in the end one, bread takes the political stage. For after eating, the multitude wants to make Jesus king (6:15).

But Jesus retreats to a mountain. The people understand fully that breaking bread can mean breaking the present political order. In our own century the Peruvian poet, Cesar Vallejo, gives powerful expression to the people's understanding in these lines from his poem "Our Daily Bread":

> You want to knock on all the doors
> and ask for anyone; and then
> see the poor, and crying quietly,
> give bits of fresh bread to everyone
> and to strip the rich of their vineyards
> with the two blessed hands
> that with a blow of light
> flew from the nails on the cross!

Completing what John resists, Vallejo senses the necessity and follows up on the bread/flesh equation, subtly linking wine with blood. The new wine-blood gift of Jesus to the poor subversively replaces the old blood-wine extracted from the poor by the rich. John resolutely holds this bread/wine symmetry in abeyance, just as Jesus holds open the past theological understanding of bread (manna) to the present, and its present political meaning to the future. In doing this he opens up a field for planting new meanings. The new bread of Jesus is like manna from heaven. But unlike manna it is his flesh.

∽

Jesus makes two forays in creating this radical redefinition of bread. His first discourse (6:35–48) expands the meaning of "manna from heaven" in order to call the past into question and include Jesus himself. This monologue, in which Jesus promises action, leaves the Jews, who know his humble origins, murmuring, incredulous at his claims. Moving from belief to touch, from the eye to the tongue, his second discourse (6:51–58) ratchets up from the first. With this radical reassessment of eating bread, the future is called into question and his listeners both repelled and transfixed. This monologue, in which Jesus demands that his listeners take action, leaves even his disciples murmuring, confused by Jesus' "hard saying." It is a watershed.

"I am the bread of life" (6:35, 48), Jesus asserts at the beginning and the end of his first discourse. The same words, but they are by the end of this first monologue transformed into a different statement. John opens up the discourse for this possibility by having Jesus tease us with a hinted closure of symmetry, saying "he that comes to me shall never hunger; and he that believes on me shall never thirst." Hunger and thirst, eating and drinking, naturally bread & wine, yet John withholds the second term as we've seen in order to create space in his discourse for expansion of the meaning of bread. The "bread" at the beginning of the discourse, then, is not the same "bread" at the end. It is transformed from the manna of God into the body of Jesus.

If manna in the desert is not the "true bread" (6:32), nor the bread collected from the grass in bits, what is the "true bread"? This bread is not in the past, as traditionally believed; and it is not in the present, as the people who would make Jesus king concluded. Instead, Jesus answers, it is belief in himself, a decision to share the immortality of Jesus, who came down from heaven and who will raise up believers. In this downward and upward movement, John echoes the angels on the ladder in Jacob's vision, which he alludes to early on in his book (1:51), descending and ascending between heaven and earth.

This dynamic of coming "down" and raising "up" creates a fine tension. The Jews are very familiar with the coming "down" from God, as did the manna, but uneasy with Jesus' claim to be such a person. The second term of the pair is also a familiar one, the Jews being accustomed to going "up" into God's presence but uneasy with Jesus' claim to be in such a place. Without his coming into the world and raising up in belief, Jesus asserts that his listeners cannot have what he calls "everlasting life" (6:40, 47). He is "the bread which comes down from heaven, that a man may eat thereof, and not die" (6:50).

Deftly, Jesus creates here a node of meaning where up and down are resolved. And he exploits this, saying that "No man can come to me, unless the Father which has sent me draw him: and I will raise him up at the last day" (6:44). Jesus has come down to draw up. Belief, which is essential to identifying with Jesus as the bread of immortality, comes only by reciprocal motion. Isolating this critical node in his discourse, then, Jesus initiates the Jews into a new dynamic of meaning, "bread" now being a body accessible by belief. Moreover, meaning itself requires their participation. They must believe in order to accept Jesus' new vocabulary which is the ground of belief. No wonder they "murmur."

Despite their resentment of his declarations, Jesus has succeeded in his first discourse in leading them down the path of redefinition. At the end of this monologue the Jews are left asking how Jesus could come down from heaven (6:42). Now he ratchets up his claims. By the end of the second discourse they are left with a harder question, one arising directly out of his redefinition: How is it possible to eat of Jesus' body (6:52)? Jesus collapses the spiritual (manna of a miracle) and political (barley loaf of the poor) meaning of bread into literal "flesh," a word he repeats in this discourse, along with "eat," until it becomes a chant.

Using the strategy of the first discourse on bread, John has Jesus make the same statement at its beginning and end (6:51, 58). A move he uses to dramatize its transformation. Jesus promises that "if any man eat of this bread, he shall live forever," radically redefining "bread" in the space of the discourse, wrenching it from the metaphoric into the literal.

Though each of the old meanings was rooted in the literal—manna fallen on the desert and bits of bread scattered on the grass—the new meaning in the future, which Jesus has pulled into the present, can only be literal. Calling himself the "bread of life" invites a metaphoric interpretation, just as when he later calls himself the "vine" (15:1). In this context, John does not link blood and wine because he wants to extend the metaphor of the vine. However, in the present context he refuses the link and eschews metaphor because he wants to open up space for the new language of bread. Jesus' insisting that "Except you eat the flesh of the Son of man, and drink his blood, you have no life in you" (6:53), makes a new invitation. One so unequivocally literal, some Roman contemporaries who grasped its fullest import accused Christians of cannibalism. It is an invitation that demands just such a radical interpretation. John pushes the literal to its breaking point: from the real loaf of bread to the real flesh.

His insistence on the literal here is shocking. Just when everyone had got comfortable with the metaphoric force of bread in the first discourse, Jesus turns the tables and insists that it's not a metaphor. A shock made greater when he has been so dismissive of the people as being distracted by literal bread (6:26).

Jesus' chant on the word "flesh" drives home the literal force of his command to "eat," destroying any vestige of the metaphoric that the incredulous Jews may be clinging to. Nothing in Jewish tradition enables them to assimilate Jesus' complete transformation of their own vocabulary, which he had inherited as well. As a result, his new way of talking can only be shocking, and we sympathize with the Jews in rejecting what can only seem to them a blasphemous invitation to practice the abhorrent rites of some alien cult.

THE SWERVE FROM THE WORD

Who would not agree with the disciples that Jesus' insistence on eating his flesh and drinking his blood is a "hard saying"? John has already shifted our sympathy to the Jews in their reaction. We are not surprised, then, that at this juncture a number of the disciples leave Jesus (6:66). Likewise, even his own brothers refuse to believe (7:5). They all steer clear of what appears to be madness, something the Jews suspect, maintaining their distrust of Jesus throughout his discourses.

On the one hand, this eating-and-drinking-the-Jesus-body conundrum engages all our powers of knowing before understanding. On the other, it strains the timbers of our mental house. Pressure builds either to shore up or open up meaning, nailing it down into a single, more manageable interpretation or adding doors and escaping its literal force, as generations have done since. Or meaning can be suspended, as John ultimately does in coming to terms with the hardest saying of Jesus.

This swerve away from Jesus' demand to eat his body and drink his blood has defined the understanding of his character ever since. The magma of Jesus' language in these discourses on bread has solidified. Uncomfortably hot words about actual flesh and actual eating have cooled over the centuries. Conventions of their interpretation have hardened. His outrageous demand simply could not stand. Trying to live with this intractable word is like having Grendel at the supper table. So it was necessary to domesticate Jesus' words in order to make his new vocabulary safe for society. And yet the Jews' question, which assumes Jesus' literal intention, their question about how to "eat" the "flesh" of Jesus (6:52), remains.

Such a hard question that even John blinks. He is, no doubt, briefly in the company of those disciples which he records as being offended by Jesus' demand (6:61). This reaction causes Jesus to attempt a softening of his own words. He retreats and blunts their literal edge by introducing the categories of "spirit" and "flesh," opening the possibility of a metaphoric interpretation of the words. And, as if he didn't quite believe this tack himself, he concludes with a sigh, "But there are some of you that believe not" (6:64).

The spirit/flesh opposition rings hollow in face of Jesus' insistent command to "eat," given even greater weight by the oracular "Verily, verily" still pounding in his listeners' ears. Four times, we remember, he demanded that they eat his flesh and drink his blood (6:53–56). And the sigh, merely admitting the obvious, is at best a plea for sympathy. At worst, in his follow up, "No man can come unto me, except it were given unto him of my Father" (6:65), it is sour grapes. Jesus is desperate. Experiencing the loss of "many" disciples as well as his own brothers, he asserts that he knew many in his audience would never believe anyway. We hear the dry throat-clearing of rationalization here and shuffling feet in the background of disciples leaving. Unable to convince all his disciples, let alone his fellow Jews, he throws the argument for eating his flesh back in their face, saying it's a given that they will not believe, and he knew this would be the result anyway.

Having felt the assault of Jesus' words, we are not convinced by this back pedaling. His discourses still whirl in our head like swords.

∾

Some of the disciples continue to follow unflinchingly; others take offense and desert Jesus. But John blazes a third path. Rocked by the full force of the new language that Jesus has unloosed in his monologues, John chooses to live on its edge. He suspends its meaning, not grasping after certainty. Familiar territory because it bears the mark of prophecy, an obscurity that "rouzes the faculties to act," in William Blake's phrase. Jesus' outrageous demand to feast on himself, masquerading as an invitation, leaves John exhilarated and uneasy. Given the strangeness of this invitation—to participate in a feast in which the eater and the eaten literally become one—it couldn't be otherwise. Even in expressing its strangeness with great power, John cannot escape a nagging sense of its absurdity.

This allows John commitment and distance simultaneously. He achieves a suspension of meaning, in short, evidenced by his parodying the feast of Jesus. The supper in the upper room with his disciples just before his crucifixion is not the feast itself but the traditional Passover meal. Its expanded meaning now includes the new lamb and new bread, of course, but their literal outworking must wait until after the crucifixion and resurrection. The true feast of Jesus, that is, held in abeyance. In this suspended moment, John uses Judas, whom Jesus had earlier fingered in his discourse on bread (6:64), to turn the supper into a parody. Referring again to the betrayal of Judas, Jesus now says to his disciples, "He that eats bread with me has lifted up his heel against me" (13:18). Rather than becoming one with Jesus, that is, the act of eating effects the opposite. Because it releases pressure in his own mind, John welcomes the irony that the bread in this context, which alludes to the "true" bread of immortality according to Jesus' redefinition, brings death.

Yet the question of how to "eat" Jesus' "flesh" continues to haunt John. For in the last scene of his book he echoes the earlier scene on the grass by the sea with the 5000, the occasion of Jesus' redefining "bread." On the shore of Tiberias Jesus invites his disciples to join him in a meal of bread and fish. Given the charge that "bread" has acquired in Jesus' discourse, his invitation here is disarmingly casual, "Come and dine" (21:12). This is the true last supper. John admits no irony, and we're moved by the compassionate and extraordinarily vivid scene. Simple and beautiful, their meal seems to promise resolution. Yet it neither answers nor dismisses the question.

Serving bread and exhorting Peter in turn to "feed" others ("lambs" and "sheep") is Jesus' definitive showing of himself. Breaking bread is his signature, and John rightfully insists that in this lies the recognition scene (21:12), despite the miracle that the disciples had just witnessed of Jesus multiplying the fish in their net (a variation on the earlier miracle with the 5000). The meal is wonderfully self-contained, then, begging the very question that John knows it raises. Because swirling around the scene is the identity of Jesus being bread. Separated from breaking bread but integral to the scene, his being bread remains present in the air like an electric field. John chooses suspension without demanding resolution, just as he never demands closure of language itself. Bread & . . . ? Bread & fish? Hardly. John leaves the symmetry broken, the doors of meaning wide open, allowing other voices to drift through.

Voices

"Mary," Jesus says, and she turns and says "Rabboni," which as John explains means "Master" (20:16). Until he utters her name, Mary mistakes Jesus for the gardener. It is not the sight of Jesus, but the sound of his voice that identifies him. A recognition scene so delicious (nothing like it until Shakespeare) that the hairs lift on the back of my neck.

John isolates and orchestrates the tender drama beautifully. He has the men leave Mary who then converses with angels in the place where Jesus was buried, which sets up her mistaking Jesus for the gardener. Mary is distraught, imagining angels who perhaps can offer hope in the face of despair (their highest function), and thus doesn't recognize Jesus whom she has known for years.

The climax in Jesus' speaking her name carries great power. We know the immediate recognition that comes with the sound of a person's voice, the tone more powerful than the sight when, for example, we're so surprised at the presence before our very eyes of a person we did not expect to see that we don't see them but instantly know them by their voice.

From the outset of his book John makes this signature power of the voice clear. John the Baptist "stands and hears" Jesus, not seeing him so much as "rejoicing" in his voice (3:29). The emphasis is on Jesus speaking and his audience hearing, not on their visually recognizing him. His essential being is in his voice.

∽

We are our voice. More than our physical features or characteristic gestures we are most essentially individuals in our voice—sighs, words, laughter—our self made public. The voice carries the inside over to the outside. It is the revelation of the inner body. Conversely, moving from flesh to voice is to push more deeply into the body, probe further, approach the life itself. For the power of the speaking voice is in its embodiment of life.

The grand opening of John's book is a hymn to this power. "In the beginning was the Speaking, and the Speaking was with God, and the Speaking was God." John's logos, commonly translated "Word," is not the word on the page but the word spoken. This is the source of power throughout John's book.

Now hear this voice, John's hymn of invocation to the word uttered, the origin of what is:

> In the beginning was the Word,
> and the Word was with God,
> and the Word was God.
>   The same was in the beginning with God.
> All things were made by him;
> and outside him was not any thing made that was made.
>   In him was life; and the life was the light of men.
> And the light shines in darkness;
> and the darkness comprehended it not (1:1–5).

The spectacular conceit of a poet: the whole world created from the word. And who is not moved by John's grand speaking in this cosmic opening. We are mesmerized by his repetition of the "Word" and stirred by his exalted correspondences: word = life, word = light. The word so potent it baffles the dark. John announces the light/darkness theme in a sublimely sweeping way, at the same time his voice carries something of a syllogistic tone. We see him making mythic philosophy and philosophic myth, no mean feat. Then rather abruptly: "There was a man sent from God, whose name was John" (1:6).

What a contrast to the cosmic opening—this single declarative. The rhythmic waves of John's voice crash on the shore and run all the way up the beach of our world, the last bit of foam falling, finally spent at the feet of this man (and us).

> The same came for a witness, to bear witness of the Light,
> that all men through him might believe.
>   He was not that Light,
> but was sent to bear witness of that Light (1:7–8)

The disclaimer is perfect. The logician's voice resumes—O that syllogistic rag. John's eating his cosmic cake and having it too. You can tell,

John's a debater. "That was the true Light, which lights every man that comes into the world" (1:9).

Back to the chant on "light," we're completely taken by John's ability to be lyrical and ratiocinative at the same time.

> He was in the world,
> and the world was made by him,
> and the world knew him not (1:10).

Entranced by repetition, John loves the emotional build of this chant. Rooted in the formal rhythm of ritual, it is intensified by John's limiting himself in vocabulary. His characteristic style, taken from and given to Jesus, isolates a word and then names it out loud, varying the context but pronouncing it again and again. He's obsessed with certain words (not unlike most poets) as if they're talismans possessing magical power.

~

As the essence of life itself, the voice has magical power against death. It is the "loud voice" (11:43) of Jesus, not his touch or gesture, that brings Lazarus back from the dead. John heightens the dramatic effect of this act of speech by having Jesus pause, just before calling out to Lazarus, and interrupt the proceedings to direct words to his Father (11:41–42). John is well aware of his artful move, establishing permission for the use of dramatic technique by pointing out Jesus' own admission that he himself used the scene to achieve a specific effect (11:42). Add suspense to magic, and the word, which we remember exists from the beginning of time, takes on immense power for life. The word is merely uttered and nature responds.

Power to triumph over death is in this voice alone. It is not in the seeing with one's own eyes or in the doing, but in the hearing that truth is apprehended. Jesus asserts that in the voice the future collapses into the present. The ear is the arena of an eternal present tense, where voices of the past and future are one in the present, and hence "The hour is coming, and now is, when the dead shall hear the voice of the Son of God: and they that hear shall live" (5:25). No action is necessary. The voice is all.

Naming in itself has an uncanny power. Lazarus comes forth at the loud utterance of his name; Mary comes into awareness at the calm enunciation of hers.

We are drawn by the one who names. Because naming out loud invokes the essential interior life, our real being is awakened. The flip side of this drawing out, however, is its pressing down. This explains why Jesus is fond of "sheep" as a metaphor for his followers, who respond when he calls them by "name" (10:3) just as sheep know the shepherd's voice. The one who names has the power. The one who names determines how we speak about the world and thus what has value and what does not, in short, reality itself.

∽

Jesus' dramatic pause to speak to his Father before raising Lazarus reveals what we've known all along, that Jesus hears voices in his head continually. Like his disciples, he too is a listener. He responds to the Father who speaks to him. At one point the people also hear this voice, interpreting it as either "thunder" or an angel's voice (12:29). Apparently a different angel than the one Mary conversed with.

The voice in Jesus' head becomes audible to those who accept his new vocabulary. As he states unequivocally to Pilate, "Every one that is of the truth hears my voice" (18:37). Hearing this voice of his "truth" is to embrace a new vision of real life, which values things differently—the law (woman taken in adultery), as well as social (Samaritan woman) and gender divisions (Mary boldly anointing Jesus with perfume), the political order itself.

John gives us many of the voices that Jesus hears. They are various, lucid simplicity as well as sublime nonsense, at times teasing or sermonizing, abrupt or tender, but always arresting.

Jesus often begins in the most disarmingly simple way: "I am the true vine, and my Father is the husbandman" (15:1), for example, then shifts to the preacher's voice. Jesus launches into a repetitious (with his numbing chant on "father"), less than joyous sermon, which irony we smile at because he's just said he won't be talking much any more (14:30). As his monologue spirals heavenward it becomes increasingly convoluted:

> I am the vine, you are the branches: He that abides in me, and I in him, the same brings forth much fruit: for without me you can do nothing. If a man abide not in me, he is cast forth as a branch, and is withered; and men gather them, and cast them into the fire, and they are burned. If you abide in me, and my words abide in you, you shall ask what you will, and it shall be done unto you. Herein is my Father glorified, that you bear much fruit; so shall you be my disciples (15:5–8).

At the same time, its centrifugal force whirls him away from the incipient parable into another analogy. "As the Father has loved me, so have I loved you: continue you in my love. If you keep my commandments, you shall abide in my love; just as I have kept my Father's commandments, and abide in his love. These things have I spoken unto you, that my joy might remain in you, and that your joy might be full. This is my commandment, That you love one another, as I have loved you" (15:9–12). What a contrast in context to the earlier admonition to "love one another" (13:34). Here it's a belaboring, almost hectoring atmosphere. Jesus' primer-like, patronizing method of proceeding exacerbates this. In the earlier context the admonition flows naturally from the warmth of his speech.

As a result, Jesus' conclusion here that he speaks so their "joy might be full," sounds somewhat hollow. Perhaps Jesus is getting impatient as his determination to give himself up to martyrdom becomes certain. He has, after all, just displayed a rather frayed frame of mind in losing patience with Philip (14:9).

Yet responding directly to the continual voice in his head, Jesus "lifted up his eyes to heaven, and said, 'Father, the hour is come; glorify thy Son, that thy Son also may glorify thee'" (17:1). Its energy in check, he modulates his voice into exquisite tenderness.

This direct address of his Father is also intended to be overheard by the disciples. With this comes a shift to a more subdued tone, a mix of humility and tenderness.

> And now, O Father, . . . I have manifested your name unto the men which you gave me out of the world: yours they were, and you gave them me; and they have kept your word. Now they have known that all things whatsoever you have given me are of you. For I have given unto them the words which you gave me; and they have received them, and have known surely that I came out from you, and they have believed that you did send me. I pray for them: I pray not for the world, but for those who you have given me; for they are yours. . . . (17:5–9)

John has his readers listen along with the disciples to Jesus' comforting supplication with its lulling, cycling rhythms and repeated words on their behalf that they might have "joy fulfilled" and, building to a climax, truth and finally glory.

The disciples must have thrilled to hear Jesus' supplication, an incantation in their honor wishing for them the radiance of Jesus himself (and John's readers wishing right along with them). Undoubtedly they failed as usual to understand what Jesus was saying, but they certainly understood the import of Jesus' gesture of speech on their behalf. They know a wish fulfillment when they hear one.

> And now I am no more in the world, but these are in the world, and I come to you. Holy Father, keep through your own name those whom you have given me, that they may be one, as we are. While I was with them in the world, I kept them in your name: those that you gave me I have kept, and none of them is lost. . . . And now come I to you; and these things I speak in the world, that they might have my joy fulfilled in themselves. I have given them your word; and the world has hated them, because they are not of the world, just as I am not of the world (17:11–14).

Having kept the "word" and in the "name" been kept, the disciples are verified as new creatures. They possess the new life of Jesus along with the "joy" that comes with it.

But this circling voice of Jesus, his reflective prayer culminating in its "world" chant, reminds us of John's voice at the opening of the book. Jesus is given a greater range of tone, and after leaving this soliloquy John rides his narrative arrow, but he has appropriated Jesus' voice. The poet has taken into himself the life of his subject, breathed in the voice of power.

∽

John makes our dependence on voice increasingly evident as his book progresses. The sheer quantity of Jesus' words, repeating and swirling around us, increases toward the climax of the book; the Word (in the beginning) becomes words even as words become the Word (in the end on the cross). John bets the world on the word. "I have been saving up my hope in language," concludes the poet Juan Ramón Jiménez at the end of his life, "in a spoken name, a written name." Like the Spanish poet, John has done the same, creating in language the figure of Jesus who creates the world by naming anew. With Jiménez, John could truly say that he has "given a name to everything."

The voice that names enables us to imagine the world differently. It confers or withdraws status. The humble are elevated; the exalted are humbled. Those formerly without power are given power, and vice versa. It is the giving or taking away of a blessing, which in the Jewish scriptures granted life itself. The blessing conferred by naming had uncanny, powerful magic. One could die without it. With it we are made new. Re-imagining the woman taken in adultery as "human" instead of "criminal," we have become new people.

But the power of naming is two-edged. Accepting Jesus' new vocabulary, which he intends to be our only vocabulary because it is the only truth, it becomes possible to name those who do not hear Jesus' voice the "damned." Once we internalize this category and place those people in it, we can legitimately act against them. For they are not human, being criminals, which excuses even murder. The power to name is the power to remake the world in your own image for good or evil.

John is drawn to Jesus because Jesus possesses this imaginative power of naming, the power to define what is. Jesus knows that whoever has the power to name the world has the power to change it. This is so because, as William Blake says, "Nature has no Outline, but Imagination has."

John's book is an extended naming of a re-imagined world, a new vision. As a writer, John taps into this power to draw new lines and make a new world. And he is supremely conscious of this project, as he boldly parallels the beginning of the world itself—"And God said, let there be, . . ."—in the beginning of his book. A book celebrating the voice as John invokes the muse of God's voice in his opening hymn, lets the voice of Jesus ring, and sounds his own. This is the line of power, a voice stream flowing from the primordial source directly into John. Like Emily Dickinson, he inherits the faith of his hero, which is also the writer's: "A word that breathes distinctly / Has not the power to die."

Wind

A WIND OF BREATH carries the voice. We can only "speak that we do know, and testify that we have seen" (3:11) by shaping the breath stream, which emanates from the literal and figurative depths of our being, into the sounds of words. Moving across the fields, words leave them "wind-addled and wind-sprung," as Charles Wright says in his poem, "Night Journal." A word pronounced is the public manifestation of a wind that swirls within us.

As the word spoken in the beginning resulted in the world, so the word carried on the breath stream creates new worlds. The spoken word is nothing less than the wind of creation, which poets have known from the beginning. Reminding us of this at the end of his book, John presents a striking act of Jesus. Appearing to the disciples after his resurrection, Jesus "breathed on them" (20:22). Power and intimacy combine in this moving gesture. It is the supreme expression of his presence both in the here & now and in the future, an affirmation that his creative spirit will remain with them after his departure, sustaining within them the new world he has made.

We detect here a whiff of the ancient Greek belief, rooted in an oral culture, that breath is all. It is consciousness, perception, and emotion. Breath constitutes the continuity of life itself. Seat of all the senses, the lungs, as the Canadian poet and Classicist, Anne Carson observes, are "organs of mind." We are connected not only to one another but to the world by breath. A poet of our own day in a culture of the written word still feels this intensely: "Windblown we come, and windblown we go away," the poet Charles Wright says, "All that we look on is windfall. / All we remember is wind."

As breath asserts the continuous, it also erases discontinuities. Thomas' thrusting hand and Jesus' breath stream of words flowing into the ear of Thomas cross the boundary of flesh and self. Familiar outlines are erased in order that new outlines can be drawn in the imagination.

The voice wind crosses all boundaries. "Breath is everywhere," as Anne Carson reminds us, "There are no edges."

In a pivotal passage, as Jesus attempts to make clear to Nicodemus the boundary between flesh and spirit, he evokes the wind. Choosing a stunning metaphor, Jesus says: "The wind blows where it chooses, and you hear the sound of it, but cannot tell from where it comes, and to where it goes: so is every one that is born of the Spirit" (3:8; NRS translation). Which Nicodemus hears as "The wind blows where it chooses, . . . so is every one that is born of the wind." A natural interpretation, of course, because Nicodemus knows that in Greek the word for "wind" and "spirit" is the same (*pneuma*). He takes literally what Jesus intends figuratively. Later, Lazarus' sister Mary will take figuratively what Jesus intends literally (11:24–25).

Like the wind, language slips and slides. It's as if Nicodemus here assumes the role of the "keeper of sheep," the speaker in a poem of Fernando Pessoa and the name that Jesus takes for himself later in John's book. When a stranger maintains that the wind speaks of "memories and yearnings / And things that never were," the keeper of sheep contradicts him, saying "You've never listened to the wind. / The wind speaks only of the wind. / What you heard it say was a lie, / And that lie is part of you." The wind has no outline except what we give it. What Jesus draws is not what Nicodemus draws. A beautiful and moving image, the wind is also wonderfully and critically ambiguous.

Jesus' words, therefore, undercut the very point he is making with Nicodemus. The image that Jesus employs at this crucial juncture in establishing the boundary between flesh and spirit is at the same time an image of boundary crossing. The categories of flesh and spirit dissolve.

The power of the wind asserts continuity, a world without edges, while Jesus ostensibly insists on discontinuity. These are no more firm categories here than they are at the end in the upper room with the disciples, where Jesus breathes on them in spirit and in flesh, and where Thomas violates the spiritual and material boundaries by a thrust of his hand. Nicodemus is perplexed (3:9) only because he sees continuity in the wind where Jesus sees outline.

Nicodemus

Nicodemus wrestles with John for his book and receives a name. Neither a believer like John, nor a teacher like Jesus, he is the questioner.

Once brought on stage, we are powerless to dislodge him from our imagination. A problem John shares. After introducing Nicodemus early in the book, John must bring him back in the middle and again at the end. Nicodemus is the man on the periphery who will not go away. He is both a central and marginal figure. Ultimately, he takes control of John's book, for we find ourselves, despite the writer's efforts, reading it through the lens of Nicodemus' questioning character. And to paraphrase Jesus, the central shall be marginal, and the marginal shall be central.

We are what we love. Character is defined by desire, and Nicodemus' desire is not for belief but knowledge. Yet desire alone is not sufficient. "The self forms at the edge of desire," as Anne Carson puts it. Desire saturates character, but the true self cannot precipitate without risk. Nicodemus risks his position in search of knowledge. Driven by curiosity, he seeks Jesus out, away from the crowd and hangers-on, away from the support of his own tribe. The questioner stands outside any vocabulary that purports to define the world in total.

While Jesus desires to die, and John desires to live, Nicodemus alone desires to know. He goes out of his way to meet with Jesus. In their colloquy by night (3:1–21), however, he stands apart as the questioner. Likewise, as challenger, he stands outside the temple coterie (7:45–52) just as he does Jesus' circle, not fully leader of the Jews and not a follower of Jesus. Yet his questions to Jesus early on haunt the rest of John's book and make Nicodemus a central figure. We are not surprised, then, when he shows up after Jesus' death to honor him with a gift of spices (19:38–42).

Call him Nicodemus the uncertain, disinterested, always engaging and disengaging; oscillating between the center and the circumference, between Jesus and those who write Jesus off, his brothers, friends, ex-followers, enemies, even baffled strangers like Pilate who encounter him purely by chance. Nicodemus savors uncertainty. He lingers in the twilight where no categories are firm, no vocabulary final, reminding us of Bulkington in Melville's *Moby-Dick*, who inspires the observing narrator and shipmate to assert that "in landlessness alone resides the highest truth, shoreless, indefinite as God." Like Bulkington, Nicodemus is the secret member of the crew.

∼

From Nicodemus' position on the periphery, when the Jews are shouting Jesus down in the temple, he brings them up short with a single question: "Does our law judge any man, before it hear him, and know what he does?" (7:51) I want to cheer. What a dramatic reappearance of Nicodemus in the middle of John's book, bursting on the scene again at this point of tense interaction and sharp interpretative interchange.

Nicodemus comes back into the story with a reaction that we didn't get when we first met him questioning Jesus. There the conversation ended with his long, almost suspended silence. We wanted more. What was Nicodemus thinking as Jesus' words echoed in the night air? (I've "discovered" three letters from Nicodemus to John that perhaps answer this question, which inventions follow this chapter, a "Fictive Interlude.") Here, as a result, Nicodemus' reaction to the crowd feels like a resolved chord. He was the cool questioner, withholding judgment, insisting like a skeptic on results, actions. He didn't buy Jesus' story, but has clearly hung around, observing him closely, and now on his behalf asks for fair play, though keeping his distance.

In the scene that follows in the same temple, however, Nicodemus chooses silence. When Jesus and Nicodemus and the Jews reconvene early the next morning (8:2), the Jews bring before Jesus a trembling woman taken in adultery. Nicodemus hovers just outside the action. A ruler of the Jews, but in contrast to the day before in the temple, Nicodemus keeps silent. He provides a ground base of questioning for this extraordinary scene of power and compassion. John reinforces our sense of his presence by invoking at the end of the scene (8:12), as he had at the end of Nicodemus' colloquy with Jesus earlier, the Prologue to his book, which contains the whole and marks both these encounters with Jesus, Nicodemus' and the adulterous woman's, as pivotal.

Though he is marginal, neither fully Jew nor disciple, friend nor stranger, Nicodemus is the speck of dust in John's eye that he can't get rid off. He wants him to believe, but John's integrity as a writer won't let him fudge when Nicodemus does not become a follower of Jesus, and he gives us the questioner. Nicodemus' resolved and detached character takes on a life of its own that cannot be made into what it is not. He chooses knowledge over belief, and even John in his own book cannot change this.

∽

A knower but Nicodemus the outsider acts boldly. We've seen him speak out, while maintaining his distance, but in the end he simply acts. And what an action, it is an unforgettable gesture. As pure and extravagant as Mary's gift of perfume, Nicodemus brings 100 pounds of embalming oil with "myrrh and aloes" (19:39) for Jesus' burial. He does not ask for fairness in the treatment of Jesus. It's too late for that. He simply acts, insisting on honor, courageously joining Joseph of Arimathea in wrapping Jesus' body for burial. Extraordinary, this last glimpse, John giving us a Nicodemus in silent, fragrant action.

And John subtly contrasts the knower and the believer in this scene. The "secret disciple" (19:38) Joseph of Arimathea does the talking, negotiating with Pilate. Nicodemus does not speak. After Joseph of Arimathea succeeds in getting Jesus' body, Nicodemus joins him. But where are Peter and the others?

It is only the two outsiders who have the courage to act, one out of belief in Jesus and one out of respect for Jesus, for the knowledge he clearly possesses. Joseph of Arimathea must speak to come clean, to declare who he is. Out of tremendous personal integrity, Nicodemus must act to pay homage, but at the same time this allows him to maintain ambiguity. Though present, his position can't be resolved. More than admirer, certainly, yet not disciple or we would have heard. And the disciples are noticeably absent. Their belief results in embarrassing absence while, ironically, Nicodemus' knowledge results in extraordinary action.

The disciples' absence, of course, heightens the power of Nicodemus' presence. Where Joseph of Arimathea appears out of nowhere, John carefully makes Nicodemus' appearance a climax, intensifying as well the drama of his gesture. He becomes bolder as he observes Jesus under a wider variety of circumstances. And possibly Jesus' defining action for Nicodemus was the forgiveness shown the adulterous woman. Witness to such manifest power, Nicodemus realizes the true depth of Jesus' understanding.

Regardless, after he meets Jesus, given continued observation, Nicodemus' emergence is inevitable. When we first see Nicodemus he speaks privately in a night scene. When we see him again, he raises a question publicly in broad daylight and, finally, joining Joseph of Arimathea, he goes beyond words and simply acts publicly.

A fine reversal of the first scene in the last epitomizes Nicodemus' stance. As John limns his progress with just a few strokes, we're aware that in the first scene Nicodemus is implicitly accused of lacking life, while Jesus is volubly alive. In the last scene, however, Nicodemus is beyond John's grasp and emphatically alive as, in silence, he respectfully touches the dead body of Jesus. And unlike Thomas and Mary Magdalene, he touches Jesus' body on his own terms.

~

Once John grants Nicodemus life, the energy of the center that for John is always the character of Jesus must be shared. We catch Nicodemus only out of the corner of our eye, but when we do, he becomes a center himself, pulling John's interest to what had been the periphery and making this figure of knowledge central.

John loses control of Nicodemus early on. The narrator begins straightforwardly to introduce his colloquy with Jesus, announcing that "There was a man of the Pharisees, named Nicodemus, a ruler of the Jews: The same came to Jesus by night, and said unto him, Rabbi, we know that you are a teacher come from God: for no man can do these miracles that you are doing, unless God be with him." But subtly Nicodemus moves to a central position in John's book. "Jesus answered and said unto him, Verily, Verily, I say unto you, Unless a man be born again, he cannot see the kingdom of God. Nicodemus says unto him, How can a man be born when he is old? Can he enter the second time into his mother's womb, and be born?" (3:1–4).

Though Nicodemus addresses Jesus with respect, conventionally as a Rabbi, his words are tinged with irony. Instead of saying simply "I know," he addresses Jesus as a representative of others, a "ruler" of the Jews in fact, saying, "We know that thou art a teacher come from God" (3:2). I hear his greeting as more a question than a declaration. As a consequence, we view Nicodemus immediately on an equal footing with Jesus, instead of an uncritical admirer come to fall at his feet in homage. Jesus' response accepts this equality. He makes clear in a rather brusque manner that Nicodemus' assumptions are unacceptable: "Jesus answered, Verily, verily, I say unto thee, Except a man be born of water and of the Spirit, he cannot enter into the kingdom of God. That which is born of the flesh is flesh; and that which is born of the Spirit is spirit (3:5–6)."

The oracular "Verily, verily" shifts our sympathy away from Jesus to Nicodemus where it remains throughout their colloquy. We identify with the questioner. For Nicodemus' remains the key question of John's book, "How can a man be born when he is old?" Rather than Pilate's, "What is truth?" The former question is about experiencing and obtaining knowledge, the latter about seeking and believing. Pilate accepts the language of Jesus, while Nicodemus explores his language. Nicodemus asks about Jesus' way of speaking, not what Jesus is speaking about.

Jesus' method is apparent. John uses this scene to make it explicit early on. He invites Nicodemus to accept a new vocabulary, not "born" of the womb as we customarily understand the term but "born of the Spirit." By this means Jesus attempts to construct an edifice of language from which there is no exit. John shows us Jesus at work building this structure: statements layered with carefully placed questions; oracular rhetoric raised on a foundation of concrete imagery; rigid categories, such as flesh and spirit, cut from steel. Jesus is the master builder.

Just as the breath of the wind through the courtyard takes his attention, however, Jesus is undercut by the disinterested Nicodemus, whose reasonable questions asked with calm, profound respect haunt us. Our sympathy shifts to Nicodemus. At the same time, he shares Jesus' power of language building, who in turn borrows his irony, "Art thou a master of Israel, and know not these things?" (3:10).

Despite John's orchestrating the scene to emphasize Jesus' power, skillfully moving from their dialogue with its threshold imagery of birth/water to Jesus' monologue with its categorical imagery of belief/truth, a counter movement undermines this power. Seen from Nicodemus' exploratory, questioning perspective, we realize that the edges of Jesus' new terms are not as sharp as they first appear. Perhaps they're modeled in clay rather than cut from steel. In the end, during Jesus' monologue, we are distracted by what might be revolving in Nicodemus' mind. And after Jesus stops, the continued silence of Nicodemus hangs over the scene like a thunderhead.

John dramatizes the fact that Jesus' power is inseparable from his mission of radical redefinition. Nicodemus' night colloquy with Jesus, then, is critical to John's book. First, because it makes explicit what is at stake. A new vocabulary is offered by Jesus, an attempt made to establish new categories, declare where the edges of things are in the new world inhabited by John's Jesus. Second, these very edges are undercut by their language, the ironies they exchange where edges blur. Just as Nicodemus is both on the inside and the outside, so none of the distinctions that Jesus makes—flesh/spirit, earth/heaven, light/darkness—remain hard. Almost as soon as these categories are defined, they begin to shift like the wind.

~

Brilliantly orchestrated, the pivotal scene unfolds in three movements of increasing length and decreasing complexity, as Jesus' vocabulary narrows to a chant of "belief" and "light" and his monologue dominates. John signals us when a movement begins and ends, using the close of each for emphasis. All three movements begin "Verily, verily" (3:3, 5, 11), the first two ending with Nicodemus' question. Significantly, the last movement ends not with a question, since Nicodemus has dropped out of the conversation, but with a declaration about "doing truth" in the light. This returns us to John's Prologue, his opening hymn to the word and the light, signaling the importance of this scene.

As we have seen, Jesus' program begins in the first movement, redefining "birth" as the necessary groundwork for the redefinition of "flesh" and "spirit" in the second. He insists that "flesh is flesh" and "spirit is spirit," attempting to draw a clear line between the two. At the same time, Jesus ends this movement with the powerful but ambiguous image of the wind, and John dramatizes the word play (wind/spirit), which together undermine any rigid distinction between flesh and spirit.

Nicodemus' question, furthermore, "How can these things be?" wins our sympathy. While we're drawn to Nicodemus, we are distanced by Jesus. For his withering irony in response, "Art thou a master of Israel, and know not these things?" betrays a lack of patience. Jesus presses his program hard in this second movement, but Nicodemus' genuine question breaks the momentum. He is no straight man, and his question dogs us throughout the rest of the book, which is why John introduces it here.

Nicodemus does not deny Jesus' assertion. Instead, he asks in so many words, "in what way are you speaking of these things"? Yet Jesus' tone shifts immediately to the hortatory with a flurry of premises, a rhetoric that Jesus wants Nicodemus to adopt because once the new vocabulary of "birth" and "spirit" is accepted, Jesus' conclusion follows.

∼

The dialogue at this point, as if to consolidate his renaming power, becomes a monologue. John gives Jesus the last word, a long speech that does not end with a question. Jesus begins authoritatively, asking a question himself, albeit rhetorical, about understanding "earthly" and "heavenly" things (3:12). At the same time, he picks up Nicodemus' irony from the opening of the scene, where he had addressed Jesus in the first person plural, "We know that you are. . . . " Likewise, Jesus shifts here from "I" to "We." More important, while driving home the firm distinction between earth and heaven, emphasizing their difference by the contrast between ascending and descending, Jesus repeatedly names the "Son of man." And he dwells in heaven as well as on earth. The Son of man participates like Jacob's ladder or the serpent that Moses lifted up (3:14) in both the earthly and the heavenly, blurring their outlines. What first seem to be hard categories prove to be soft.

A similar dynamic operates at the end of Jesus' monologue. Working himself into a fine chant on the word "belief," he climaxes with a demand for belief in the "name" (3:18) of the Son of Man/God. Anyone, not just Nicodemus could be confused, for by now this name signifies God and/or man. Jesus breaks the law of the excluded middle. In building language with Nicodemus in their contra-dance, Jesus dissolves the categories of flesh and spirit, earth and heaven, even man and God.

Returning at the end of his monologue to the primary categories with which John opens his book, Jesus makes a final attempt to draw the edges clearly. He turns to the consequences of not accepting his new vocabulary, such as "birth," and its concomitant binary categories of thought and life, such as "flesh" versus "spirit." What opposition could be clearer than light and darkness? An ancient dualism, Jesus turns it to his own ends, redefining it in terms of a person "come into the world" who courts the world and is either loved or rejected. In a wonderful move Jesus turns an abstract, traditional metaphysical duality into a drama of desire. Earlier Jesus has said he is not concerned to "condemn the world" (3:17) for not believing on the "name." Now we understand why.

For the world, if it rejects the lover named light, suffers a condemnation that arises from within:

> And this is the condemnation, that light is come into the world, and men loved darkness rather than light, because their deeds were evil. For every one that does evil hates the light, neither comes to the light, lest his deeds should be reproved. But he that does truth comes to the light, that his deeds may be made manifest, that they are wrought in God (3:19–21).

A deft move, Jesus avoids condemning, as does John throughout his book, by simply pointing to the condemnation that dwells in all who do not choose to inhabit his new edifice of language. And self-condemnation, we know, is the worst damnation.

This strategy enables Jesus to avoid the trap of dualism, inherited from the tradition of light/darkness, while constructing new categories with which to understand the world. Yet this advantage cuts both ways. Turning back on him, his strategy erases any sharp line between the categories. For light is reality, a bodily reality, the light in the beginning and in the end, while darkness is defined wholly in terms of this reality. Darkness ultimately has no substance in itself. The one who does evil does not finally, therefore, love darkness. Rather, he "hates the light." Thus darkness is fundamentally the absence of light.

Jesus speaks of desire that forms character, those who "come to the light" like lovers. With John we appreciate the irony of Nicodemus the lover of light coming to Jesus by night. Later John uses the word symbolically, noting pointedly that Judas, after betraying Jesus, goes out into the "night" (13:30). But John clearly savors the night scene here for its dramatic effect. Using it counter to convention, darkness reinforces the note of affirmation at the end of Jesus' monologue, where in a lesser writer we would expect condemnation. In the silence that John gives Nicodemus, we become aware that he knows but does not believe on the one "name." For Nicodemus resists a single all-defining vocabulary with its rigid categories by which we are intended to understand our experience.

As a lover of knowledge rather than belief, Nicodemus is content to visit Jesus' house of language and learn, but not to move in because it is ultimately too confining. The one Word by which "all things were made" and "without him was not any thing made that was made" (1:3) is profoundly and disturbingly exclusionary. No spiders or Visigoths need apply.

Nicodemus' questions lodge in our mind for the remainder of the book. Their bringing language into account, riding the edge of figurative and literal, categorical and ironical, ultimately results in their going unanswered. That is, we find ourselves viewing all that John presents subsequent to this scene through Nicodemus' eyes. His blurring the edges with irony that Jesus picks up and adopts, his silence as the categories dissolve, not light versus darkness but light and absence-of-light, finally prevails in this pivotal scene that forms the climax to the first part of John's book.

Nicodemus, in short, consistent with his desire to know and his disinterested character, obliquely revises Jesus' language and with it John's book. Fittingly, in a scene that forms the climax to the last part of his book (19:38–42), before the resurrection and reunion, John brings Nicodemus and Jesus together again. And true to character, the ambiguous Nicodemus' very presence questions the language of John's book. If as the disciples say, they "believe," why aren't they present? So he continues to haunt us as we last see Nicodemus, now by daylight, bent in silence wrapping the dead body of Jesus.

The Nicodemus Letters to John

a Fictive Interlude

FIRST

YOU ASK ME TO confirm your account. You ask me as if records could be true. I answer let both the lettered and unlettered have his voice. In the main you've followed my relation of that night, though I note you've left out the moon and the locusts, as well as my disinterested . . . but you know this. I'll not niggle over small omissions and additions. Foremost is that you let his voice sound, and I make allowance knowing how you loved him and how he took your head in his hands.

Our Vocalisimus he was. If as legend has it we Jews found the stops, and the Greeks the vowels, then he invented the word. Without breath, as they say, the letter is dead. So why are you still obsessed with belief and water? This is a dry land but we're deluged, God knows, with belief. The very word swims before my eyes.

Let him speak in your text, yes, where words rise against words. The language streaming from his mouth carried us like leaves—leaping, plunging, erratic—remember? Let him say all the letters out loud. I can only be grateful for what you've resurrected of that cataract. You give us his riddling. And you let us be swept into his maelstroms of monologue. Manic interpreter, frothing talker, he had to be, like our old inspired prophet-poets, of God.

SECOND

How explain his effrontery? You ask as if I knew. He'd offer clear, cold water and just as we drank, shatter the vessel of interpretation. He reveled in pushing figures of speech off the precipice.

I'm still puzzled by his taunting us like some Dionysiac to cannibalism, offering his breadflesh and wineblood. I found myself at times uneasy, as you know, passing in deja vu from the white room to the red, seated with The Cook, the Thief, His Wife & Her Lover before the served body, as in Peter Greenaway's 1989 film. Then, just as we reached to partake of understanding, his figures swerved, and we stumbled.

And the opposite. Bending the literal into figure. Outrageously inviting Thomas to try on his body like a bloody glove. As if that could prove anything. Belief suddenly become as pointless as unbelief. He delighted in making us uncomfortable in our own language. And in our bodies, as if we needed new ones, morphing letter into figure like some mathematics of the spirit. Lazarus sleeps.

Then bending down beyond his bright and dark sayings, finger to the ground. In that tense moment we looked at each other empty. I still remember the paralyzing clarity of his act. Now I know what it must have been to see Ezekiel in the tree. The teacher simply bent down before that poor woman and inscribed on the ground. The hostile mob surrounding, struck dumb as a tree. Who could interpret. Who dared? The talker of all time silent.

Writing or drawing we didn't know. Was he inscribing a sign or simply a glyph in the ground to make of that mark his point, nothing more? I remember thinking "he's stalling for time." But what a spell when we saw in the dust that speaking picture.... The look in your eyes, who could forget, said we'll never know keener sounds than on that day under a metal sun.

THIRD

Having been drawn again to your account, as if by a whirlpool, I remain grateful for your fleshing his speaking in letters on the page. As always we'll disagree about signs. But I respect your honest admission of selection and understand your wine-to-blood arrangement in a frame of light. More important, you get the glint and grit of the sand in his voice.

A voice so insistent in the dark I have to close your book to sleep. Awake, I return to my texts, and they suggest other texts, and they in turn gesture beyond the desert where a raven marks the edge of many circles. I can't escape that son-of-man's voice. Explain. How in his brief time on earth had he come to shepherd such a flock of words?

Age can resent this, but instead I was exhilarated, as you know, going out of my way for his way of speaking. Taking words in his teeth, confronting and evading at will, just as he moved deliberately from place to place like a guerilla. Immortal magnet? Jack, joke, sly son?

The man's mouth could taste its own fate. His unnerving certainty, his radiance like the firefly's—uncanny, as if the circumference were within. Exuberance of youth? Maybe arrogance and recklessness come with the conviction of immortality. I only know that the circumference still expands going forward to eternity.

All these years John, and you've called me reprobate on occasion, but in this we're one: being close to him, the spray of his voice in our face, we were most alive.

Light

Light is time thinking about itself.

—Octavio Paz

LIGHT WALKS THE EARTH wanting to be courted like a lover. He does not oppose darkness because darkness has no real existence. For light, who has come into our world to be desired, darkness is not even a question. Light being wholly light cannot conceive it. Light is not opposition but attraction; he draws all to himself. Those who reject the lover, however, give darkness existence because their state of rejection is called darkness. The body of light knows only radiance. His name is Jesus.

John has fallen in love. And he writes a book about this being, whom he quotes more than once declaring: "I am the light of the world" (1:8; 9:5). In gesture and word, Jesus is for John incandescent. We can easily imagine him saying of Jesus, as Guy Davenport remarks about a character in one of his stories, "He eats light and his droppings are copper." John's dream of sharing light with Jesus at the table is fulfilled. And in an epilogue to his book he projects himself into a most moving scene of breakfast on the beach: Peter and Jesus breaking light together at daybreak. By an act of adoration John partakes of this light, feeding on the nourishing light, just as John the Baptist became by his love "a burning and a shining light" (5:35).

From the beginning, as John makes clear, light is life that gives life. Light is not a moral category but the substance of life itself. When the "Word was made flesh," light became a body. And in the Word "was life, and the life was the light of men" (1:4). This answers the main question of our age, posed succinctly by the Argentine poet Roberto Juarroz, "Where is the light of a god propped against nothing?" And it is John's fervent desire that those who witness this light walking the earth might like John himself fall in love with Jesus, which is to "believe" (1:7), and thereby share in the fullness of life that radiates from Jesus.

John's yearning here extends throughout his book. He savors light in his prologue, repeating the word in an incantation, "and the life was the light of men; and the light shines in darkness" (1:4–5). Jesus echoes this in his own incantation at the end of the colloquy with Nicodemus (3:19–21) and later as the knowledge of Jesus' imminent, gruesome death oppresses him (12:35–36). In John's mind light and life are inseparable. John wants what we all want, as A. R. Ammons describes it in "Summer Place," nothing short of a land "where tenderness would be so high it would transmit / light . . . and the rivers would / be flowing light and trees would sway with the fruit of light."

∼

John in love is why he refuses the traditional opposition of light and darkness. He inherited a dualism that pitted light against darkness. And the writer of Genesis reinforced this tradition. John, however, returns to the profound intuition of light not only as the very ground of life, but as the primal reality. Light did not drive out original darkness; instead, darkness was only given a name by the absence of light. Light came first in the creation of the world and in the radiant person of Jesus.

Rooted in this assumption is John's emphasis on the love of light rather than the traditional war between light and darkness. His is a radical move. This is evident when we contrast John's understanding of light to that of a contemporary community, the Essene's. Their apocalyptic fears were projected into a war between the "Sons of Light" and the "Sons of Darkness." Jesus, however, under great stress, implores his disciples at the end, "While you have light, believe in the light, that you may be the children of light" (12:36). John portrays this as an admonition to a personal act of love. The Essene community's *The War of the Sons of Light with the Sons of Darkness* (c. 60 B.C.), in contrast, moralizes becoming "children of light," turning the act into one of communal hatred. It demands that its disciples "Love all the Sons of Light" and "Hate all the sons of Darkness," the basis for all genocide before and since. The traditional symbolism of light/darkness is used here as an incitement to war.

Jesus rejects this, as does John, and pushes back beyond the inherited symbolism to employ light as an inducement to a fuller life. The ethical overtones are still present, but they are inward and derived not from opposition but unity. By contrast, *The War* thrives on the traditional opposition, separating and demonizing, inflaming the passions of hatred rather than generating love.

The character of Nicodemus saves John and thus Jesus from this black-and-white fate. Nicodemus who came by night in the beginning of John's book comes by day at the end loaded down with spices for Jesus' body. A half-lit figure, he is to the moon's "white fire" in P.B. Shelley's phrase as Jesus is to the dawn, cooking breakfast for his disciples over a charcoal fire on the beach. Nicodemus and Jesus share this threshold existence between light and dark.

John, consequently, cannot bring himself to condemn those who do not love, for he knows that they are condemned already by their own lack of love. This is why Jesus is so ambivalent about judgment, stoutly maintaining that he has not come to judge, yet often sounding like the accuser. John underscores this ambivalence. He shuns absolutes, the easy binary categories of morality, as in his portrayal of Jesus bending down to write in the dust. Once John introduces Nicodemus, his love for this ambiguous figure will not allow him to judge. Thus darkness, though used symbolically on occasion, as in Judas' going out into the "night," is not absolute. There is no hell in John's book. And this is owing to Nicodemus, the creature of John's reporting who in turn shapes John's creation.

To be "children of light" is to have within oneself, like Jesus and John the Baptist, light. John does not desire to follow the light, so much as partake of the light. For then this light emanates from the person. There can be no darkness, then, for the child of light. When "there is no light in him" (11:10), the result is night. It is left to Dante, a poet the equal of John, to continue the exploration of this phenomenon in his *Divine Comedy*. With sublime subtlety he leads us from the poor bastards in hell, doomed to seemingly infinite variations on a darkness of their own making, to the vision of Beatrice in paradise pouring from her the fire of love, the river of "living light."

∽

Power is the emanation of living light. John gives us a dramatic demonstration of its power in Jesus' healing the blind man. John sets the scene, introducing us to the man and having Jesus, just before he heals the man, proclaim: "I am the light of the world." What follows is another of Jesus' wonderful gestures, which John has an eye for. Immediately, he reports, Jesus "spat on the ground, and made clay of the spittle, and he anointed the eyes of the blind man with the clay" (9:6). John brilliantly alludes to the creation act in Genesis, making this explicit by turning his camera on the clay here and again presently (9:14). He draws up into this image of light all the power of the primal act. Not only does this magical power heal, bringing fullness of life, but it restores life itself. For just as Jesus announces his identity with light before healing the blind man, so he reminds us that the light resides within him before raising Lazarus from the dead (11:10).

Light draws into itself not only the beginning of creation but its end as well. As the ground of all being, light is the reality containing space and time, which has proven to be not only figuratively but, according to our cosmologists, literally true, as Octavio Paz alludes to in the epigraph. Obsessed with his end, Jesus continually remarks about his "hour" not yet come. By speaking of it, though it is in the future, he places it in the present. In reflecting on his mission, he discovers in each present moment his future.

In every instant of his life Jesus dreams of a death in which finally he will be truly loved and, as he says, "draw all men unto me" (12:32). The light at last loved by all. Not unlike Shelley who voices the yearning of all poets for "memory" to give his "living name" wings on time, alighting in the hearts of his readers and so "making love an immortality." An aside to his readers makes clear the importance to John of the fact that when Jesus says he must be "lifted up" and draw all men, he refers to his own death (12:33). John wants us to understand exactly what psychological pressure Jesus is under. It is the same kind of pressure that we are all under, a function of being conscious that as humans we must die.

But John recognizes that what sets Jesus apart is the intensity of this pressure, so great in fact that it produces a strange radiance. He feels more acutely than anyone, even Socrates, his agonizing end contained in any given present moment. Understanding this pressure, which John ensures, contributes to our being the more greatly moved by Jesus' remark to his disciples, "yet a little while is the light with you" (12:35).

Jesus

*The exceeding luster and the pure
Intense irradiation of a mind.*

—P. B. Shelley

I

THE MIND OF SAMUEL Taylor Coleridge, that is, as Shelley describes the English poet to his friend Maria Gisborne in 1820. And the poet-painter William Blake had the same effect on people, friends as well as complete strangers. While still in his teens, the patrons of a literary salon came under his spell and raised the money to publish a volume of his poems. In Blake's last years, the painter Samuel Palmer gathered with other disciples regularly in the "House of the Interpreter," as they named his apartment and workshop, kissing the bell handle each time before entering.

So too Blake experienced the visionary power of Jesus, as manifest in John's book, declaring that "Jesus & his Apostles & Disciples were all Artists." But Jesus was the supreme figure of imagination. For Blake "The Eternal Body of Man is The Imagination, that is, God himself / The Divine Body, Jesus." He is a multitude of imaginative possibilities, Blake insists, not a single theological or moral or social notion. We are the "Members" of this body which "manifests itself" in "Works of Art," such as the books of John and Dante and Blake.

And before Jesus, Socrates. Subject to intense mental irradiation, the ex-playwright Plato gives us a version of the man bent on death who acted as midwife to the life of his followers, bringing into the world the fullness of a life examined. Socrates in the dock is incandescent, intellectually brilliant and supremely confident. Likewise, drawn by the luster of Jesus, John writes a visionary account of the man dedicated to martyrdom who offered everlasting life. Both were provocateurs, neither a writer. And both owe writers, who were also drawn to be followers, their existence.

II

Only a few are privileged in every generation to experience this gift of incandescence in another. Dante felt it in the presence of his beloved teacher Brunetto Latini whom he called a "radiance among men." This light is not necessarily goodness. And it's certainly not fame, though that can result. Blake worked in obscurity his entire life, unknown except by a small coterie. Nor is it always manifest in a body of work. Coleridge left us only a handful of poems; by all accounts it was in his conversation that he glowed with a white heat.

Yet those around Coleridge and Blake, and in our time Ghandi and Einstein, recognized a force of personality and an intellectual brilliance orders of magnitude beyond the commonplace. When this coincides with the ability to make works of art (like Blake) or devise writings of power (like Mohammed and Joseph Smith), or by chance to attract a great writer, as did Socrates and Jesus, then we can stand at the end of the ages in their light.

Incandescence is the central fact of Jesus' character. Illuminating all those around him—followers as well as enemies—it could also burn. John shows us the light dawning within the Samaritan woman. But we imagine smoke rising from the temple, as tables crash to the floor and coins scatter, and from the crowd of Jews left to smolder, having heard yet another blasphemy.

III

Inciting to love, incandescence invites risk and fulfillment. Its presence threatens and welcomes. We are attracted by it, wanting to merge with the incandescent one and burn with a new knowledge.

In short, we find what we most desire—life at its fullest. The adventure of knowledge becomes inseparable from the adventure of love. And I confess with Anne Carson, that "These two activities, falling in love and coming to know, make me feel genuinely alive."

The experience of uncanny power carries with it the conviction of coming into extraordinary knowledge. We want to embrace its source and at the same time express the power of this encounter. John makes his book; his successors make a cult and ultimately a culture.

The kernel of all subsequent transformations, however, is John's experience of being fully alive in the presence of incandescence. This is the core of the appeal of Jesus.

IV

Incandescence is not charisma but concentration. Absolute conviction brings the rays of personal energy to a focus like a burning glass. And anyone with certain knowledge of what they're about in this world draws others. One who knows where they come from, where they are going, and what the future holds exerts a centripetal force on all those around. Derived from intellectual confidence, the single-minded focus of the incandescent character, however, is double edged. Jesus knows exactly where he is going and why, but so do fools and sociopaths.

Hitler too was incandescent. He had the same powerful effect on his followers, as an early adherent to Hitler admits: "I do not know how to describe the emotion that swept over me as I heard this man. His words were like a scourge. . . . His appeal . . . was like a call to arms, the gospel he preached the sacred truth. . . . I forgot everything but the man. Then glancing around, I saw this magnetism was holding these thousands as one."

All who have experienced the incandescent character testify to this feeling. It's a high. It's life beyond life, an overwhelming sense of being at the center of life, which cannot be defined any more than love can.

Incandescence like love promises the fullness of meaning, a plenitude at once beyond meaning and, in rendering it irrelevant, the end of meaning. This experience, as we have it from witnesses as disparate as Plato and John, Dante (on Beatrice) and Nils Bohr (on Einstein), is like the eclipse that Annie Dillard describes, "The meaning of the sight overwhelmed its fascination. It obliterated meaning itself." An incandescence so bright it is darkness. An experience so full of possibilities, that is, so thick with life, we are overwhelmed. As a result, the visionary whole has all too often been abstracted to something more easily assimilated.

V

Dostoevsky exclaimed in a letter to his niece Sophia Ivanova that "There is only one positively beautiful person in the world, Christ, and the phenomenon of this limitlessly, infinitely beautiful person is an infinite miracle in itself." The meaning of Jesus for Dostoevsky, contained in that appellation "Christ," overwhelms his fascination.

The reason Dostoevsky got it wrong is rooted in his reducing Jesus' character to a single trait—beauty. Reduce the visionary possibilities to a label or category, a title like "Christ," and the electricity of the man is short circuited. Ostensibly a gesture of homage, the title's real motive is the need for refuge, to find a defense against the power of presence. Jesus' incandescence so blinded Dostoevsky that he went reeling from John's portrait and turned Jesus into an abstraction.

Obsessed with the problem of portraying the pure, completely good man, he idealized Jesus in his notion of the Christ. There is infinite beauty in Jesus' forgiveness of the Samaritan woman and in his tenderness with Mary Magdalene. But Dostoevsky simply does not see the infinite arrogance of Jesus. He understandably ignores minor lapses, which we all share, such as Jesus' peevishness with his disciples on occasion (6:67), and rudeness to his mother at the wedding party in Cana and to Nicodemus. But he also ignores more serious flaws, such as his meanness in gratuitously testing Philip (6:6) and viciousness in accusing his fellow Jews, when they merely questioned his new way of speaking (8:41), of being sons of the devil himself (8:43–44).

In fact, John's visionary Jesus is often not very likable as he patronizes his disciples and baits his enemies, boasting and blaspheming— "Before Abraham was, I am" (8:58). Even large character flaws remain invisible to Dostoevsky and the church that solidified around the Christ, namely, his toying with people or using them outright as objects (signs), like the blind man, to achieve his own ends.

VI

The visionary character that John portrays in his book is exasperating and exhilarating at the same time. Jesus' outrageous claims infuriate even while we celebrate his smashing the cherished categories of his culture: the social (speaking with the Samaritan woman), religious (breaking the law by healing on the Sabbath), and political (claiming a higher authority than Rome). By his actions Jesus violates all manner of thresholds.

Even his disciples cannot be comfortable in their categories. It is apparent that the Jesus they have constructed is not concerned with things of this earth or given to the sensual, but rather spiritually concerned and politically engaged. Thus the disciples are certain of their ground when they criticize Mary for anointing Jesus with the oil of spikenard. But he rebukes them, "Let her alone: against the day of my burying has she kept this. For the poor always you have with you; but me you have not always" (12:7–8).

Self pity aside, the sensuality of the scene is evident. Hair brushing Jesus' feet, house filling with the fragrance, John specifically points to the sensuous particulars, Jesus clearly enjoying them. The concrete, sensuous experience is more important than the abstract class called "the poor" (its abstraction reinforced by the irony of Judas, future betrayer and thief, complaining that the poor should benefit instead of Jesus). Jesus affirms the sensual here and now, shattering the disciples' categories. The senses, he knows, are the only hold against our day of burying.

The threshold-crossing actions of Jesus epitomized in this scene are dramatic. More than brilliant performances, they define his essential character. His defining moments occur at crossing-over places: a marriage, a political trial, a shore at dawn. But he occupies the thresholds of the culture in order to redraw them. He is not so much concerned to usher his listeners across as he is to obliterate and rebuild thresholds. In fact, he is not the keeper but the threshold itself. Hence Jesus calls himself the Door (of the sheepfold, 10:7).

His violation of conventional categories manifests itself most profoundly in his use of language. By this Jesus makes himself the door to all understanding. Taking a word, for example, like "lamb" that belongs to a well-defined and widely accepted category, Jesus wrenches it loose and applies it to a different category, redefining "sacrifice." He keeps his listeners off balance. This is a poet's way of speaking. And it is, as Kenneth Burke defines the verbal "atom-cracking" perspective-by-incongruity method of poets, with regard to definitions established by custom, "impious." Jesus is no respecter of categories. Many simply do not exist for him, like the door he walks through without opening (20:26) or the book belonging to John that he walks right out of. Locked doors cannot contain him. Books cannot hold him. Jesus is larger than any of his theatres.

He creates his own arena and in so doing continually violates our understanding of center and periphery. For him these categories do not stay still but oscillate. He makes the Jewish establishment peripheral. He renders Rome peripheral. At the same time, he brings working-class men and outcast women from the periphery to the center, making disciples out of fishermen and privileging Mary Magdalene with inside information about his resurrection. In an ironic act meant to point up the radical nature of this identification with the outsider, Jesus washes Judas' feet (13:5). And Jesus thereby makes him central, all the while knowing that he is the betrayer who defines the peripheral.

VII

Jesus glows with contradiction. He is grand and pathetic, magnanimous and petty. Capable of righteous or self-righteous indignation, harassing the moneychangers in the temple, he is also capable of sour grapes, sulking like a poor loser (6:66).

Jesus can contain contradictions because he is a field of energy. He is drawn to Peter because like him Jesus acts from "impulse," as Blake asserts, "not from rules." Jesus is the figure of energy that breaks the bounds of his body and pours into the world, pushing water into wine, prodding the body from death into life.

From this energy comes his power over people and events, as Jesus turns angry mobs away from stoning him to death. And derived from his power with the people, he obtains power over nature, walking on water or right through a wall.

VIII

Yet Jesus blends power with tenderness. Though Jesus knows from the beginning who will betray him, he is still "troubled in spirit" (13:21) each time he voices the realization. On occasion John underlines this with a wonderful camera shot: "the disciples looked one on another, doubting of whom he spoke." Their perplexed looking at each other puts us in the scene, convincing us that Jesus was "troubled." Poignancy and oracular arrogance (13:18) clash here in a scene with the enemy betrayer to reveal the complexity of this character Jesus.

The same is true of his interaction with a friend. He is deeply moved by the death of Lazarus, weeping even as he prepares to bring him back to life. But at the same time, Jesus invests the scene with another emotion. Layered with his warm response to Martha as a friend is his coldness as a man on a mission. Bent on higher ends, he can't resist a performance opportunity that will further his ultimate goal. Does he weep for the benefit of the Jews looking on?

After all, Jesus knew what he was going to do (11:15), use this act as the ultimate sign to bring about belief in the Jews, so we can't help but be suspicious. We know Jesus is capable of playing with the feelings of even his disciples. A part of John like Dostoevsky, however, wants us to view Jesus' motives as pure, emphasizing that he was in fact deeply moved (11:38) as if anticipating a reader's suspicions. The fact remains that John is self-conscious about Jesus' using this event for effect (11:40–42), which reveals the complexly disturbing effect of Jesus on John himself. This becomes apparent to his readers as well, for we too are uneasy.

IX

Jesus wields the word of power. He calls out Lazarus' name, and Lazarus comes forth from the grave. Angry crowds are quelled. And great gusts of power swirl from Jesus' spiraling monologues with their mesmeric cadences rising stepwise to a crescendo. They have the energy of jazz improvisation. Laying down a word, adding a line, taking up the same word like an eagle gyring into the sky, Jesus becomes the sun itself.

Yet even this power is paradoxical. For Jesus demands a response from the very ones to whom he denies understanding. His audience is characteristically puzzled. They greet Jesus with bewilderment, even consternation, followers accustomed to his "hard" sayings (6:60) as well as enemies. Furthermore, when Jesus proposes to clarify, he uses figurative language, such as the parable of the shepherd, that mystifies his listeners or moves John to interpret for his readers. The spirals of Jesus' speech unfurling like a continuous peel from an apple (such as chapters 13–17), promising the fruit of meaning, often fall to the floor and collapse.

At the end of one of his monologues, for example, Jesus concludes, "I have yet many things to say unto you, but you cannot bear them now" (16:12). His disciples can "bear" it, as we learn later, but to their ear he's speaking gibberish. Jesus has covered all bases—sin, righteousness, and judgment—and thus no bases are safe. He has worked himself into a fever, which is psychologically convincing because John shows us a Jesus come into an increasing certainty about his own decision for death that brings with it, of course, an increasing emotional strain.

Continuing, Jesus tells his disciples that when "the Spirit of truth is come, he will guide you into all truth" (16:13). Then he rips off a stunning metaphor: "A woman when she is in travail has sorrow, because her hour is come: but as soon as she is delivered of the child, she remembers no more the anguish, for joy" (16:21). Jesus demonstrates his powers of language in this seemingly casual development of his idea, taking his disciples where they didn't ask to go. Nonetheless, they can't help but marvel at his powers of observation and elaboration. He may be under stress, but he's lucid.

More subtly, Jesus shifts to a direct address of the Father that is also directed at his disciples, "These words spoke Jesus, and lifted up his eyes to heaven, and said, Father" (17:1). With this also comes a modulation to a more subdued tone, a mix of humility and tenderness. Jesus can be tender when his disciples overhear him, if not when speaking directly to them, especially under the pressure of his circumstances. He is, after all, about to enter the Garden of the End (Gethsemane) where he'll be betrayed (18:5), making the final commitment.

John has us listen along with the disciples to Jesus' cycling rhythms, making his hypnotic supplication on their behalf that they might have "joy fulfilled" (17:13) and, building to a climax, truth and finally glory. The waves of the words of Jesus build toward the end of John's book. The Word becomes words spraying us in the face, even as words condense in the one Word and ultimately pass beyond language to the final sign, his body hanging on the cross—threshold of life and death—and standing on the shore—threshold of death and life.

The disciples must have thrilled to hear Jesus' supplication, an incantation in their honor wishing for them the incandescence of Jesus himself (and John's readers wishing right along with them). Undoubtedly they failed as always to understand what he was saying, but they certainly understood the import of Jesus' gesture on their behalf. It's doubtful that they "murmured" among themselves here, grousing about how hard Jesus was to understand, as they had on earlier occasions (6:61). They knew a wish fulfillment when they heard one.

Yet, as much as the torrent of Jesus' language rushes out into the world, misunderstanding pushes back. The great power of the word meets an equal force. Talk countered by query and silence (Nicodemus), or challenge (the Jews), or incomprehension (disciples, friends, enemies, strangers, acquaintances) is a principal tension of John's book. In the field of response invited by Jesus' monologues, we are always buffeted by the forces of incomprehension.

X

Jesus' contradictions, above all, evidence an incandescent intellectual power, something beyond charismatic and obsessive. Just being with this man Jesus gave one a sense of being alive, not an uncommon experience in the presence of genius. While in this euphoric space, his followers clearly felt that they knew more than they understood.

Within the first few chapters of his book, John succeeds in creating a complex, many-faceted character in Jesus that engages our attention and emotions. John takes us on an emotional roller coaster: Jesus introduced by a charismatic figure in his own right, who is awed by his "fullness" and pushes him to the foreground; Jesus on the road attracting followers by his very presence; Jesus at a wedding party impressing friends with his superhuman powers and for the first time revealing part of his character unguardedly in reaction to another person; Jesus in a temple, furious, demonstrating his considerable human powers; or Jesus exhibiting impatience with a stranger who comes asking questions in the middle of the night.

And John gives us defining moments, such as Jesus with the woman taken in adultery, where his courage and power are demonstrated beyond a reasonable doubt. For all his ambivalence about judgment, a theme he returns to throughout John's book, Jesus affirms in the end mercy.

The beauty of his mercy shines on strangers, like the trembling woman, as well as followers. With tender forgiveness he reverses Peter's threefold denial in the courtyard, which Jesus overheard as he was being slapped by Pilate's soldiers, in his graciously serving Peter breakfast on the shore of Tiberias. He simply asks Peter three times whether he loves him and without mentioning the previous scene gives Peter his threefold blessing.

XI

More than love, Jesus desires death. His power in life is fueled by death. Obsessed with his own dying, Jesus calls our attention to its weight on his life. From the outset, even celebrating at the wedding feast in Cana, Jesus makes clear that every present moment includes his end. At the heart of Jesus' character, this fact becomes the core irony of John's book. Jesus, who for John is the figure of blazing life, views himself as a sacrifice for the entire world: animal (the lamb slaughtered), vegetable (the bread eaten), and mineral (the temple destroyed), a body promised to death from his very birth.

Feeding the fires of Jesus' incandescence, this death wish drives John's book. Death deferred to the end (his "hour" not yet come), like the knowledge deferred that Jesus always promises, builds tension. Jesus' edginess, turning on friends in frustration or disappearing suddenly to be alone, so much a part of his character, results from this pressure. And the grace of Jesus' last act of forgiveness with Peter, as the sun dawns on the beach, flows from its release. Great psychological pressure builds inexorably as John's book moves closer and closer to the crucifixion, and is then released in death—Jesus' wish come true.

XII

Why did Jesus call Judas as a disciple? Even as he chooses Judas, Jesus knows from the beginning that Judas will choose betrayal (6:64; 13:21). In choosing Judas, Jesus chooses death. Now we know why after washing the disciples' feet, including those of Judas (13:2), he asks them if they know what he's doing (13:12). They don't, of course, because as only he knows, his gesture drips with unbearable irony.

Jesus' magnificent act of humility, a model he recommends (13:15), is also a breathtaking act of arrogance. Not the first time, since Jesus used the innocent blind man for his own ends, namely, "that the works of God should be made manifest in him" (9:3). And after learning that Lazarus was sick, Jesus waited two days until he died (11:6, 15), which understandably angered Mary (11:20). He does this for the express purpose of making the miracle of raising Lazarus from the dead more dramatic in order that the Jews would be impressed and believe on Jesus (11:45). Just as he uses the blind man and Lazarus, so Jesus uses Judas as a tool to accomplish, literally, his own end.

XIII

Jesus follows two death scripts: one spoken and one written. The spoken is his father's voice making his will clear (5:30), informing Jesus of his sacrificial mission (6:39), which is proof to Jesus of his father's love (10:17). The written is scripture, the words of the prophets. The voice tells Jesus what he must do, while the text informs him in detail about how to carry it out.

Jesus obeys the voice of his father. Like Socrates and Blake, Jesus follows the dictation of voices. He could say with Blake that he converses with "friends in Eternity" and writes from "immediate dictation," some things "even against my Will." At the same time, Jesus imitates the actions of the Messiah described in the Jewish scriptures. Like Don Quixote, Jesus models himself on the stories he finds in books. He lives the prophet's vision of the Messiah as recorded in these texts, which he knows by heart, quoting them often and acting them out.

The voice centers Jesus in time. His Father's voice is the voice by which the world was created and the promise that Jesus' future death will not be in vain. It centers the past and the future in each present moment of Jesus' living. At the same time, he acts out the text of the past prophets in the present, down to the specific words that he is required to utter at his death as the "Messiah." This text centers Jesus in space, where lifted up on the cross, all the world collapses into his body. He is the space of all life, the one Lamb and the one Vine; and the space of all sacred places, the one Temple. As the spoken word expands time, the present moment, to include Jesus' death, so the written word expands space, the locale of his actions, to include all the world and ultimately the heavenly city.

The spoken and the written word are finally the same word, of course, the one Word Jesus himself. Just as he construes and misconstrues the text of the prophets, his Father interprets him in turn, "the Father that sent me bears witness of me" (8:18). Their relationship, "Father, the hour is come; glorify thy Son, that thy Son also may glorify" (17:1), involves reciprocal interpretation. But meanings converge. Both the voices and the text chart the same path for Jesus, the way of death.

XIV

The voice continually sounding in Jesus' head, which he calls "the Father," gives extraordinary confidence. From this comes his unswerving character, single-mindedly pursuing his mission, emitting sparks along the way.

Only Jesus hears this voice, no one else, not even his disciples (5:37), except on one occasion where the people thought it sounded like thunder or an angel (12:29). They heard but couldn't understand what it was saying. Outside Jesus' head, it's just noise.

Yet everything that Jesus does he does at the dictation of this voice. As he admits, "whatsoever I speak therefore, just as the Father said unto me, so I speak" (12:50). Grounded in this "Father" voice is his unshakeable belief that he offers "life everlasting." And from this conviction comes his remarkable ability to convince others of what he offers.

Viewing Jesus from outside his head, the disciples (1:45) as well as the Jews (6:42) casually remark that his father is, of course, Joseph. But he's strictly off stage. And for all the talk to/with/about Jesus' "Father," ironically, it's his mother we picture. By contrast, Jesus invokes his Father like a mantra, but we can't picture him. Where we see Jesus' mother in Cana and at the cross, we're forced to imagine both his fathers, just as he does. We hear rumors of Joseph, who hardly seems more than this to Jesus himself, since he doesn't mention him even once. And we hear constantly about the Father that only Jesus hears.

Like all sons, Jesus carries the father-authority voice with him all his days. But amplified by the prophets, it becomes the voice of thunder from heaven (2 Sam 22:14; Ps 77:18) resounding in the chamber of his head. The action of Jesus' life, before it shows itself in the world, plays out first in this small theatre—just he and the Father. Here the Father/Son voice reverberates, as a laser is pumped before it bursts into a single coherent blaze of light.

Because it's easy to forget, given the way Jesus speaks about the Father, we're reminded many times that the Father and Son are one person. Jesus declares, "the Father is in me, and I in him" (10:38). And he makes clear that this is not only a spiritual but physical identity (14:9). Accordingly, they project each other's job of work (5:17): raising the dead (5:21), giving eternal life (10:28), and passing on their spirit (15:26). Jesus speaks, and the Father listens (11:42). And vice versa, Jesus feels intensely that the words he speaks are not his own but the Father's who lives in him (14:10). The voice never ceases for Jesus, as the Father continuously oscillates inside-outside his head.

They revolve around each other like those Asian eagles that whirl in mid-air, talon-to-talon, tumbling and sparing in an aerial dance. The Father/Son exchange generates power. Taking leave of his disciples at the end, "his hour . . . come" (17:1), he lets them overhear for the first time his side of a conversation with the Father. The mesmerizing voice swirls rhythmically—doubling phrases back on themselves (17: 4–5), repeating the word "world" like an incantation (17:5–6, 9, 11, 14–18, 21, 23–25). Jesus insists that the Father "glorify" him (17:1) but then circles and assumes it (17:22). Likewise, he regards himself as both the one sent into the world and sender (17:18).

Throughout his stately lead & retreat, a mine-are-yours-and-yours-are-mine dance (17:10), Jesus again reminds his disciples that he and the Father are "one" (17:11, 21–23). As if they'll mistake his gyring soliloquy of self-preparation for self-abnegation. When this last dance ends, Jesus has induced a state of power—an odd mix of tenderness (17:13, 26), insistence (17:14–18), and inner peace (17:23). Now the disciples are prepared to bear the world's hatred (17:14). Now Jesus is ready to enter the Garden of the End (18:1).

An earlier crisis has enabled him to achieve this eerie calm. Under stress and deeply "troubled" (12:27), Jesus pumped himself, arguing, "What shall I say?" Should he ask, "Father, save me from this hour?" which by voicing at all becomes a question directed to the Father. Jesus considers it, but stops. Hearing the voice of the Father (12:28), he answers himself, it's "for this cause came I unto this hour" (12:27). Gathering power, his voice resounds with absolute certainty.

Though he seeks death, he never wavers from his belief. The voice assures him that his sacrificial mission, the losing-one's-life-to-save-it "cause" (12:25), will succeed: "And this is the Father's will which has sent me, that of all which he has given me I should lose nothing, but should raise it up again at the last day" (6:39).

XV

Jesus blazes with a self assurance derived from this voice, just as Socrates had before him and Blake after. It is similarly responsible for Socrates' "absolute unlikeness to any human being that is or ever has been," as Plato remarked. Both Jesus and Socrates put great stock in what he calls his "internal oracle." They were both about their Father's business, obedience to God enabling them to defy the powers of the state. Both had a talent for antagonizing their enemies. And, finally, both were in Plato's words martyred "to fulfill the will of God."

Remarkably similar in their circumstances and mission, both forged on virtually alone, steeled by the voice in their head to face down death. Though married, Socrates lived an unmarried life, as did Jesus. Socrates like Jesus had no visible means of support, depending on friends and disciples. How did Jesus make a living? We never see him making a table or fixing a door. John seems as unconcerned as Plato. Their real occupation was in dialogue and debate, both professional wordmongers mesmerizing and offending their listeners.

What they have in common highlights the difference in their characters. Though their fathers were tradesman, Socrates' a stonemason and Jesus' a carpenter, Socrates dismissed them, while Jesus chose them as companions. Similarly, Socrates seeks out male companions, perfunctorily dismissing his wife at the end in the presence of his disciples, while Jesus seeks out the company of woman from the beginning. More important, while both fulfilled their desire in self-sacrifice, Socrates martyred himself to the present life, Jesus to the life beyond.

XVI

Both hear a voice in their head and obey it, but Socrates' typically says "turn back," warning him from some act, while Jesus urges him to "go forward," to act. A large difference in focus and method results. Socrates' objective was to invite doubt that leads to self-knowledge in the present; Jesus' was to invite belief that leads to future knowledge. This contrast in focus on the present and the future, respectively, reveals a profound difference in their understanding of the very nature of knowledge itself. For Socrates knowledge was primarily the recovery of ignorance for use now; for Jesus knowledge was the discovery of truth for later.

Both understood knowledge as a birth. Jesus insisted on a second birth, however, viewing himself as the mother-creator, while Socrates brought about self-knowledge in the role of "midwife," bringing to light rather than creating. Socrates based his life on the knowledge that he lacked knowledge; Jesus the opposite. Socrates said the wisest man is "He who has realized that in respect of wisdom he is really worthless." Jesus asserted, "I am the way." Clearly, Socrates reveled in uncertainty, while Jesus exalted certainty.

Where Socrates sought to assist at the birth of knowledge, Jesus acted to give birth to belief. Socrates as the midwife, then, leads us into using our own language in order to demonstrate that we do not know what we think we know. On the other hand, Jesus as father/mother gives us a new language in order to convince us that we will know the truth. In short, Socrates stakes all on self-examination. Despairing of any truth, he asserts the value of the act itself. But Jesus directs the gaze of his followers outward, toward the Way.

Both used irony as a method. A powerful tool for recovery or discovery, it could be cruel as well. Socrates showed up the ignorance of his followers while claiming to be ignorant himself. But no one was fooled; it was an obvious pretense, no doubt offensive to some. He used irony to strip away. The nothing that was left was the nothing that one could confidently know. His listeners had to pass through darkness before they could enter into the light. Jesus had a similar penchant for asking questions to which he knew the answers, testing his disciples. However, he used irony to redefine what they thought they knew. In so doing, Jesus built a new house of language, brightly furnished with all the desires of one's heart, which he invited his listener to enter.

This divergence in method accounts for why their own voices reveal such different characters. The voice that Plato gives Socrates at his trial in *The Apology* is wholly convincing. Wonderfully ratiocinative, it builds inexorably to an unarguable conclusion. It's a voice we ride like a strong and steady horse. The voice of Jesus in contrast, as John recreates it for us, swirls and rushes like rapids. It is often unconvincing in its headlong plunge but always overflowing with meaning.

We admire the willfulness and intellectual strength of Socrates, proceeding inexorably to a conclusion, as Plato depicts his mind masterfully moving over the chaotic waters of contention. We want to walk beside Socrates, hang out with him in the grove. But we want to be Jesus. Capable of crystalline statements, such as "He that loves his life shall lose it; and he that hates his life in this world shall keep it unto life eternal" (12:25), Jesus can also trail a bright cloud of sublime nonsense. We're attracted and repulsed by Jesus. In contrast to Socrates, who with the utmost cool completely inhabits the present moment, Jesus is hot, the past and future blazing within him.

XVII

Jesus is unpredictable. Socrates says he does not judge, and he doesn't. Jesus, however, wrestling with himself, claims not to judge yet judges. He dwells in fantasy and dust. His voice tells him that he must die, for only in his death is forgiveness. He is contradictory and dies full of holes, haunted by the cock crowing. Socrates is of whole cloth and dies with a last request that the god of healing be given a cock as a gift.

"If Morality was Christianity," as Blake says, "Socrates was the Savior." Ethically, Jesus and Socrates obey the same voice. Neither seeks vengeance and both refuse to flee when they have the chance. The former, however, associates with the marginal and outcast people of society, while the latter associates mainly with the rich and the sons of the rich. Socrates' last gesture is one of acceptance, but he does not forgive his accusers.

A strain of mercy sounds in the voice that Jesus hears. He forgives the woman taken in adultery, a capital crime, as Lincoln would later forgive the man who fell asleep on sentry duty. Jesus forgives and gives his believers the power to forgive. Who can gainsay this power in Ghandi and Martin Luther King, Jr., standing in peace unmoved against hate-contorted faces. How otherwise to explain Nelson Mandela's commitment to peace after being tortured and imprisoned for 27 years by an apartheid regime or to comprehend South Africa's Truth & Reconciliation Commission, an entire community of forgiveness.

XVIII

Obedience to the voice in his head, which Jesus calls the "Father," impelled him to a death that he was convinced would result in life. But how to become this sacrificial figure, called the "Messiah," how to carry out his own death and ensure its efficaciousness posed another question. The answer came to him, as it did to Don Quixote, through the voice in a text. Jesus took instruction from the prophets as recorded in the Jewish scriptures. While he could passively accept his Father's mission, Jesus actively sought and followed the guidance of Ezekiel and Isaiah to carry it out.

Don Quixote of Cervantes' great novel understands this project. For it is his own. After decades of steeping himself in the old books of chivalry, exhilarated by the adventures of gallant knights and awed by the wonders of soothsayers and magicians, Don Quixote determines to be a knight. He models himself on the knight as described in the old books and becomes that character. His mission is to right all the wrongs of the world. Faithful in carrying out knightly deeds, such as aiding the oppressed, he even arranges to die in the way the books prescribe that a knight should die.

Jesus is also enamored of old books. He grew up reading the scriptures. He admired the character of the prophet they describe. He is awed by the prophet's magical powers like Elijah's, turning water into blood or making it burn; his visionary powers like Ezekiel's, seeing eyed wheels within wheels in the sky; and, of course, his political powers, forcing kings to quail at the mere pronouncement of his word. Thus one day Jesus determines to devote his life to emulating the heroes of his beloved books. Just as Don Quixote decides to turn himself into a knight errant, so Jesus decides to turn himself into an heroic prophet called the "Messiah."

And Jesus follows his script(ure). So closely, in fact, that for him Isaiah's book could be called *Life: a User's Manual* (novel by Georges

Perec), and he devoured Ezekiel and Jeremiah and Zechariah, the entire company of prophets. Don Quixote's head was filled with "numberless Amadises, of that multitude of famous knights." So Jesus' head was filled with numberless prophets. Don Quixote plays the knight in *Tirante el Blanco*, and Jesus plays the role of prophet exactly as described in Isaiah. Starting with the necessary accompaniment of every true prophet, Jesus appropriates "signs" (Isa 7:11–25). In his first sign, which John is careful to point out, Jesus turns water into wine. Later, Nicodemus, knowing the prophets' writings as well as Jesus did, acknowledges what he is doing, fully aware that Jesus is consciously keeping to his script(ure).

Following the prophetic texts, he cleanses the temple (2:18; Zech 14:21), heals the blind man (9:7; Isa 42:7), and finds a donkey that he rides into Jerusalem to his death, carrying out instructions in the script(ure) that the Messiah must be mounted on a young donkey (12:14; Zech 9:9). By imitating the prophet's actions, Jesus becomes the hero. He comes to identify himself as the Shepherd, just as Ezekiel had before him (10:11; Ezek 34), and as the true vine, just as Isaiah had (15:1; Isa 5). Jesus doesn't miss a detail. And John is explicit about this program, commenting after he describes the soldier piercing Jesus' side, "For these things were done, that the scripture should be fulfilled, A bone of him shall not be broken" (19:36). Even in his last moments on the cross, he self-consciously fulfills his role as prescribed by the books: "After this, . . . to fulfill the scripture perfectly he said: 'I thirst'" (19:28; Ps 22:15).

In the act of reading, therefore, Don Quixote and Jesus radically change themselves. They burn with desire to be what they read. The reader continues to read like a flame consuming the page. The word, in turn, incarnates the reader. They become what they read.

XIX

Jesus is the Quixote. Not Vladimir Nabokov's Don Quixote who "stands for everything that is gentle, forlorn, pure, unselfish, and gallant." Jesus is too cranky, unpredictable, even forgiving, in short, too outrageous to stand for purity or gallantry. No more than he could stand for Dostoevsky's beauty. Yet viewing him as Quixote, clarifies Jesus' character.

Don Quixote appeals to us in his refusal to adjust the "hugeness of his desire," in the Spanish poet and philosopher Miguel de Unamuno's phrase, to the "smallness of reality." It is just this refusal in Jesus that appeals to John. Jesus burns with desire for life, wanting more life out of our one life, a life everlasting. This grand desire lasers through the reality of suffering and death. It has a powerful attraction because we all feel the disparity between our desires and the world's willingness to grant our desires.

As a result, we spend a lot of energy devising ways to defend our huge desire for life against the small, nasty fact of death. We interpret and reinterpret the world around us in this effort. And to one degree or another we manage to transform it into a world that accommodates our desires.

This involves a range of magic, from finding enchanted things like quarks in the world to making enchanted things like Don Quixote, who is himself aware that he is in a book. Don Quixote finds the world to be an enchanted place where giants are changed to windmills; Jesus makes the world a magical place where he changes water to wine, reads a man's mind (2:25), and wakes the dead. For both, enchantment serves to preserve desire intact against the world's most corrosive agents. Its strategy is simple. Breaking down conventional categories and rendering reality uncertain—bread can be body and death life—makes possible the construction of a new reality. Sancho Panza sees windmills where Don Quixote sees giants, and the disciples see death and departure where Jesus sees life and return.

Both Jesus and Don Quixote have the capacity of not only defending desire but extending it. They contain within them all of life, including our lives. Jesus like Quixote extends his self outward to encompass all of life. And all its books—the Word. Jesus embraces all of Palestine, its countryside and sea and city, all the world, until he is the cosmos itself—the Light.

Our Lord Don Quixote and our Lord Jesus of Ridiculous Desire, they must both travel this far, for they have chosen a preposterous mission. Who can be the knight errant of our wildest dreams? Who can be the ultimate prophet, the Messiah of our fondest desires? Who can right all wrongs, reinvent the world, banish death?

Volunteering for missions such as these inevitably leads to the absurd. So Jesus declares he is God (8:48–59). To defend huge desires in any age appears to those without desire to be madness. Unamuno viewed Don Quixote's madness as the embodiment of wisdom and faith. The world that mocked Jesus and Don Quixote has disappeared, but they live on. Jesus the Quixote, the fool, even mad, proves to be the sanest man in a mad world.

XX

Like Socrates, then, Jesus hears voices. His Father's voice continually resounds in his head propelling him toward his heroic destiny. And like Don Quixote, Jesus looks to the old books, the script(ure)s he grew up with and memorized, for guidance about how to become his own hero. Yet Jesus is not Socrates and not Don Quixote.

Only Jesus launches into a monologue like that after the woman taken in adultery has left the temple. It begins calmly, then escalates, getting nasty and finally dangerous. Jesus manages in his blustering to provoke the Jews by echoing the great "I Am," Jehovah himself (8:58), declaring, in effect, that he is god. He could very well have spoken the words that D. H. Lawrence gives him in *The Man Who Died*, "I tried to compel them to live, so they compelled me to die." Jesus pushes all their buttons and then hides. What are we to make of his exasperation, argumentative flimflam, and seemingly gratuitous provocation?

The answer, in short, is a prophet. John gives us Jesus the prophet in all his human complexity. Intellectually powerful, quick in debate, he is a maker of brilliant images and metaphor in sparring with the Jewish teachers and turning the words of their scriptures to his own ends, as in his disquisition on bread (chapter 6). And he is capable of brave, sometimes selfish, and even bizarre actions. He is as provocative as Ezekiel, in fact, who lied on his left side for 390 days and on his right for 40 to make a point (4:5–6). And as much the poet as Isaiah, using the full range of language to whine, skewer, patronize, command, provoke, deduce, cajole, expatiate, and delight.

His interrogators, Jewish or Roman, can't keep up with him, nor his friends. He keeps Martha off guard with his word play at a highly emotional time when she has just lost her brother (11:24–25). She misinterprets him, taking figuratively (death) what Jesus means literally (sleep), while the disciples had just taken literally (sleep) what he had meant figuratively (death). Hard to keep up with Jesus' maneuvering, but that's part of John's design. Jesus is dazzling and infuriating at the same time, a bit of a trickster, the convincing sign of the prophet.

XXI

But how does Jesus vouchsafe the prophet's authority? Listening to voices and following models is not enough. It's one thing to claim to be the ultimate prophet, the Messiah, another to convince others to accept your claim. The best answer is an oblique sentence in one of Emily Dickinson's letters: "To be singular under plural circumstances, is a becoming heroism." The hero must needs be somewhat obsessed. It not only suits the hero, setting him apart, but is in itself a hero-making strategy. Single-mindedness will get you a long way. In Jesus' case to stand alone against the culture, to adopt Ezekiel's prophetic stance and set his forehead like flint, was a most powerful form of self-authentication.

The prophetic character alone, then, would seem to carry its own authority. Attracting followers, awing the establishment, and engaging the opposition ought to be testimony enough. Even Jesus' enemies, as John quotes them, admit his singular brilliance: "And the Jews marvelled, saying, How knows this man letters, having never learned?" (7:15)

But quixotically, Jesus tries to establish his authority. Even the self-confidence of a Jesus can waver. So he puts forth a criterion for judging whether anyone claiming to be a prophet truly speaks for God or merely for himself. "He that speaks of himself seeks his own glory," Jesus says unequivocally, "but he that seeks his glory that sent him, the same is true, and no unrighteousness is in him" (7:18). The claimant, therefore, who operates not from the desire that most men have for fame, money, power, and the love of women (as Freud once observed) speaks from God.

But this begs the question. Jesus' criterion seems to establish the principle of "right judgment" (7:24). The context of feeding the multitude, however, subverts this principle because it is manipulated for Jesus' own "glory." For John admits that Jesus' asking Philip what he should do as the "great company" descends upon them is only a test, because Jesus "knew what he would do" (6:6), raising questions in our mind about his motives and as a consequence his authority.

Ultimately, Jesus relies on a single argument to establish his authority, one that reduces to self-authentication. "I am one that bear witness of myself, and the Father that sent me bears witness of me" (8:18). That is, he counts two witness on his side, which the Jewish law required—he and God his Father. Such an argument is, of course, specious. Jesus is the

Father; the Father is Jesus (10:30). By inviting us to debate, Jesus disappoints us. Yet it's completely in character.

Wanting to simply assert and, at the same time, to logically justify is a characteristic of Jesus which he did not find in the prophets. Their mode was to assert, and in the end Jesus falls back on this. Real authority is power. He bends down to write on the ground, the trembling women beside him silent, and the angry crowd is unable to raise their arms to stone him. This scene defines what it is "to be singular under plural circumstances." He bends down, scoops up some mud, spits on it, and applies it to a blind man's eyes. Immediately, the man sees and tells the world his story, simply, straightforwardly, with courageous power. His experience is authentic and to Jesus' enemies, despite their strenuous efforts at cross examination, unarguable.

By silent action Jesus radiates an unquestioned public authority. He can vouch for himself and get away with it. In private recognition scenes, also, we observe authentic moments of power. A simple exchange of words glows in the night with authority: Nicodemus acknowledging a fellow Rabbi who in turn acknowledges Nicodemus. Begging off Mary's touch in the cemetery, Jesus observes himself as if in another's body, being with Mary, and we see the arc struck between them. Jesus glows with this same light in that moment when the disciples recognize a dim figure on the beach, and Peter leaps out of the boat to join him.

So coy with Mary in the garden, so tender with Peter on the beach, Jesus lights the way with his personal authority. At the same time, he is fiery in his political face off with Rome and the Jewish establishment. He calls into question the most cherished political and religious values of society, reexamining the rules about whom to associate with and what laws to follow, which to ignore. Socrates is a conservative; Jesus and Don Quixote are radicals. Socrates obeyed the law in the end and died to affirm old values. Jesus broke the law and died to assert new values—forgiveness and everlasting life.

When Jesus sets his forehead like flint he strikes sparks against an obdurate culture. Playing his authentic role and becoming the prophet, he can rightfully claim: "I am the light of the world" (8:12; 12:46). This is the incandescent Jesus of whom others exclaimed: "That was the true Light" (1:9). Sheer presence and power, he is life itself. But he can only achieve this authentic self as he incarnates, as the "Word," the speaking of his father and of the prophets.

One Big Word

In the beginning was the Power. In the beginning was the Thought. Reason. Mind. The Truth, Wisdom. In the beginning was the Preaching, the Law, the Speaking.

So the "Word" or logos of John's opening hymn has been variously and legitimately translated. John's Greek listeners/readers would hear in this word strains of Heraclitus, who posited logos as the cosmic ordering principle, akin to what we regard as natural law, while his Jewish audience would hear a reference to the revealed Law of the Torah. Both traditions, however, the Greek thread of thought/mind/power and the Hebrew of truth/wisdom/proclamation, have their origins in the fact of speech, the voicing of language.

Both rooted, that is, in the ancient and primary experience of language as power, evoking that past age when "They stopped the sun with a word, / a word burned cities to the ground," as the Russian poet Nikolai Gumilev describes. The word, then, contains a dream of power.

> In the beginning was the Word,
> and the ... Word was God. ...
> All things were made by him;
> and outside him was not any thing made that was made
> (1:1–3).

More fundamentally, the Word is the ground of creation. Words not only beget words, but the world, our laws, our heroes, our cities of desire. What now is was once only language. All that we know is constituted by language. The active word, then, is personified as the creator God in this first strophe of John's hymn. And, of course, like the epic poet calling on the muse, John invokes its creative power at the opening of his book. As he sets out to make a new book, he appropriates the long tradition of the word as the generator of life and light. Word is both creative force and result of that force. Word = Wor(l)d.

As a writer, John resonates with the word as the creative principle because he knows the power of the word voiced. He may hear notes of Heraclitus and echoes of the Jewish Law, but the resounding voice in his ears, overwhelming all other music is the formula that the prophets like Hosea use to open their own books, "The Word of the Lord." Sounding in John's head is the Hebrew word *nabi*, which means not only "prophet" but "mouth." Speaking out against their prevailing culture, the prophets continually invoke the "word of the Lord." It is the source of their power. And their own people as well as their foes are understandably in awe of this speaking, even as Jesus' enemies say of him, "Never man spoke like this man" (7:46).

∼

John draws on traditional materials for his hymn, establishing in its first strophe the ground of his creative powers as do the prophets before him: the Word is the Creator. But he departs quickly, asserting in its third strophe something radically new, as St. Augustine was the first to point out:

> And the Word was made flesh,
> and dwelled among us,
> (and we beheld his glory,
> the glory as of the only begotten of the Father,)
> full of grace and truth (1:14).

The Word is a body. As a writer, John knows the experience of being filled with the word, inspired, and at the same time, being created by the word. Just when he believes that he controls his words, they take over and control him, leading him down unforeseen paths. The writing becomes a body in its fullness of sensation and perception, in its willful disobedience.

All writers know this experience. In being spoken and written, the word takes on a body and makes its own way in the world. John can only marvel at what he creates that in turn creates him, enabling him to make his self out of hitherto unknown images and desires, an experience of nothing less than "grace and truth."

The Word takes on a body in the act of speaking and writing. John like Emily Dickinson uses his experience as a writer to comprehend the incarnation. Acutely aware that the body of a poem can only be born by what she calls the "consent of language," Dickinson extends this notion. The word, the ground of creation, embodies itself according to its own will in a poem. The Spirit of Language, that is, condescends to become a physical work, spoken or written. And the "condescension" of God, she says, is "Like this consent of Language / The loved Philology." Language or "Philology" embodies itself in the poem's flesh, as God embodies himself in Jesus' flesh.

We are exhilarated by his opening hymn because John both courts language, seeking its consent, and revels in its power. As Jeremiah says, words are a "burning fire shut up in my bones" (20:9). But this roaring fire also gives light. The word makes "grace and truth." Aware that he follows in John the Baptist's footsteps as a maker of a "record" about who Jesus is (1:19), John well knows the magnitude of his task. And after hymning the Word, he also knows that the Word has responded to his declaration of love. It has granted him consent. He then delights in his own power, being filled with the spirit of language. He will make a lasting thing, the desire of every writer. For John knows the truth of Gumilev's poem that "only words / Stay radiant among earthly troubles."

It is by his book that John creates himself as well. His (contra)diction reveals himself to himself a believer. As he selects, arranges, and describes, making and interpreting the words of his central character, he imagines himself into the body of Jesus, whose radiance he wants as his own.

By the same token, he talks himself into the mind of the other that serves to sharpen the lines of his self. He incorporates the counter characters: the man at the margin, like Nicodemus; and the women who burst the constraints of their culture, befriending and understanding them; as well as the imaginatively intractable ones, the man asking for and accepting an outrageous invitation, like Thomas.

Writing his way into Jesus' character, John makes up his own character. His book is the book of Jesus, yet the Jesus we are given is first and last, despite his walking in Palestine some two millennia ago, made from words. He is incarnated in John's book. And it is the body of this book that John becomes in order to be Jesus. It is a new body, one that will glow always. "If I make a word, I make myself into a word," he can say with William Carlos Williams in *The Great American Novel*, "one big word."

Signs

Inspired by a voice—the "Word of the Lord"—the prophet speaks with power. But like Ezekiel by the river Chebar the prophet also sees visions. And the prophet shows forth his visions. The people stand in awe. Kings quake. Inspired by what he saw, Ezekiel lies on his left side for 390 days and on his right for 40. You can look it up (4:4–6). Signifying his battle against the "iniquity" of Jerusalem, this "sign to the house of Israel" is imbued with power.

Verbal power braided with visual. The prophet speaks and acts from knowledge of a visionary power accessed by the ear and by the eye.

Hearing voices and seeing visions, the prophets convey this knowledge to their people. Their vision counters the prevailing culture, and it sustains as well as unnerves. It taps another world that calls into question the "real" world. The prophet's words attest this power. As do the prophet's extraordinary actions, called "signs," like Moses striking the rock and bringing forth water. If the people cannot hear, let them see. The ear prophet and the eye prophet intertwine.

Drawing on this tradition of prophetic signs, John presents Jesus performing public acts that attest his power. These miraculous "works," as Jesus refers to them, such as changing water to wine or walking on water, point to an uncanny world that exists beyond the bounds or at the center of our everyday world.

It is one of power that he appropriates to make the world we all know conform to the world we all desire. No one is hungry here, no one is sick. In this world the lame walk, the blind see, and the dead rise up.

∽

Self-consciously selecting his signs from the many he had observed or heard about, John orders them according to his purpose of showing the power of Jesus. Seeing is believing. John is explicit about this (20:31), convinced that whoever sees the miraculous works of Jesus will believe that he offers everlasting life. If we see the sign, we'll not only see what the sign points to but be convinced that Jesus possesses the power to make good his promise of eternal life.

John maintains this conviction about the potency of signs, despite the fact as he himself records, being a writer of integrity, that seeing is not necessarily believing. He admits they don't always work (12:37).

But John is not deterred from his program even when Jesus' family (7:5) and friends, including some disciples (6:66), as well as his enemies, including a traitor, see the signs and don't believe. Enumerating the signs he has chosen, the metamorphosis of water at Cana being the first, John arouses our expectations.

And he obliges, giving us Jesus' signs in climactic order. Jesus moves from performing party tricks (changing water to wine) to defying death (raising Lazarus). Determined to display the prophet's complete power, John selects a strategically inclusive group of signs. They demonstrate power over the human (healing the cripple) and the natural worlds (walking on water). Moreover, he demonstrates Jesus' virtuosity, healing at a distance (nobleman's son) and at a touch (blind man), and not only healing the body but triumphing over death, first in bringing his beloved friend back to life (Lazarus) and then himself.

∽

Jesus like his models in Jewish scripture speaks and acts with power. His speech throughout the first half of John's book is woven with his miraculous works. Verbal and visual prophet like Ezekiel, who laments and exhorts as well as sets out an "iron pan" between him and the city as a "sign to the House of Israel" (4:3), Jesus balances both. But John extends our understanding of "sign" to include the word (12:33; 21:19), which he affirms to be an act in itself, a work (14:10).

In the second half of the book, the series of miraculous signs ceases even as Jesus departs from his models and becomes himself a sign. John lays the groundwork for this earlier in Jesus' monologue on bread, where he equates himself with the miraculous manna (6:36). But words, repeating and swirling around us, increase toward the end of John's book until they ultimately pass beyond language to the final sign on the cross (death) and on the Tiberian shore (life).

All signs collapse into The Sign, the one sign which is life. Jesus the signifier, pointing to everlasting life, becomes the signified, eternal life itself.

Brilliantly selecting and arranging his signs, John collapses the traditional verbal and visual prophets into one Messiah (1:21; 6:14). His handling dispenses with signs altogether. We find ourselves in the uncanny world that transcends signs because of John's power as a writer in demonstrating Jesus' power. Jesus is the ultimate prophet, not using signs but becoming himself the sign, which is not a sign but the thing itself. The world of desire—neither sickness nor death—not pointed to but realized.

John has subtly prepared us for this. He is insistent about what signs do: induce belief. Yet, paradoxically, he reports that they are not always efficacious. He builds his book on an armature of signs, yet he casts suspicion on them. Even as he depends on their power, they shimmer with ambiguity and arch their backs threateningly.

Implicit in this paradox are four complications leading to three propositions about signs. Yet they're still elusive. Though Jesus' chasing the moneychangers from the temple occasions his identifying himself as a sign, the act is ordinary anger, justified or not. And while the seamless coat that gives rise to the soldiers casting lots is not in itself a sign, being an ordinary article of clothing, John implies its miraculous nature.

Signs remain elusive because complications arise from these actions. When is a sign a sign? What John enumerates does not exhaust the category of acts that Jesus performs. And the question is sharpened by Jesus himself. His extraordinary act of writing on the ground before the hostile crowd that surrounds the woman taken in adultery is not a miracle, though it causes belief in his authority, while his commonplace act of spitting on the ground becomes a miracle.

FIRST COMPLICATION: DRIVING OUT THE MONEYCHANGERS

After Jesus "had made a whip of small cords" and drove the moneychangers "out of the temple, and the sheep, and the oxen," scattering their money and upsetting their tables (2:15), the Jews asked him: "What sign do you show unto us, seeing that you are doing these things?" By what authority, in other words, does Jesus drive legitimate businessmen from the temple, who provide a necessary service to the people in selling animals and birds so they can make religious sacrifices.

He answers with a miracle. He himself is the sign, his body resurrected from the dead. But he answers obliquely: "Destroy this temple, and in three days I will raise it up." He knows that the Jews will think he is talking about the temple he has just trashed, and they oblige. In other words, he does not answer them with a miracle that they would recognize as such, being thoroughly familiar with the prophetic tradition. He does not take the opportunity to be straightforward about a sign with an audience that understands the nature of signs.

Instead, he is arrogant. He doesn't care if the Jews fail to understand his metaphoric way of speaking. Even his disciples fail to understand, John reminds us (2:22), until after he performs the miracle of rising from the dead. Jesus sidesteps a direct question about signs. Both the Jews and the disciples are left in confusion. The Jews give up; the disciples remember later and piece the puzzle together. As with the seamless coat, which conflates past and present, only we as readers know now and only because John tells us.

He intentionally complicates the sign with time. Jesus' body as temple collapses the present and future, which obviates the declared purpose of a sign as causing present belief. John says that later the sign caused the disciples to believe the "scripture" and Jesus' "word," but of course they already believed by then, as he makes amply clear earlier in his book. John reinforces Jesus' sidestepping of the sign.

SECOND COMPLICATION:
GAMBLING FOR THE SEAMLESS COAT

As Jesus hangs on the cross, four soldiers on the ground below him split up the spoils. They have no trouble dividing his other clothes among themselves, but Jesus' "coat was without seam, woven from the top throughout" (19:23). They realize that it only has value if left intact. So they decide to cast lots for it, rather than cutting it up. In accordance with Jesus' model, that "the scripture might be fulfilled," John adds this delightful fairy-tale element to the grisly crucifixion scene.

Wonderful how the soldiers could care less whose spoils they're dividing, pausing only to preserve the coat's resale value. On this level, John restores the reality of the working world (like the soldiers with Peter before the fire in the courtyard). They're completely unaware of its significance, giving it no interpretation at all, oblivious of the sign above Jesus' head with which Pilate in a pique has goaded the Jewish establishment.

On the level of politics and pedagogy where John's program pivots on the sign, however, he must interpret the coat for us. Though it is neither a sign for the soldiers nor for the onlookers, John makes it a sign for us. It carries prophetic power. For John explicitly calls the coat a fulfillment of the scripture that includes this detail of casting lots for the "vesture" of the Messiah (Ps 22:18).

The "seamless" coat, however, is John's invention. He invests the mundane with uncanny power. It does not need to be a coat, let alone a special coat to fulfill the scriptures. But to sustain John's program it must be seamless, as if the integrity of the coat were bound up with the completeness of Jesus who becomes at this climactic moment a sign pointing to himself.

THIRD COMPLICATION: WRITING

When the woman taken in adultery is brought before Jesus, she believes she is about to die. The crowd expects this, and the Jews believe that Jesus has no choice but to concur with what the Law says. Instead, ignoring the mob and the leaders, "Jesus stooped down, and with his finger wrote on the ground."

The woman stands, trembling, and Jesus doesn't say a word but writes on the ground. She expects the worst, but Jesus' gesture quiets the crowd, their anger ebbing. The sign he makes changes her world, for in the end the people put down their stones and struggle off. It is a sign charged with the power of the prophets, like Ezekiel lying on his side or Isaiah making himself a sign (8:18). It is a miracle, a power to open us to understanding. As the South African poet, Lionel Abrahams, who is dismissive of Jesus' pain as "common squalid stuff," admits, "I open to the writer in the sand."

Extraordinary, but it is a purely human miracle. John invests the human act with superhuman power. Though it evokes the Word in the beginning, John does not label this a sign. But we are meant to understand it within the prophetic tradition of signs, particularly when a few verses later he precisely parallels it with another human act that ends in a miracle.

FOURTH COMPLICATION: SPITTING

The act: Jesus "spat on the ground, and made clay of the spittle" (9:6). The tip off: making mud from the dust on the ground with his saliva is purely gratuitous, as was making his coat seamless. Jesus has healed at a distance as well as up close by merely pronouncing. He doesn't need to spit on the ground to heal the blind man; he does not need a clay poultice to apply to the blind man's eyes. He could have performed the miracle simply at the touch of his hand.

But John goes out of his way to select this act from the many that Jesus did and invest it with great resonance by heightening its drama. Not simply a miracle over and done, but a magical ritual of spitting, making clay of the spittle, and anointing the eyes of the blind man. Not a single act in one scene but three acts: outside the temple, at the pool, and in the old neighborhood. Why are clay and water necessary, why the breaking of the law in spitting, anointing, and washing?

Writing on the ground and spitting on the ground are both signs in themselves, of course, the former natural, resulting in human compassion, and the latter supernatural, resulting in a superhuman miracle and belief, the genuine mark of a sign. Here we have two very different public signs, but the audience of Jews accepts each as an act of power.

John invests them both with cosmic resonance by identifying them with the original act of creation where man is formed from the "dust of the ground" (Gen 2:7). In the beginning was the Word, which Jesus writes in the dust before the adulterous woman, and also the Light, which Jesus incarnates, as he reminds us after he dismisses the woman (8:12) and before he spits on the ground (9:5). Pointedly, Jesus positions himself at the moment of creation (9:32). In this theatre both ordinary and extraordinary acts, a sign of human power and a sign of divine power—writing and spitting—shatter the vessels of tradition, scattering the old laws and writings to the wind.

John places both acts squarely within the prophetic tradition, wellspring of new vocabularies, from signs, such as Ezekiel's iron pan, to visionary metaphors, such as his four-faced man with four wings. Yet these acts muddy the miraculous nature of the true sign. John complicates our conventional understanding by skillfully mixing the natural and supernatural modes, keeping us a little off balance.

Now that John and his Jesus have stirred the dust up, we can make three propositions about signs:

PROPOSITION ONE: SIGNS ARE AMBIDEXTROUS

Presence is a sign—the present wine which once had been water. Absence too is a sign—the body absent from the tomb. Those who believe in the sign receive power. They can be healed. They have access to the unseen world.

Unbelievers, on the other hand, do not know that the sign passes by like a pickpocket, deftly lifting meanings from the secret places of the world. The sign unrecognized appears to another, offering its meanings.

Miracles are signs only to those who believe (6:26). "Jesus could not do miracles where unbelief hinderd" is Blake's succinct summary. Yet John relies on signs to bring his readers to belief.

They have power, we're assured. They are powerful both in themselves, effecting healing, and in their influence, bringing about faith. "This beginning of miracles did Jesus in Cana of Galilee," John sums up, "and manifested forth his glory; and his disciples believed on him." He has just told a wonderful story about water being changed to wine, but he has designs on us. Though attempting to reinforce the power of Jesus' miraculous sign, strangely, he seems to lose faith in the power of his own story. His need to underline its moral, signifying "glory," and its success, causing belief, belies a lack of confidence in the power of the story on his readers. Also, his didactic statements render it anticlimactic. For like Nathaniel they already believed.

Even Jesus doubts the power of the sign. When he feeds the multitude, they are impressed and follow him. We assume that the miracle has had its effect. However, he knows their motives. We can hear the sigh in his voice when he says to them, "You seek me, not because you saw the miracles, but because you did eat of the loaves, and were filled" (6:26).

The people persist in wanting a sign (6:30), as if they had not just seen a most impressive sign. It doesn't point to anything for them except their bellies because it had not yet been interpreted. Hence Jesus interprets, explaining at great length the "bread from heaven."

Signs are signs because Jesus, or John himself, interprets them as signs of something. In his right hand Jesus holds a miraculous loaf of bread that points to something else; in his left he holds bread, just a loaf of fragrant bread. And they are the same bread.

PROPOSITION TWO: SIGNS ARE SUSPICIOUS

Thomas draws his hand from Jesus' side and exclaims, "My Lord and my God" (20:28). But Jesus splashes cold water on his ardor, "Thomas, because you have seen me, you have believed: blessed are they that have not seen, and yet have believed." Even here, after all they have gone through together, Jesus doesn't give the disciples credit. They come to the right belief but for the wrong reason.

They have been taught the power of signs. Yet Thomas must have more than a sign. Seeing is not enough. And Jesus insists that the "blessed" are those who need less than a sign.

John at the end of his book finds himself caught on the same hook. The sign falls short; it is after all only a pointer. And, at the same time, the sign exceeds because it is so seductive. It can take on symbolic power, drawing all into its orbit and radiating everywhere. Yet it is somewhat arbitrary. For he admits that Jesus performed "many other signs" which John did not record in his book (20:30), underscoring his work of selection as a writer. On the one hand, this is the author's humility; on the other, it's his boast meant to overwhelm the reader.

Yet it's a puzzling move because Jesus has exhausted the sign by becoming the ultimate sign, which obviates the need to see. This is the supreme irony of his encounter with Thomas. Jesus concludes that signs are a crutch (20:29). There won't be any more signs which is, in fact, the more "blessed" state.

Explicit in the end, Jesus reveals this attitude earlier. He is the reluctant performer of signs. A certain nobleman, for example, finds Jesus in Galilee and asks him to heal his son who is near death. The request catches Jesus at a bad time. He does not sympathize or inquire about the boy's circumstances, but turns on the man, saying, "Unless you see signs and wonders, you will not believe" (4:48). This is hardly the point.

Signs are complicated, potent but dangerous. Jesus is nagged by their two-edged nature. He knows they are useful, and so indulges his audience who expects signs. But on this occasion his ambivalence surfaces. His nagging suspicion of signs breaks through, and he responds abruptly without human consideration. He doesn't want to perform.

Jesus' reluctance is affecting. Even though he well knows that "signs" are a trap, Jesus goes ahead and performs the miracle anyway. The father, of course, is not fussy. And John rather satisfied with himself notes that the man and his whole house "believed," didactically enumerating the miracle as Jesus' second sign. Yet there remains an exasperated note in Jesus' parting words to the nobleman, "Go your way; your son lives."

Having doubts, Jesus acts. He is still conflicted. But then John blunders in and tallies one more sign, underlining the very thing that makes Jesus uneasy. To John's credit it makes us uneasy too, makes us consider that Jesus is right to be uneasy, and John is right to point this up.

We know that Jesus knows more than John writing, yet John wrote what Jesus knew. This irony creates a fine tension, something of that which Jesus strained under when he replied so abruptly to the nobleman's earnest request.

PROPOSITION THREE: SIGNS ARE VORACIOUS

Did Jesus heal the man's son ultimately out of human concern? Or, alternatively, with signs on his mind, Jesus' initial reaction in ignoring the man's distress extended into his work. Performing the miracle as a means to an end, using it as a tool to secure an expected outcome, perhaps Jesus was not at all interested in securing the man's relief and happiness but instead the man's belief.

The sign as vortex, sucking all into its insatiable center. Metamorphosing from prolific to devourer, the sign bares its teeth. The prophetic act radiating human meaning becomes a tyrannizing abstraction. The human devoured by the purposeful.

A man born blind passes by and the disciples, assuming that he's either blind because of his own or his parents' sins, ask Jesus which was the cause. Jesus answers neither. The man was struck blind from birth, Jesus says, so he could serve as a sign. He is blind for this very occasion "that the works of God should be made manifest in him" (9:3). A chilling proposition.

Can it be that a man is made to suffer merely to be used as a sign? The sign becomes simply a technology for bringing about one end. And to Jesus, therefore, the man becomes an instrument for realizing this purpose. He is not a man but a sign to be interpreted.

Jesus' is the most disturbing of the three hypotheses proposed for his blindness (though we're repulsed by the other two as well). John doesn't flinch from its cruel implications. Jesus' objective subordinates the man's life. And John has Jesus underscore this with a note of urgency, saying, "I must work the works of him that sent me, while it is day: the night comes, when no man can work." More of an indictment, Jesus ignores the man himself and his suffering, and interprets the man's state in blithely symbolic terms: "I am the light of the world."

Even the miraculous raising of his beloved friend Lazarus becomes an act to be interpreted. Jesus insists that his act is a sign (11:4). In this event Jesus shows a genuine concern that he hasn't evidenced before, but the sign devours the work. Jesus shifts focus away from Lazarus and makes himself the one raised, the one to whom belief by the power of the Lazarus sign must be transferred (11:25). He is no longer primarily friend but pure sign. As such, Lazarus doesn't get to speak, his words being swallowed up to preserve the mysterious power of the sign, which Jesus appropriates.

∼

Lazarus climaxes John's sequence of signs: changing the water to wine (chapter 2); healing the nobleman's son (c. 4) and the cripple (c. 5); feeding the multitude (c. 6); walking on water (c. 6); and restoring the blind man's sight (c. 9). In the Lazarus sign (present) is the Jesus sign (future), which climaxes John's book itself. The thing interpreted becomes its interpretation. Thus the family's actual anxiety, grief, and subsequent joy are lost. As the sign (Jesus appropriating Lazarus) becomes the signed (Jesus himself), all human meaning is devoured.

In his orchestration of signs John is right to show us Jesus revealing their danger. As they successively demonstrate increased power and scope, they become farther removed from their human context. John knows the danger here at the climax of his miracle series that Jesus doesn't fully comprehend, as he turns even his friend into a sign. Jesus is not primarily concerned about Lazarus but about what he means. Yet Jesus well knows the complications of signs. In John's dutiful enumeration and touching faith in their efficacy, even when they prove to be ineffective or even dangerous, is a sweet irony. Which revelation to the reader only shows that like any true poet John is capable of thinking against his own thought.

These ironies add up to the wonderfully ironic fact that only the reader knows the sign's real character. Only we know the whole story. And we're uneasy. Its status and power are ambiguous. Neither the thing itself nor the thing pointed to, the sign occupies a threshold world. Both act itself (miraculous "work") and presupposed act (work of belief), the power of the sign is two-edged. It expands the human, challenging prevailing cultural assumptions, even as it contracts the human, sacrificing desire and compassion to abstraction ("glory"). That John's poetic imagination can comprehend this paradox tells us much about his power as a writer and character as a man.

John

The stutter is the plot.

—Charles Olson

Counter thought thought out.

—Susan Howe

I

To open your book in a way that invites direct comparison with the magnificent opening of Genesis is supreme confidence. Only Dante and Blake share John's authorial chutzpah. Born partly of his passionate desire for more life, it is also born of a single-minded need to convince his readers of the reality of this life everlasting. Energizing the present and promising an everlasting future, "eternal life" is for John the ground of all being and hence evades the law of death. A life embodied in Jesus.

Radiating immortality, Jesus inhabits what the poet H.D. calls the "over-conscious world" in contrast to the "sub-conscious" realm of "sleeping dreams" and physical love. This is the visionary "world of waking dreams and the world great lovers enter, spiritual lovers, but only the greatest." Imagination and desire reign here. It is a world of paradox: the way up is the way down, the last shall be first. Opposites resolved. The split in our consciousness between who we are and what life makes us is healed.

This world, that is, mediates the private and public. While night dreams remain inward, daydreams extend outward. They are yearnings let loose in the conscious world of our common life. Waking dreams are desire that changes the world. The prophets were most familiar with these dreams—visions—and derived power from them.

II

John portrays Jesus as a hero of the spirit. A great spiritual lover, Jesus lives a waking dream. His desire for life is so great, it appears outwardly to be a death wish. His love for the world is so great, it can easily be mistaken for judgment and rejection of the world. His desire is a whirlwind sweeping all into its vortex. The hero Jesus rides this great wind like the Son of Man rides Ezekiel's chariot. John's hero is large. Jesus encompasses friend and stranger, rich and poor, male and female, loved and unloved. And John is in love with his hero.

Like all heroes Jesus is irascible and arrogant. He can be ridiculous, talking nonsense. At the same time, he weeps over Lazarus and loves Peter the impulsive one and John the smitten one. His beauty manifests itself as he shows compassion for the woman at the well and humility in washing the feet of his followers.

The waking dream he lives is all encompassing. It includes the natural as well as the human world. John gives us Jesus as a force of nature. He can make water do what he wants, become a floor to walk on, without waiting for it to freeze, or wine to celebrate with. He is, after all, the vine. It is no great stretch to see him as "the grapes that hung against the sun-lit walls," as H.D. does.

Bursting our sunny reverie, John confronts us with the Jesus of force. His torque like a tornado's, as John's book nears its end, displayed in swirling monologues and wild mind swerves is unnerving. Not without some justification, H.D. concludes that "He was the gulls screaming at low tide and tearing the small crabs from among the knotted weeds."

III

Great was Jesus' desire to remake and center the world in himself. So great, we are convinced that it will not be thwarted. A typical hero's or child's desire, we could easily dismiss this colossal daydream. Summoning all his powers as a writer, however, John gives us the flesh and bones of Jesus' waking dream.

IV

For it is John's as well. His greatest wish is to live forever, and we recognize his motives as our own. "Because death is built-in," as the artist Jacob Landau observes, "we seek immortality through identification with ideas, movements, heroes." In short, "we are figure-oriented, we are narcissists, we want to live forever," provided, of course, that our body and curiosity remain intact. Not since John has such a passionate desire for immortality been expressed, save perhaps in the Spanish poet Juan Ramón Jiménez' naked cry of longing prompted by an ordinary sunset, "Serene last evening, / short as a life, / end of all that was loved, / I want to be eternal."

John pushes the envelope of a desire we all share. More than any of the gospel writers, John emphasizes Eternal Life. He stakes his whole book on its reality. He gambles with nothing less than his own life. John's desire for immortality, however, is no more extreme than some current technoptimists, such as Ray Kurzweil, whose fantasy is that "we will be software," and "the essence of our identity will switch to the permanence of our software." We will never die because "our immortality will be a matter of being sufficiently careful to make frequent backups."

The difference is that John does not look to some future technology to fulfill his longing for eternal life, but to a living person within his own experience. As a technician of the sacred, one who has learned to leverage his encounter with incandescence, John seeks to lay out for his readers the way to satisfy their longing. John gives us Jesus' new language, confident that we will make it our own and that it will transform us. More than identifying with the figure of Jesus, he undergoes a metamorphosis, his body becoming the Jesus body. And so he experiences immortality.

The emanations of Jesus' life in his signs and breathstream of language lift John toward life like a newborn baby, even as Jesus is lifted up on the cross. His is radiance so bright that in John's mind it cannot be allowed to end. Thus, as Jesus is lifted up to death, so he is lifted out of the ground to life. Thus John wants us to appropriate this life for ourselves, just as he has made a new self out of this life.

Or viewed from the outside, this incandescent character is strong enough to ameliorate the fundamental shocks of being human: first, the glorious fact that the world exists at all, which is why John opens his book with a hymn, "In the beginning." Second, the tragic fact of our absolute knowledge that the world is temporary. It will be gone, ultimately burn up in an apocalypse of our own making—war (humanity having devoured itself); or of the innocent cosmos' making—star death (our sun having consumed all its helium fuel). Like us, John is desperate to hold on to the world, insisting that the spirit will never pass away. The Comforter, eternal life itself will always be in us and we in it.

V

The child's desire to remake the world in his own image is woven with the hero's desire to flout death. Jesus is beautiful and ridiculous. The writer who sets out to depict an experience of radiance finds himself, if he is a great writer, presenting the ridiculous. For the figure of beautiful compassion and vision, one who lived the waking dream of life and more life, must in the world that is ours have an aspect of the ridiculous.

In this respect John shares with Cervantes a singular achievement, who set out in Don Quixote, according to Dostoevsky, "to present a positively beautiful man." This is the "most difficult subject in the world," he explained to his niece Sophia Ivanova, "because the task is so infinite." To Dostoevsky, John and Cervantes were the only writers to succeed in presenting a "positively beautiful person in the world."

Approaching the infinite, however, John approaches the absurd. He is transfixed by "the manifestation of the beautiful," the incarnation of a waking dream in Jesus. This is the true subject of his book.

And as a writer committed to pursuing this infinite goal, to present his experience of a radiant "manifestation," he accepts the possibility of the absurd. In literature Jesus' only rival, Dostoevsky reminds us, is that "beautiful individual" Don Quixote, whose bizarre behavior is well known. Understandably, John suffers considerable anxiety about the possibility of his hero appearing to be ridiculous (e.g., 6:6). But Jesus, like Don Quixote, is "beautiful only because he is ridiculous." Furthermore, like Jesus, "it was by making himself ridiculous," Miguel de Unamuno insists, "that Don Quixote achieved his immortality."

VI

This realization binds Nicodemus to Jesus. And John develops their relationship to dramatize an aspect of his own stance toward the hero. Nicodemus must visit and observe this Jesus who lives the life only dreamed of, that of a "teacher come from God" (3:2). Though for this very reason they can only exchange ironies, leaving their dialog forever open. More important, Nicodemus must defend the necessity of Jesus' outrageousness, his absurdity, in the eyes of those who do not understand his mission, insisting that they observe and hear (7:50). Finally, Nicodemus must honor the man who accomplished his beautiful and ridiculous mission (19:39).

This difficult glittering man is in the eyes of most dedicated to an absurd end. Given Jesus' stubborn provocation of his enemies and cryptic explanation to his followers, it is an end more comic than tragic. In this John agrees, for he has made a comedy like Dante's book, ending in life and light.

VII

Yet Jesus' response to an individual woman met at a well or brought to him in the temple, having been caught in the act of adultery, is far from absurd. Nicodemus, who was doubtless on the periphery of the crowd surrounding this woman, knew the beautiful Jesus as well. John gives us a hero who insists that as individuals we're special, not just as a people. Jesus' beauty is manifest in this insistence. John responds with love to love. Jesus gives the individual significance and meaning, not primarily political or social but personal.

John does not merely follow or even believe. He depicts a hero who invokes in us something more. This hero, unlike those John knew from the stories he heard as a child or read as a man, such as Plutarch's *Parallel Lives*, perhaps, confers value not on politicians or generals who have won fame, but on a particular fisherman or crippled beggar or despised foreigner or woman of the streets. It is a fundamentally anti-aristocratic stance.

VIII

Jesus never explains his motives. John does not present us with a Jesus who pauses for moments of self examination or even reflection. He is not Hamlet. We know Jesus by reaction. His center is hidden, and John can only place him in circumstances of social bombardment, observe the ricochets, and construct his character based on the pattern of deflections.

We know Jesus by John's crab-like progress in constructing the character of his hero. This method of proceeding arises from his anxieties. We are never far from his explanations rooted in a fear that his hero may appear absurd. His narrative hiccups, halting suddenly as he pauses to underline or interpret. John is concerned that we not miss his point and, in fact, come to believe. Interjecting, he excuses the high priest of the Jews from personal culpability and explains the real meaning of Caiaphas' words (11:51). More boldly, he tells us what Jesus really thought (11:38). Jesus, however, is simpler. Though women become more important to him as he comes into a fuller sense of his self, and monologues become more frequent as he comes into a fuller realization of his imminent death, he remains relatively unchanged from the beginning of the book to the end.

But John does change. He comes to respect Nicodemus, even needing him. He finds himself bathing Thomas in irony, taking him less seriously than at first. Conversely, he takes Jesus' mother more seriously. Paralleling these, as Jesus' authority is solidified in his signs, John's anxieties about authority become increasingly acute. But there's no question about his growing affection for some of his fellow disciples. The buffoon Peter, awkward at first in love, becomes the graceful recipient of a love that exalts him in the rising sun on the beach. And John, though envious, is exalted with him.

IX

John is the strong persuader. Infused with the force of the character he portrays, John makes his book of Jesus. His is the confidence of the lover. And John accepts the waking dream of Jesus as his own. Or Jesus' waking dream happens serendipitously to be John's. How can we know? He can say with Cervantes, substituting Jesus for the knight, "For me alone Don Quixote was born and I for him; it was for him to act, for me to write, and we two are one."

The next step is that their waking dream becomes ours or that ours finds congruence with theirs. John desires to change his mortal self to immortal. Having done this, he wants to create desire in us, desire to be one with Jesus, that is, to believe and thereby to change ourselves. Thus John becomes seducer.

Persuasion and seduction are married. The story of Jesus is a love story. John's Jesus loves him as he loves Jesus. By definition, the lovers in a love story face obstacles. John makes it clear that Jesus is going to achieve his objective but "not yet," his hour not yet come. Full understanding of his love for John will come later.

Likewise, complete knowledge of Jesus' love for death comes later, in the moment of death itself and its happy resolution in resurrection. The obstacle to Jesus' love for John and to his love for death, keeping them apart, is the same: lack of knowledge. Overcoming this creates the suspense of John's love story as well as its meaning. In the end John experiences Jesus' full love, as does Jesus' mother and his disciple Peter. In the same moment, Jesus experiences union with death. John is rightfully confident he can seduce his reader as he himself has been seduced.

X

John's confidence is matched only by his anxiety. Following the twists and turns of the man Jesus is not easy. John's purpose is simple, but in the writing of his partial life of Jesus, which relates selected events only, the execution becomes complex. On the one hand, he writes from an understanding born of love; on the other, he writes from within love's mystery. He finds that Jesus is habitually less than straightforward. As a result, John stutters in the telling, pausing to interpret, backtracking, repeating.

To ease his anxiety, he adopts an ironic posture. We do not get just the hero. We also get the ironic counter hero; John gives us Jesus and Nicodemus. The counter is the complement of the hero, not the antithesis. The anti-hero, such as Judas, provides a perfect foil for the hero. This symmetry is useful as well as pleasing. It is easily handled and causes John no hesitation.

But the counter hero nags John. He's of two minds whether to include him or not and oscillates between accepting and rejecting the character. Judas is necessary to his hero. He enables John to dramatize Jesus more effectively and paint him in bold strokes. Nicodemus, however, is unnecessary. He can only fuzz the picture and reveal John's handling his anxiety about exactly what kind of hero he's portraying.

XI

John explicitly states his purpose of bringing us to belief, seducing us into loving his hero, which is to say believing on his name. He clings tenaciously to this persuasive program, enumerating the signs and reminding us of his designs on us, but at the same time his moves belie another purpose.

He proceeds like a pamphleteer, but discovers like a writer. In the telling of his story he discovers what is counter to his conscious intent. This is not opposed to his intent, so much as oblique to it. His discovery cuts across any single path forward. Having integrity, he must fold this truth into his story. Hence he includes in addition to Nicodemus the counter hero Caiaphas and, as we'll see, the counterplot of deferred understanding versus immediate knowledge.

John's thought as a writer is counter thought. In this respect John needs Caiaphas. An unlikely candidate for John's program, he uses this counter hero for his own ends. He consciously includes him in the tale, giving him a pivotal role, which could well have remained implicit in his narrative. In the figure of Caiaphas John brings to the surface of his consciousness a thought counter to his program, which must be enfolded into it if it is to be true.

XII

One of John's most dramatic scenes presents Jesus before Caiaphas, while outside in the courtyard Peter denies any knowledge of Jesus. John introduces Caiaphas by reminding us that we've met him before and telling us why. He draws our attention to the man, the same Caiaphas who "gave counsel to the Jews," saying, "that it was expedient that one man should die for the people" (18:14). Why does John bring Caiaphas back and train the camera on him?

A brilliant move on John's part, Caiaphas enables him to dramatize and expand his arena of persuasion. He moves beyond a personal relation with the hero of his book. It is aesthetically satisfying that John bring this character back because he provides a social, even mythic perspective on the action (Jesus as fulfilling the traditional role of scapegoat). And our being taken from the garden, Peter brandishing his sword and the servant bleeding from the side of his head, to the pinnacle of political power in one fell swoop is a heady experience.

But it is necessary to John that we view the action from inside and from outside. Caiaphas allows John to show us the truth of the situation. Caiaphas is not an anti- but counter-hero. He is not the negation of Jesus like Pilate but his shadow. A lesser writer would have kept the focus exclusively on his hero.

The camera shifts to the courtyard scene:

> Then says the damsel that kept the door unto Peter, Are not you also one of this man's disciples? He says, I am not. And the servants and officers stood there, who had made a fire of coals; for it was cold: and they warmed themselves: and Peter stood with them, and warmed himself. (18:17–18)

And a lesser writer would have left this out, a wonderfully moving scene. The servants and officers, Peter trying to mix unobtrusively, all standing around the fire, all is so cozy. But it's a lie; we know Peter's anguish. He doesn't feel like he blends in. He only wanted to please a pretty girl in an unguarded moment, relishing her attention and not wanting to shut down conversation right away, to say nothing of not being particularly brave. And who can blame him. Who would have done differently under such highly charged circumstances?

Back to the inside, a shot of Caiaphas:

> The high priest then asked Jesus of his disciples, and of his doctrine. And when he had thus spoken, one of the officers which stood by struck Jesus with the palm of his hand, saying, Do you answer the high priest so? Jesus answered him, If I have spoken evil, bear witness of the evil: but if well, why do you smite me? (18:19–23)

As we experience this confrontation and violence, which John alone among the gospel writers reports, the previous scene haunts us. John deftly counterpoints the inside and outside scenes. He forces us to see both at the same time. We can't forget for a moment Peter in the courtyard warming his hands, feeling more and more miserable, while inside Jesus is being struck with a hand. Jesus is as direct as Peter is evasive.

XIII

I'm awed by John's ability to get us to identify with Peter, then Jesus, and then both at the same time. We can't help respecting and thus believing a narrator who cares equally for the hero and the coward, and stirs in us equal empathy.

Then John raises the stakes, as the scene moves outside again:

> One of the servants of the high priest, being his kinsman whose ear Peter cut off, says, Did not I see you in the garden with him? Peter then denied again: and immediately the cock crowed. (18:26–27)

John times the discovery exactly right. We're in his hands all the way. A fine dramatic move to have the servant seemingly in innocence (with a rhetorical question) but clearly in revenge query Peter. And the cock crowing is the perfect climax. John milks the irony that the bird associated with dawn and light (and with sex, sounding the overtones of Peter's encounter with the girl at the start of the scene) is the one to announce Peter's failure in the night. And, of course, on the beach later as the sun rises Peter accepts Jesus' forgiveness.

Now once more inside, shot of Jesus with Caiaphas fading in the background:

> Then led they Jesus from Caiaphas unto the hall of judgment: and it was early; and they themselves went not into the judgment hall, lest they should be defiled; but that they might eat the passover. (18:28)

The counterpointed scenes, the questioning of Jesus and Peter, are neither foreground nor background. John's counter thought erases these categories, for both scenes are equally prominent. John could have kept the camera on his hero, but instead shifts back and forth, giving the hero and the coward equal time. He increases the dramatic tension by emphasizing contrasts.

XIV

But what of the counter hero Caiaphas? John cuts alternately from outside (courtyard) to inside (judgment hall). This spatial alternation corresponds to John's psychological state, resisting and accepting Caiaphas as necessary to the truth of the story. The girl questions Peter. Cut. Caiaphas questions Jesus. Cut. Caiaphas' servant questions Jesus. Cut. Jesus is led away from Caiaphas. We find that Caiaphas, in fact, is present in each scene, as we realize that in the second scene his servant has been present with Peter from the first. At the same time, John doesn't give him any words, reporting only indirectly his questioning Jesus about his beliefs and followers.

Yet Caiaphas swags over the entire drama. We feel his shadow across each scene. His presence makes us uneasy like a huge awkward bird sitting in the middle of our living room, watching. Then we realize that John has made it clear why he includes Caiaphas in the drama. Ironically, he alone knows what the drama means. Caiaphas carries the meaning that John discovered but resists: the identification of Jesus here as the sacrificial scapegoat.

John's thought is the hero achieving his objective heroically, which ostensibly the scene dramatizes: to stand and die. Jesus' defense appears unassailable. He turns the tables on Caiaphas and asks a question himself, one that goes to the heart of the matter. Can Caiaphas produce witnesses to support his charges or not. Our hero stands boldly, meeting question with question.

In contrast, Peter accepts the lead of his questioners, following the path of least resistance. Counterpointing them, John makes Peter the perfect foil for Jesus. Peter makes the hero look heroic. He also stands as an equal with the hero in our affection, owing to John's skill as a writer. This relationship enhances the hero's stature by tying him to life, rather than making him larger than life, while at the same time evoking our admiration and empathy.

John's counter thought is Caiaphas. This character does nothing to make the hero seem more heroic. In fact, Caiaphas has him humiliated. By the same token, he does not come into direct conflict with the hero. Instead, Caiaphas dogs the entire proceedings with a dark meaning. He bears John's covert thought that this scene dramatizes an impersonal force dedicated to defeating the hero by amputating him from the body politic like a gangrenous leg. The hero does not act on his own, but was set up by something more powerful, more heroic. John's counter thought thought out. We witness John of two minds in oscillation, both necessary for truth to be finally stammered out.

XV

"For neither did his brothers believe in him" (7:5). Why would John stop to point out that Jesus' own brothers didn't believe his claims? He did not need to report what seems on the face of it, at least in part, a failure of his hero's program. If Jesus can't convince his own brothers, what chance does he have in convincing strangers? Jesus' brothers, along with Caiaphas and others, constitute a whole group that counterpoints the believers which Jesus collects along the way. And John insists in his book on this party of disbelief.

It is a shrewd move, aside from its honesty, because John is able to incorporate two views of his hero simultaneously, at once creating and dispelling his own perplexities. Just when we think Jesus most outrageous, even ridiculous, John performs a mental judo move. He encourages us to let our own doubts surface and face the same question the audience of strangers (Jews), followers, and family face, namely, whether Jesus is a "good man" or "deceives the people" (7:12). John forces us to take counter heroes like Nicodemus seriously in a way that we don't have to take a traitor. The party of disbelief is not only key to the dramatic success of John's story but essential to its truth.

That John imagines fully all possible stances with regard to Jesus is an astounding writer's feat and the principal aspect of the book that keeps us interested in this many-faceted man who is the subject of his tale. He embeds within his book its own criticism, a disarming strategy, just as he continually raises the problem of its interpretation: the disciples' interpretation of Jesus' words, Jesus' interpretation of the prophets' words as recorded in the Jewish scriptures, and both parties' interpretation of the "signs" that John selects for us.

Like science and poetry, John's book succeeds in incorporating doubt. The true artist incorporates what is different from oneself in building the self. John is more lover than believer and to this degree more a man of knowledge than faith, closer to Nicodemus than Thomas.

XVI

Lodged deeply in the story, furthermore, is what I call John's Inverse Law of Belief. Not growing up with Jesus (as a brother) or knowing his father (as did the Jews) correlates with belief. Jesus himself senses this, admitting that he has "no honour in his own country" (4:44). In short, though not absolute, belief is inversely proportional to distance from Jesus. His own brothers don't believe, and many disciples turn away (6:66). At the middle distance, an acquaintance like Nicodemus and Jesus' countrymen (Galileans, 4:50; neutral rulers, 12:42) neither believe nor disbelieve. While at the farthest remove from Jesus, complete strangers believe, like the Samaritans (4:39).

More than merely a rhetorical move, this is radical. It is lodged like a splinter in John's story, irritating and calling attention to itself, so we can never rest easy with his telling the tale. Bluntly put, to those who know his family and origins, Jesus' claims seem to be grandiose or simply not credible. John himself doesn't seem easy with this, and it becomes a source of anxiety. For who could better judge Jesus' credibility than his brothers?

John may have raised a tougher question than he intended. As a writer, he takes a great risk. We may identify more with Jesus' brothers and those disciples who left him than John wants us to.

Yet we are experiencing John's own identification. For he oscillates between giving us a man who's annoyed by the crowd, like any celebrity, and an otherwordly Jesus, the Logos who exists outside history. We see the Jesus who lives in the moment while a woman brushes his feet with her hair, and the Jesus who floats in some other realm where he inhabits the hour yet to come. He's the victim, discovered on the shore by a persistent, jostling rabble of people, and he's the magician able to escape unnoticed through the middle of a crowd. Genius often appears magnetically exhilarating and ridiculous at the same time.

Up close and personal, Jesus could well come off as a comic figure making grandiose claims about himself and living out his own fantasies. His personal waking dream having about as much relevance to the world as a wet dream. Familiarity seems to be a great antidote to hero worship.

XVII

As a writer John has no choice but to adopt this double point of view, not Jesus accepted or rejected but both at once. Yet incorporating the party of disbelief creates anxiety about his own authority in relating Jesus' story that manifests itself in John's inclusion of counter heroes and a counterplot.

If John is anxious about his own authority in telling his hero's story, he is doubly anxious about establishing his hero's authority. The beleaguered pamphleteer, trying to establish the truth of his tale, reveals his own uncertainty by continually insisting that he's telling the truth (19:35; 21:24). Rather than proceed with the confidence displayed in his opening hymn, narrating smoothly and swiftly, he breaks off unexpectedly or shifts his point of view abruptly. He also interrupts his trajectory with asides and repetitions.

Unlike the authors of the typical hero stories of his time, John cannot tell a black-and-white, straight-ahead tale because his task self-destructs. His telling and all its tricks of verisimilitude, such as the exact number of fish caught (153), must fall away before the hero who transcends such a story. After all, coming back to life Jesus escapes the story that John tells, returning to the disciples as the "Comforter" after the story ends. He manages to free himself of the writer John at last.

More disconcerting, as John proceeds authoritatively in the manner of most narrators, he must establish the credibility of a self-authenticating hero who offers himself as principal proof for his claims about himself. Jesus is not joking when he says he has two witnesses that will attest who he is: his Father and himself. John is of two minds about this and stammers. One part of him nods assent, muttering "Yes, Jesus is Jesus and God is God," the father who can vouch for him. Another part coughs, looks down and admits with Jesus, in a speech John gives him, that Jesus is in fact God. Two become one gutting the claim of two. Owing to the circularities of John's task, we are not surprised that he is anxious. The waking dream proceeds less like an arrow than a snake.

XVIII

Yet all the things in his book, he says, "are written, that you might believe that Jesus is the Christ, the Son of God; and that believing you might have life through his name" (20:31). John's purpose could not be more overtly stated and targeted. He does not merely want to tell a story or teach us. Rather, like Blake and Kafka he wants nothing less than that his book change our lives.

Consciously continuing in the line of the prophet-writer, he wants his word to be more than words. He makes his book the last sign pointing to the last prophet, the Messiah who obviates all signs. He wants the sign of his book to have the power of magic, transforming our lives through its presenting the life of the ultimate prophet. Pronouncing its words in us, John trusts his book to turn the water of our ordinary life into the wine of everlasting life.

Yet this clearly stated purpose is whistling in the dark. It is a hopeful tag appended to what has already been wrought. So John moves on briskly. And because he has succeeded in presenting with such uncanny presence the figure of Nicodemus, we recall him and read what has come before this perfunctory statement of purpose through his eyes.

We cannot help but compare John's one-sentence assertion of purpose, that is, with his preceding book's embodiment of purpose. What he says and what he does are different. At the end of his book he brings himself back to a conscious purpose that was no doubt the initial impulse for the book. Yet in the meantime his book has taken over. For he has in reality done a lot more than his stated aim, and he knows it. His writer's instinct and his personal integrity have asserted themselves, as he uses a skillful interplay of narrative and drama to reveal with great force believers and unbelievers, hero and counter hero.

His own words subvert his intent. When John tries to confine himself to a single meaning, as if "belief" was simple, he blossoms with meanings like petals.

XIX

A writer, John is set apart like the prophet. His book like his hero goes against the grain of an aristocratic culture. Furthermore, as a member of a tiny group of outsiders (followers of Jesus) within a minority (Jews) on the fringes of the Roman empire, John is understandably anxious to establish his credentials.

This is exacerbated because John's authority, he realizes, ultimately rests on the authority of the hero he depicts. He has Jesus bluster, when pressed by the Pharisees who dismiss out of hand his circular claim to authority, "Though I bear record of myself, yet my record is true: for I know whence I came, and whither I go; but you cannot tell whence I come, and whither I go" (8:14). No attempt to argue the point, no elaboration let alone explanation. He merely asserts once again that he is privy to a reality they are not. In short, he inhabits a waking dream, his own, which they do not.

Not very satisfying and thus guaranteed to give John pause, but in fact this is the sum of Jesus' claim to authority, as it is for anyone who pursues their waking dream. The blunt and unarguable response of the world has always been and will be that of the Pharisees: "You bear record of yourself; your record is not true." As Blake says, however, it is futile to ask of records, historical or otherwise, that they be true.

Yet hounded by this implicit charge, one John accepts, he continues his convoluted and increasingly desperate attempt (through chapter 19) to establish his authority. Jesus himself is on the defensive because he realizes, as does John, that he's ultimately vouching for himself. This is John's most difficult problem because this type of claim is always suspect. John himself knows he is on shaky ground.

XX

The problem won't release its grip. John returns to it at the end of his book, claiming to be witness to Jesus' actions, "And he that saw it bare record, and his record is true" (19:35). And he attempts to back up his claims by putting them in the context of what the prophetic books said should happen "that the scripture should be fulfilled." Yet this is the author's own version of his hero's circular argument.

To compensate, John is often hyperspecific, causing his story to stutter like a blade drawing through a sharpener. In the scene where Peter cuts the servant's ear off, John gives us his name, Malchus (18:10). This is a strange detail, smacking of John's overeager attempt to establish verisimilitude. It is an awkward move. On other occasions he is overly fastidious about time, noting when he descended from a mount, and place. He mentions Bethabara (1:28) as if to reassure us that he was there, for example, yet the name itself means "the place of crossing over," potentially useful as a symbol, though he refrains. The naming is gratuitous, distracting us. He simply attempts to localize out of his anxiety.

John seems at times not to trust his tale. He succumbs to an anxiety about who he is and who his hero is and whether his reader will catch the argument for Jesus as Messiah. Thus his true argument is not as Dostoevsky claims, to give us a "positively beautiful man," but to present an encounter with incandescence.

XXI

And John's principal method of presentation is irony, which he uses with such dazzling effect in the early dialog between Jesus and Nicodemus. John's is a fundamentally ironic mind, as in this later scene: "Much people of the Jews therefore knew that he was there: and they came not for Jesus' sake only, but that they might see Lazarus also, whom he had raised from the dead. But the chief priests consulted that they might put Lazarus also to death" (12:9–10). Yes, of course, he could die twice. What a macabre possibility that John can't resist.

Throughout his book we are privileged with John (and Jesus) to know how the story ends, knowledge that the disciples do not have. John characteristically employs dramatic irony. And it's not confined to the reader and writer. Sometimes John is blatant about Jesus' own love of irony: "Judas then, having received a band of men and officers from the chief priests and Pharisees, comes to there with lanterns and torches and weapons. Jesus therefore, knowing all things that should come upon him, went forth, and said unto them, Whom seek you?" (18:3–4). It is not, of course, difficult to surmise, given the nature of the band and their bearing weapons. And we remember Jesus' previous provocation. John savors the irony of Jesus asking them when he knows both the answer and the fact that they know him.

Did John get his irony from Jesus or impute his irony to Jesus? Either way, irony is clearly John's habitual mode. Woven into the details of dialog and scene, irony is the warp of the central drama of understanding and misunderstanding, belief and disbelief. It threads the entire book, counter hero calling the hero into question and vice versa, as it must, given John's anxiety about his subject and role as narrator.

Irony, in short, enables John to handle complexity, namely, the ecstasy of his encounter with Jesus. The paradoxical and the absurd combine in the character of Jesus. John is fully aware of the beauty and absurdity of a Jesus who lives the waking dream of eternal life. Irony is John's strategy for coping and exploring. And ultimately it enables him to present his hero's waking dream, which has become his own, that "you may believe."

You

The "you" at every turn in John's book is targeted by the word. Some duck, many succumb, all squirm. They feel its force in Jesus' formula, drawn like a bowstring, "Verily, verily, I say unto you." The recipient "you," Jew or disciple, skeptic or traitor is confronted. Jesus does not so much appeal to the "you," as loose his word in the world, continuing to speak when the "you" he addresses has fallen silent (Nicodemus) or even exited (the woman taken in adultery). Yet he demands from the "you" an action in response, not merely rhetorical assent or dissent.

Jesus does not ultimately aim to persuade but to present. John gives us a Jesus who comes to announce not to argue. Nicodemus grasps this perfectly and falls silent. Neither believer nor nonbeliever, still Nicodemus responds as the "you" whom Jesus succeeds in striking with his word. John records, however, that many hearers chose not to respond. Not out of malice or considered rejection, they simply heard and walked on by (the position of many in our own age for whom "God" is not even a question).

Jesus acts on the assumption, nevertheless, that what he announces will elicit from the "you" a response. John establishes this paradigm early in his book. Jesus speaks and the "you" seeks: "And the two disciples heard him speak, and they followed Jesus. Then Jesus turned, and saw them following, and says unto them, What do you seek?" (1:37–38). The word is simply spoken and the listener responds. With characteristic irony, Jesus pretends not to know the force of his announcing. And his own response in turn underscores the power of his speaking, as if it were beyond him.

John invites us to observe this speak-and-seek drama within the frame of his book. In fact, it is a principal drama of his story. We identify first with one character then another, substituting ourselves for the "you" at any point in Jesus' "I say unto you." We are the Jews challenging. We are Peter denying or Mary entranced. We are resentful Judas or Jesus' brothers disgusted with his posturing. We are Nicodemus engaging Jesus in a conversation by night and being rebuffed. But John has a surprise for us. He introduces another "you."

Accustomed to observing and variously identifying with others caught up in the speak-and-seek drama, we're shocked when John breaks through the frame of his book. As free-floating participants in the "you," identifying with each of Jesus' addressees, we have become comfortable within the frame. Then John turns the tables on us, speaking for the only time directly to another "you," the reader. At the end of his book, he addresses the reader within the frame of a future time and distant place, explaining that all the scenes of the drama he has presented have been "written that you might believe" (20:31). We're stopped in our tracks by a searchlight. This "you" includes his readers—us—arrested in the act of reading.

∼

Included in the "you," we cannot avoid John's demands. We can no longer stand outside his scenes, but have now become part of the drama. Within both frames, that of the book and that of the reader reading John's book, we are characters in the scene. And as participants, John expects a response.

His breaking the frame of his drama is a bold strategy for changing us from observers to participants. John's addressing us directly is as disconcerting a move as would a character's suddenly turning toward us in a painting. We are forced to reexamine all that we've seen and heard throughout the course of John's story. Like Cervantes in the second half of his book, making Don Quixote into a character in a book that Don Quixote the character in Cervantes' book hears about, John shifts and collapses frames of reference on us. Thrown off balance, we're made vulnerable. As a result, we're more susceptible to making a response. Our desire to respond crosses a threshold like the point where water turns to steam.

Because Jesus is for John the author of language itself, he lacks Jesus' confidence in the power of language to create desire and effect an action in response. There is a disarming humility in John's "might believe." His fervent desire builds and suddenly surfaces. It is all the more convincing for its breaking out almost as a confession. All the more do we feel that the force of the personal demand he makes reinforces the objective demand of his dramatic scenes and language. He desires and hopes for belief, a response Jesus assumes.

So susceptible are the hearers of Jesus' words that even he is astonished, as in this scene where having never met Nathanael, he greets him as someone he knows, a friend without guile:

> "How do you know me?" Nathanael asked. "Before Philip called you," Jesus answered, "I saw you under the fig tree." Nathanael replied, "Rabbi, you are the Son of God; you are the King of Israel." Jesus answered, "You believe, do you, just because I told you that I saw you under the fig tree? You will see far greater things than that" (1:48–50; trans., R. E. Brown).

Jesus is not only amazed at the power of his simple words, "I saw you under the fig tree," to effect belief, but somewhat disappointed as well. He seems to say, "words are one thing but just let me show you true power." He's boastful and crestfallen at the same time, like a boy whose thunder is stolen as he's about to deliver wonderful news.

Despite what Jesus has just heard, the desired response having already been elicited, Nathanael declaring his belief, Jesus presents his vision of power anyway. Nathanael has just acknowledged that Jesus is the "Son of God" and "the King of Israel," yet Jesus presses right on: "Verily, verily, I say unto you, Hereafter you shall see heaven open, and the angels of God ascending and descending upon the Son of man." His insistence, despite any rationale for it having disappeared at the moment Nathanael responded with belief, is touching. Particularly since the vision he goes on to present is introduced portentously, "Verily, verily," and is not original. It can only be off the point and, even more dispiriting, anticlimactic to Nathanael who already knows Jacob's dream well, an old story.

Jesus doggedly links belief here with a sign. Later in the book, however, he accepts Nathanael's way of coming to belief as equal with the way he favors in this scene. Responding to skeptics, Jesus demands: "Believe me that I am in the Father, and the Father in me," the way of Nathanael; "or else believe me for the very works' sake," the way of signs. Either way, the result is power. "Verily, verily, I say unto you, He that believes on me, the works that I do shall he do also; and greater works than these shall he do" (14:11–12). The act of belief in response to Jesus' demand makes the believer a prophet in his own right who makes his own demands.

The prophet spawned by Jesus can do even greater signs than the prophet himself. Belief must ultimately be divorced from signs, however, because John knows that signs don't always work (10:25–26). Or they're not always recognized as signs. The crowd who has witnessed the feeding of the 5,000 asks Jesus, "What shall we do, that we might work the works of God?" He answers that they must "believe on him whom he has sent." And despite the miracle they have seen, they ask him, "What sign do you show then, that we may see, and believe you?" (6:28–30).

∼

John is clear about the demand for and the outcome of belief, namely immortality, everlasting life. Also, Jesus promises that we'll become prophets in our own right, even gods (10:35). Jesus confers this power as God himself, claiming, "Before Abraham was, I am" (8:58). By believing in the ultimate prophet, who is God, we can according to John be transformed.

John's language of promise creates in us the desire to act, who must finally become the "you" that he and Jesus address. John manipulates our desires by presenting scenes and speeches to achieve the end of belief, a relationship with the one who invites belief. Always it is belief "on" a person, a movement toward the one demanding belief. The model is the lover. Does John's love for Jesus, then, constitute belief? Does his knowing Jesus, as Jesus "knows" his Father, constitute belief? Is John's writing down the words of Jesus belief? Or is his recreating in language the speak-and-seek drama of Jesus belief?

Clear about the demands and rewards of belief, John is curiously oblique about the act of belief itself. More disconcerting, he complicates the possibility of the "you" acting at all. "No man can come to me," Jesus declares at one point, "unless the Father which has sent me draw him" (6:44). John compounds this by maintaining that "Jesus knew from the beginning who they were that believed not, and who should betray him" (6:64). (Thus sadly making Jesus incapable of astonishment, an essential and glorious human trait.) A painful irony results: John constructs his book to create in the "you" of all times and places a desire to believe, that is, creates this desire in the "you" who is incapable of acting with belief because perhaps the Father does not "draw him." Though ultimately unacceptable to John, this irony does reveal the complexity of belief. The truth of the matter involves a paradox. On the one hand, to believe is to will, the thrust of John's book; on the other, it is to succumb to another's will.

But this is the familiar paradox of love, where we find ourselves both intending and falling. John recognizes the mysterious nature of believing. Belief, like love, involves push and pull. We move toward the beloved, but the beloved draws us as well. If this is not understood, John's entire program is futile because any action by the "you" does not matter in a foreordained world. In such a world there is no point in John writing. And hearing Jesus' statement that "no man can come unto me, unless it were given unto him of my Father," we're ready to join those disciples who as a result "walked no more with him" (6:66).

Like Jesus' authority and love itself, belief is self-authenticating. Anything can be believed just as anyone can be loved. For this reason, belief often appears to be madness. A relationship rather than an object, the act of believing is unassailable. Believers are as difficult to understand as the insane.

John recognizes that the act of believing demanded of us must remain elusive. The relationship created by this act cannot be reduced to a formula, but it can be explored, as he does in this dialogue:

> Then said Jesus to those Jews which believed on him, If you continue in my word, then are you my disciples indeed; And you shall know the truth, and the truth shall make you free. They answered him, We be Abraham's seed, and were never in bondage to any man: how say you, You shall be made free? . . . Jesus said unto them, If God were your Father, you would love me: for I proceeded forth and came from God; neither came I of myself, but he sent me. Why do you not understand my speech? even because you cannot hear my word (8:31–43).

We must keep in mind here that Jesus is speaking to Jews "which believed on him," who have responded to his demand and acted. But given their shared tradition with Jesus, they understandably question him further. Jesus is nonetheless increasingly exasperated that they don't understand, as if he wished for a moment at least that belief were a state rather than a relationship. As a result, we become increasingly sympathetic to the Pharisees, who are after all trying to understand, as Jesus loses patience: "You are of your father the devil, and the lusts of your father you will do. He was a murderer from the beginning, and abode not in the truth, because there is no truth in him. When he speaks a lie, he speaks of his own: for he is a liar, and the father of it" (8:44).

Throwing this in their face (they're sons of the devil) is tantamount to throwing in the towel. Then he takes another tack, saying, "And because I tell you the truth, you believe me not." A bitter tone enters here. Jesus had overreacted to their lack of understanding and called them nasty names, but now he is simply sad, shifting to the unwarranted position that they lack belief. The relationship of belief that the Jews have with Jesus is a lover's quarrel. John reveals by this drama that belief is not a substance, not static. Jesus talks himself out of the relationship that John stipulates at the beginning of the dialogue: "Which of you convinces me of sin? And if I say the truth, why do you not believe me? He that is of God hears God's words: you therefore hear them not, because you are not of God" (8:46–47).

Finally, Jesus resorts to this resoundingly circular argument, a rationalization for the conviction he has talked himself into. He's escalated legitimate questions into disbelief. As a result, he concludes that they cannot believe because they are not believers, unable to hear because they don't hear. Jesus is now not surly or bitter, just strangely helpless.

∽

John skillfully creates sympathy for the Jews while inviting us to feel sorry for Jesus who sputters and resorts to name calling—those lying murderous devils—and ends in utter frustration. He seems to want the magic belief that worked with Nathanael, where seeking was the inevitable outcome of speaking. Both parties are strangely equal in this quarrel; neither bests the other in argument and both retain our sympathy, Jesus frustrated and the Jews earnest. Having created in us an even-handed sympathy, John can leave the question of belief open. Do the Jews continue in the relationship of belief that John points to in the beginning of the dialogue or do they break off the relationship as Jesus claims at the end? John forces us to question Jesus' assessment. It is difficult to judge belief without act.

Although John attends to "truth" in his book, this is why truth is irrelevant. Insofar as it has a doctrinal content, that is, he empties "truth" of meaning. For it is the relationship of believer and believed—the "you" moving toward and Jesus/John drawing the "you" —that is the core of belief, an action rather than abstraction. By whatever means established, however desire is manipulated, doctrine is immaterial. Once established, the beliefful relationship, like love, can in and of itself change "you," make us act like immortal beings, personally cared for in the world we're passing through. And who can gainsay this waking dream, anymore than the sustaining fantasies of the mad.

A hard saying, but William Blake is right when he declares that "Every thing possible to be believ'd is an Image of Truth." Aristotle had come to the same conclusion, and William James gives us the working version for our own times: "The true is the name of whatever proves itself to be good in the way of belief." We cannot become the "you" of John's fervent "that you believe," which could as well be translated "that you continue to believe" (in which case, he makes his book for believers and even more emphatically presents belief as relationship rather than doctrine), unless we hold with Blake and Nicodemus.

Missing this fact, many Jews conclude understandably that Jesus is mad (10:20). John answers their slander not with argument but a scene. While Jesus walks in the porch of the temple, the Jews surround him and ask: "How long dost thou make us to doubt? If you be the Christ, tell us plainly. Jesus answered them, I told you, and you believed not . . . because you are not of my sheep, as I said unto you. My sheep hear my voice, and I know them, and they follow me" (10:24–27). Jesus at last speaking "plainly" about belief. Significantly, he considers plain speaking to be parable. He does not debate or even explain when he's forced to respond directly, but tells a story, to his mind the most truthful form of speech. Jesus attempts to gloss this after the pressure is off, as he has a number of times before, saying, "though you believe not me, believe the works: that you may know, and believe" (10:38). But this misses the heart of the matter, the relationship itself. His exhortation merely restates the paths to a relationship of belief, which we know are numerous, as John has made clear, desire being variously and wonderfully aroused. Nathanael only needed to hear; the noblemen needed to hear and see; Thomas not only had to hear and see, but also to touch.

Only in action and parable does Jesus capture the essence of his relationship with the "you." In it he avoids both fatalism and magic. More important, he eschews doctrinal content. Jesus simply says that belief depends on who "you" accept as shepherd. Accept the shepherd, enter into the relationship, then you'll hear his voice, its breath fanning the flame of your belief.

The simplicity of this is beautiful, and it is the key to John's speak-and-seek drama. As a visionary writer, John is attracted to parable, appreciating the power of figurative language, but he is also wary, attempting to explain time and time again. Yet he knows that only parable can capture an inexplicable relationship because it resists translation into any other language, such as the philosophical or theological. Plainly, John reinforces Jesus' preference for figurative language, baffling though it may be to many, and guides us into seeing that the truth cannot exist apart from a relationship. True or not, speech/signs (words/works) move "you" to act and "follow." It is only the truth of the relationship itself that frees "you" to act in belief. And John insists with Jesus that the act frees "you" into more life in this world, breaking down the walls between tribes, genders, and classes; and in the next as well, erasing the threshold between life and death.

House of the Interpreters

BAFFLEMENT PERVADES JOHN'S BOOK. The disciples are puzzled and ask Jesus to speak plainly. The Jews are confused and then angered by Jesus' pronouncements. Jesus himself is perplexed by the seeming stubbornness of the Jews and obtuseness of his disciples. John assumes, furthermore, that his readers will be confused, pausing to explain Jesus' motives (6:6), metaphors (2:21), and even the meaning of his death (12:33).

Confusion derives in part from the tradition, which goes back to Socrates, of the master whose words are necessarily cryptic in order to spark in his followers a desire for the knowledge he wishes to lead them into. There is also the inevitable difficulty of language found for a necessarily public expression of an essentially private vision, Jesus' waking dream. And, not to be underestimated, it's a personal penchant as well. At times Jesus revels in obfuscation, as when he takes leave of his disciples (e.g., chapter 16), using it to heighten his power in keeping with the prophet's role. And on one occasion Jesus seems to delight in baffling a disciple. John implies that in teasing Philip, Jesus enjoys the game for its own sake (6:6).

The confusion that reigns in John's book is mainly rooted, however, in Jesus' program to seduce the listener or reader into embracing and finally inhabiting a new vocabulary. He builds a new language and invites all to enter. A new way of speaking brings with it a new way of understanding and, it is the fondest hope of both John and Jesus, a new way of being in the world. And true novelty, because it does not fit our preconceptions, is by its very nature incomprehensible.

Committed to furthering this program, John's strategies reinforce those of Jesus. On the one hand, his book creates a new language. On the other, it undermines the old language of the Jewish writings, breaking ground for the new. We're reminded of Cervantes, who wrote Don Quixote with the express intent of "overthrowing the authority and prestige which books of chivalry enjoy in the world." Likewise, John wrote his book in order to destroy the authority that the Jewish scriptures have in the community he addresses. Once undermined, he can leverage them, transforming old language into new by reinterpretation.

So interpretation goes hand in hand with Jesus' mission of building a new language. He introduces strange new terms like "born of the spirit," and redefines old ones like "sacrifice." From birth (the twice born) to death (the hero as sacrificial lamb), Jesus must interpret and reinterpret, laying the foundation for the new. As we'll see, John often depicts Jesus in the act of interpreting his own words or those of the scriptures, or correcting various misinterpretations of his words.

Jesus uses interpretation to tease and cajole, shock and comfort, anything to further his program. At the same time, head to head with professional interpreters, the teacher-preacher-lawyer rabbis, Jesus earns respect as well as resentment, causing consternation and ultimately his death. They recognize Jesus' utterances within the tradition of "sayings of the master," which were assumed to be perplexing and thus to require interpretation, but he radically extends this tradition to include his own body. John makes clear from the outset that Jesus is himself an utterance—the living Word (1:14).

Not only does he engage with his followers and enemies in acts of interpretation, participating self-consciously as a teacher-preacher-lawyer himself, but as the "Word" he is an object of interpretation. Is this Word from God, to be accepted, as John the Baptist as well as some family, friends (his disciples), and strangers (the woman at the well) conclude; or is this Word from the Devil, to be rejected, as other family members (7:5), friends (6:66), and strangers (the Jews, 8:48) conclude? The latter interpretation leads to Jesus' death, the former to a new body, his own and that of his disciples and ultimately John's readers, interpreters of the acts and words of Jesus that John chooses to report.

Interpreting Jesus' words is to interpret the Word itself. Not only is meaning at stake, then, but the body. In John's story the death of Jesus consolidates the death of the old language, the received interpretation of the Passover sacrifice as a lamb whose bones were not to be broken (Exod 12:46; Num 9:12). At the same time, his death is the triumph of the new language, John's new interpretation of this sacrifice as the body of Jesus whose bones, John takes pains to point out, are also not broken (19:36) and who lives again. From the words of Jesus to Jesus the Word, John raises the interpretive stakes.

DUELING INTERPRETERS

A matter of life and death, Jesus performs great feats of interpretation. These are at the heart of John's story. Right interpretation inculcating right language which produces right belief leads to life. But it also leads to death. Belief in the long run, John assures us, brings everlasting life. But in the short run, interpretation giving rise to the new language of the "way" (14:6) brings about Jesus' death. His reading of scriptures leads directly to the hero's end.

Tragedy is inevitable because Jesus' reading can only be understood by the Jews as misreading. Yet his tactic, which results in a scene of dueling interpreters, is necessary to break ground for construction of the new edifice of language. After what to the Jews is an outrageous claim, equating himself with God the "Father" (10:30), they pick up stones to kill Jesus. But he answers: "Many good works have I showed you from my Father; for which of those works do you stone me? The Jews answered him, saying, For a good work we stone you not; but for blasphemy; and because that thou, being a man, makest thyself" God (10:32–33). Ask a question, get the enemy talking so they forget the weapons in their hands. Jesus is a fine talker, and John a fine dramatist here, preparing us for the central interpretive drama. He makes us very much aware of the tension in the air. Jesus is talking for his life.

But he is also talking for his death, consciously taking another step in carrying out his mission of self-sacrifice, which he had accepted from the Father, and goes on the offense. Almost in the same breath, he interprets a key passage from the scriptures, answering them, "Is it not written in your law, I said, you are gods" (10:34)? A bold and risky move, Jesus takes the words they know so well from the Psalms (82:6) and uses them for his own ends. This is clearly not how the Pharisees interpreted these words, believe and you'll become gods.

Why would professional interpreters like the rabbis buy this flagrant misinterpretation? Does Jesus really believe that he can get away with it? He keeps talking so it seems for a moment like he's won, which is a nicely dramatic touch, but he only buys a little time and in fact they do not ultimately buy his interpretation, as John's readers surely know from the beginning.

But Jesus' move is understandable. Balancing on a knife-edge, he must both defend and offend. His hour of death has not yet come, so he doesn't want to precipitate immediate self-sacrifice. Thus he engages in debate, defending his interpretation and with it his life. At the same time, he knows this clash of interpretations is a necessary step in ultimately effecting his martyrdom. So he goes full tilt, as John presents the scene, right through blasphemy to something else. Breathtaking argument, but a sustained misinterpretation that can only infuriate: "If he called them gods, unto whom the word of God came, and the scripture cannot be broken; Say you of him, whom the Father has sanctified, and sent into the world, You blaspheme; because I said, I am the Son of God? . . . the Father is in me, and I in him" (10:35–8). The atmosphere remains heavy with Jesus justifying his assertion of being a god, continuing from the Jews' point of view his willful misuse of their sacred text. But, of course, this is what he's about (as is John): to proceed from misusing to reusing to using a new text. The Jews read one way, Jesus another. He can say to them with Blake, addressing the teacher-preacher custodians of received interpretation in his time, "Both [of us] read the Bible day and night / But thou readst black where I read white."

Jesus goes directly against the grain of the rabbis, challenging their received interpretation. He opens up the original text to new meaning, metamorphosing it into a new language and applying it to himself. The Jews, having institutionalized a standard interpretation of the text, condemn this blossoming of meaning as blasphemy. "Therefore," John comments dryly, "they sought again to take him." And we come full circle.

Interpreting scripture, as Salman Rushdie discovered in our own day, is dangerous business. For John this scene of rival interpreters squaring off is irresistible. Not only because of its dramatic possibilities, for the scene reveals what is at stake in the act of interpretation—life itself (the present physical as well as the "everlasting" spiritual).

NESTED INTERPRETERS

From the announcements of John the Baptist, whom we meet assiduously countering misinterpretation (1:19–26), and the dialogue with Nicodemus, which hinges on misinterpretation (3:4), to the farewell speeches of Jesus that his disciples strain futilely to interpret (14:5, 22; 16:17–18), John is preoccupied with interpretation. Self-conscious about his interpretive act of selecting materials from the life of Jesus (20:30; 21:25), John also interprets Jesus' life by artfully arranging these materials. He moves the scourging of Jesus, for example, to the middle of his trial before Pilate (19:1–3), contrary to the accounts of Mark and Matthew and to Roman judicial practice. All according to his overriding purpose "that you might believe" (20:31) or, in other words, that the reader might accept a new interpretation, which is a new language.

John is the last interpreter before his readers take up the task. We're reminded of this constantly in his interpreting Jesus' words, such as the bold statement Jesus makes in reference to himself, "out of his belly shall flow rivers of living water" (7:38). Rightly assuming that we are baffled by this utterance, John immediately explains, "This spoke he of the Spirit, which they that believe on him should receive." Jesus himself does not feel constrained to interpret for his listeners, we notice, but John is anxious for us his readers. Because we have the statement itself, we do not have to accept John's interpretation, but Jesus stands interpreted.

Just as Jesus himself interpreted the words of the Jews and their scriptures. And his listeners respond in kind, as we've seen. For along with the Jews, the disciples interpret Jesus' words from the very beginning, as John goes out of his way to show. The fourth disciple becomes a follower, in fact, because he leapt to an interpretation of Jesus' words that Jesus himself implies is dubious (1:48–50).

An ensuing dust-devil of interpretation whirls through John's book, interpretations eliciting counter interpretations of perceived misinterpretations. Nicodemus questions Jesus based on an intelligent construal of his words, who shuts him down with a commentary (3:10–21). A crowd having been fed by Jesus misunderstands him, misinterpreting his actions, which result in Jesus' interpretation of his own multiplying-the-bread sign (6:32–58). And like the crowd, his own disciples misunderstand, which results in Jesus correcting them with yet another interpretation (61–65).

So with bafflement comes pressure to clarify. Jesus has broken ground by strategically misusing the sacred language of the Jews, as we've seen in his interpretive duel with them. Continuing his project, he lays the foundation for the edifice of his own language of "eternal life" by reusing their language. Interpreting and reinterpreting his interpretation, much to the consternation of the disciples, some of whom give up on this nesting of interpretations and leave him (6:66), Jesus is a carpenter of language.

It only remains for Jesus to complete his program, namely, to deliver his new language from mystery and reveal the gleaming construction of the "way." Yet an irony like a troll, always ready to challenge the unwary, crouches beneath the bridge between mystification and clarification.

The figurative double language of puns and of parables exfoliating their meanings is the source of both. Despite the great pressure that his disciples as well as the Jews put on Jesus to speak "plainly," he insists that his new language be built with puns and parables.

DOUBLE LANGUAGE

In fact, it's curious how much of Jesus' mission to inculcate a new vocabulary rides on puns. His word play carries a tremendous burden in John's book, beginning with the pivotal colloquy between Jesus and Nicodemus. We soon realize that this is because puns allow the expanding of an old language, extending its range of meaning as a necessary step in creating a new language for new purposes. Their conversation turns, of course, on Jesus' pun on the word *pneuma*, meaning "wind" and "spirit" (3:8). Like all puns, this play on words can be taken as humorous. (Not as funny as the marquee I once saw on a country church announcing Sunday's sermon: "The Pneumatic Christ." The pun in English is unfortunate and was doubtless unintentional, bringing to mind some wind bag or surreal buxom Christ.) John's subtle humor lies in the way language intrudes on the scene itself. Nicodemus sits feeling the wind on his face, while Jesus emphasizes the word *pneuma*, alluding to its double meaning. Jesus saying, in effect, "Get it?"

A fleeting moment of humor, for in dead earnest Jesus has transformed the night. It is not the same night that Nicodemus set out in. The word *pneuma* now has a foot in two worlds, the visible one of the courtyard where they talk and the invisible one of transformation. Nicodemus has a new vocabulary, unable to pronounce the word now without conjuring in his mind the second world and what Jesus has elaborated about it. By means of the pun Jesus modulates from one language to another. The visible becomes a sign for the invisible. We're not allowed to forget this, a basic part of the new vocabulary that Jesus creates. For wind/spirit proves critical later in John's book, as it becomes the bearer of promise (14:16–17).

The "water" that Jesus alludes to in this scene is redefined in the same way and drives the next dramatic scene. Jesus meets a Samaritan woman at Jacob's well and says, "If you knew the gift of God, and who it is that says to you, Give me to drink; you would have asked of him, and he would have given you living water" (4:10). The phrase translated "living water," *hudor zoe*, primarily denotes "flowing water." So Jesus offers what on the face of it is impossible, and the woman responds accordingly, having heard "flowing water": "Sir, you have nothing to draw with, and the well is deep: from whence then hast thou that flowing [living] water? Are you greater than our father Jacob, which gave us the well and drank of it himself, and his children, and his cattle?" (4:11–12). Jesus, as he did with Nicodemus, now modulates to another language, pivoting on the *hudor zoe* pun to the language of an invisible world of everlasting life: "Jesus answered and said unto her, Whosoever drinks of this water shall thirst again: But whosoever drinks of the water that I shall give him shall never thirst; but the water that I shall give him shall be in him a well of water springing up into everlasting life [*hudatos . . . zoein*]" (4:13–14).

Now the woman gets it. She picks up on the second meaning of "flowing water," understanding Jesus' play on the words: "Sir, give me this water, that I thirst not" (4:15).

Nicodemus understands Jesus' new language but maintains his disinterestedness. In contrast, the Samaritan woman understands and accepts. Jesus has an advantage here that John dramatizes. Where Jesus and Nicodemus operate in the same arena of class and power, Jesus and the Samaritan woman do not. Jesus puts her off guard by the very act of addressing her, a female and a foreigner, which he takes advantage of to inculcate a new vocabulary. The language here, in contrast to the former scene, is already charged in its crossing of male/female and Jew/Samaritan thresholds. But Jesus takes control of the language and employs it not to cajole, as with Nicodemus, but to court. Jesus wins this woman over to a new vocabulary, who is disposed to accept it wholly.

Two dramatic scenes driven by puns. More important, two pivotal words redefined. "Wind" and "water" cannot be, from this point on in John's book, simply wind and water. Puns have enabled Jesus to remake the language. We see him attempting this with Nicodemus, which dramatizes Jesus' method, and succeeding with the Samaritan woman, which demonstrates its power. These crucial puns at the outset have opened up language, renewing it for the rest of John's book.

So skillfully does Jesus use the pun and so critical is it to his program, he dreams of a language where every word has a second meaning that he can use to make a new language. We catch glimpses of this from time to time, as in his play on the word "sleep," referring to Lazarus who has died (11:11–12). Jesus only reluctantly acknowledges that this term in the language does not also denote "death."

The same desire for double meaning informs his most radical claim as well. As Jesus nears his end, Philip asks, "show us the Father, and it suffices us" (14:8). Jesus answers gently, "He that has seen me has seen the Father; and how say you then, Show us the Father?" After their time together, Philip's asking can only have been a great disappointment. With all his being, Jesus wants the word "Father" to be for Philip a pun denoting both Jesus and God. The dream of double language is Jesus' discovery of the freedom necessary to build a new language, having broken ground by misinterpretation (dueling with the Jews) and established the foundation by interpretation (nesting within interpretation).

BLOSSOMING LANGUAGE

In parabolic language Jesus exploits the freedom he has discovered, pushing beyond double language. The parabolic unfolds myriad petals of meaning. This is why when the Jews press him on one occasion to come clean and speak "plainly," Jesus turns to parable, saying, "My sheep hear my voice, and I know them, and they follow me" (10:27).

His rejoinder follows on the heels of Jesus' interpretation, for the Jews' benefit, of his own "parable." And unlike those reported by other gospel writers, this parable is strange in that it directly invites the listener to be the protagonist of the story. John takes this departure from the traditional parable even further in the later story of the vine, when Jesus, responding to his disciples, casts himself as the protagonist (15:2–6). The shock of his answering the Jews' request for plain speaking with a parable is reinforced by the fact that before relating it, Jesus had shifted abruptly from the image of blindness to sheep (9:41 to 10:1). This unexpected move was a way of waking his listeners up, pointedly calling their attention again to his project of redefinition. Shock of change in imagery reinforces the shock of new vocabulary, his all-important consolidation of redefining and reinterpreting. Parabolic language goes beyond the pun because it is not tied to the meaning of any single word, enabling Jesus to expand his radically new language.

And Jesus' commitment to its newness, knowing that his language carries power only when confronted in all its strange and even off-putting novelty, is why he explains the parabolic with the parabolic. Jesus embraces the irreducibility of parable; it cannot be simplified to argument or doctrine. It must be inhabited. This new language stubbornly resists translation into the more familiar language of ideas, as his own interpretation and the Jews' frustration with it demonstrate. Here's the "parable" in question:

> Verily, verily, I say unto you, He that enters not by the door into the sheepfold, but climbs up some other way, the same is a thief and a robber. But he that enters in by the door is the shepherd of the sheep. To him the porter opens; and the sheep hear his voice: and he calls his own sheep by name, and leads them out. And when he puts forth his own sheep, he goes before them, and the sheep follow him: for they know his voice. And a stranger will they not follow, but will flee from him: for they know not the voice of strangers (10:1–5).

John reports, "This parable spoke Jesus" and, as we would expect by now, his audience "understood not what things they were which he spoke unto them." This bafflement gives Jesus a chance to interpret and drive home the tenor of the story: "Then said Jesus unto them again, Verily, verily, I say unto you, I am the door of the sheep[fold]" (10:7).

Surprise, this is not the direction that the story seemed to be heading. Rather, it contrasts the shepherd and the thief; the former enters through the "door" or gate, the latter over the wall. More important, the sheep know the shepherd's voice but not the thief's. What of the porter, however, who opens the gate to the shepherd himself? Another character introduced for no discernible purpose, which muddies the distinction between believers and unbelievers. (Perhaps this character who's neither shepherd nor thief is Nicodemus.) As if this were not enough, when Jesus delivers his punch line, his immediate interpretation, he does not say "I am the shepherd," as we've been led to expect, but instead, "I am the door." His listeners, with Ezekiel's parable of the shepherd rattling in their heads (Ezek 34), where David is the shepherd acting for the Lord himself, would also expect Jesus to declare himself the shepherd. They think they know the story. But their expectations are initially thwarted. They must reflect on a new story. For a moment they're suspended between the familiar language of what they think they know and the new language of what they've just heard. Is Jesus the shepherd or the door?

Continuing to interpret his own parable, Jesus declares that he is both (10:7, 11), but introduces yet another character, the "hireling" who flees at the first sign of a wolf. In short, Jesus interprets his parable with another parable. As a result, the Jews split into factions, one side concluding that Jesus is mad (10:20), the other that they must abandon the enterprise of interpreting his words and fall back on his signs (10:21).

Jesus thus complicates what he ostensibly sets out to clarify. By this strategy he preserves the integrity of parable, his new word, despite pressure from the Jews. Bound up with this, as John has led us to expect from the opening sentence of his book, is the integrity of the Word—Jesus' body. Jesus reminds the Jews that he alone has life-and-death power over his body (10:18). Accordingly, John depicts them here as merely divided among themselves (10:19), not determined to kill him as in a later scene (10:31). Just as Jesus' new language must be accepted on its own terms, so his body must be accepted.

OBLIQUE PLAIN SPEECH

This new language, resistant to reduction or translation, must also be preserved intact for his followers. As with the Jews, when at a crisis of clarity he insists on the parabolic, so with his disciples. Baffled by his talk of going "to prepare a place" (14:2), they want to know exactly where Jesus is going and the "way" (14:5) to get there. In his patient answer Jesus' tonal range is astounding, as he promises a "Comforter" (14:16–17) and ends his first farewell to them on a note of concern in place of declamation (14:27). It is a most moving leave-taking heightened by the irony that the disciples don't fully understand that it is a farewell (14:22). At the same time, Jesus avoids responding in the way that his disciples desire. He does not explain where he is going or how to get there; he simply points to himself (14:6).

Despite his obvious compassion and concern for their understanding, that is, he proceeds obliquely. For at the climax of Jesus' disquisition, which has circled around explanation like a dog on a bone, he again points to himself, though now the bodily self, declaring, "I am the true vine, and my Father is the husbandman." He then extends this metaphor, launching into a shockingly personalized "parable":

> Every branch in me that bears not fruit he takes away: and every branch that bears fruit, he purges it, that it may bring forth more fruit. . . . Abide in me, and I in you. As the branch cannot bear fruit of itself, except it abide in the vine; no more can you, except you abide in me. I am the vine, you are the branches: He that abides in me, and I in him, the same brings forth much fruit: for without me you can do nothing. If a man abide not in me, he is cast forth as a branch, and is withered; and men gather them, and cast them into the fire, and they are burned. (15:2–6)

Speaking to his disciples, believers in contrast to the Jewish unbelievers to whom he addressed the parable of the sheepfold, he casts himself as the protagonist of the story. This is not the conventional way of parable. In fact, throughout his book John avoids the traditional parable in order to make clear that Jesus' disciples are present at a radical remaking of language. To them the form of the vine story seems to be a parable, but a strange one in that Jesus inserts himself and swerves from the expected story. He progresses by surfacing its metaphoric core—his body the vine. He daringly personalizes the germ of a parable that he and his disciples knew from Ezekiel (17:6–9). This gets their attention and roots them in familiar language while leaving them suspended among the meanings of a new language. Jesus' story is transparent, but the terms are opaque.

In this way the disciples come face to face with the radically novel. And Jesus bears down, addressing them directly and making it clear that they must be grafted as branches into the vine of Jesus himself in order to "bear fruit." Though a richly suggestive image, open to many interpretations and thus rather puzzling, the consequences of not bearing fruit are clear; they will be pruned, cast to the ground to dry up, and finally burned. Jesus counts on his new language being understood before it can be grasped. He demands a visceral receptivity to his words, a grafting into his living body that is the ultimate Word.

Parable and metaphor are, in short, as clear as it gets. Jesus brings his disciples through bafflement into bafflement, using parable to elucidate parable. But they have entered the house of his new language. Consequently, continuing his very moving farewell, he shifts them to the future, saying, "A little while, and you shall not see me: and again, a little while, and you shall see me, because I go to the Father" (16:16). Once again they are puzzled: "What is this that he says unto us, A little while, and you shall not see me: and again, a little while, and you shall see me: and, Because I go to the Father?"

In his response, Jesus plays on their assumption that his destination is death, coming clean in a less than a forthright way. And they react as we'd expect with "we cannot tell what he says" (16:18). Finally, Jesus admits that he continues to speak in figurative language (16:25). But with pressure from his disciples increasing, he promises to speak "plainly" in the future (ironically, after his death) and seems to compromise, explaining, "I came forth from the Father, and am come into the world: again, I leave the world, and go to the Father" (16:28). But this simply repeats a statement he has made already (16:17) that is no clearer now than before.

Surprisingly, however, the disciples answer, "Lo, now speak thou plainly, and speak no proverb" (16:29). Either they give up in frustration, mollifying Jesus, or they convince themselves that his talk of the Father is plain speech. Their light-bulb-goes-on reaction is not the tone of resignation, so the alternative must be true. Intent on knowing in the here and now, they overlook the fact that Jesus has deferred their understanding to the future. They comprehend his tone of ultimate concern like music but do not grasp his meaning, as their perfunctory response shows. That is, they have entered the language that Jesus has built but still have the many rooms, which he has prepared, to explore. Meanwhile, owing to the unbearable pressure of the moment—a farewell, death looming— they convince themselves that this is plain speech, finally getting what they've pressed for all along.

What they actually get John also gives us, which we can evaluate, and we see clearly that it's figurative language, the old father/son trope. Nothing new here. But Jesus' language in itself exerts pressure. If he is pressed to speak plainly, the disciples are mightily pressed to understand, even if they don't. They feel constrained to acknowledge that Jesus speaks "plainly" simply to signal that they are his sheep. They want desperately to "hear" him, to understand what he's saying, as opposed to the Jews who don't (10:27) and thus accuse Jesus of not speaking "plainly" (10:24). They don't want to fall into this trap. And they're still smarting from a misstep in "hearing." At a rather inopportune moment, earlier, the disciples had got tangled up in Jesus' figurative language, a pun on "sleep" (11:11), and Jesus finally had to speak to them "plainly," blurting out, "Lazarus is dead" (11:14). They don't want this to happen again, especially when the stakes have risen. For in their mind, the very ability to understand is a test of whether they are sheep or goats.

Nonetheless, the disciples are fooling themselves about Jesus abandoning "proverb." John in effect asks us to judge for ourselves. Like any writer, he insists on language at its richest. And John supports Jesus in this, who knows he must replace our accustomed vocabulary, our habitual way of seeing the world with another.

His mission is not to banish language but to break up the old and give us a new language built on a foundation of new interpretation. Our only conclusion can be that metaphor ("I am the vine") and parable ("the shepherd of the sheep"), which brings from Jesus another parable in response as interpretation, are in fact speaking plainly. The way to tell the truth, to borrow Emily Dickinson's phrase, is to "tell it slant." The disciples can only declare from within their beliefful relationship with Jesus, "Now are we sure" (16:30), knowing how they feel about the hero who stands before them but not precisely what.

So just when the disciples thought perhaps they could fly free of words that insist on their own integrity, free of parable to some pure realm of meaning, they are left with the intractable word, ultimately the physical Word. What began in the clash of interpretations, then, and puns on wind and water, ends in the body. Ironically, this is what Philip wanted, not the telling but the showing (14:8). The integrity of Jesus' language, John makes clear, is bound up with the integrity of his body. Both resist death, insisting on their irreducible power. Jesus lays down his life as the old sacrifice only to exercise his power and take it up again (10:17) as a new, radically redefined sacrifice. For his is the body of "eternal life" (17:2) breathing the wind of "spirit" and drinking the "water of life" that is the new language of "the way" he created—the word/Word (17:8). He is himself interpreter and interpreted, the indestructible parable.

The Book of Water

Meditation and water are wedded forever.

—Herman Melville

John's book begins by a river and ends by the sea. And many are the shapes of water in between, from pool and spring to well and basin. Like Jonah, John immerses himself in water and makes a poem. Like Noah, he navigates waves lashing the ark of his book, at last coming to rest on dry land where a promise is given for the future.

From John the Baptiser to Jesus the foot washer, water is a central fact. The Jordan is a presence throughout the book, as it is in the imagination of Jesus, his followers, and countrymen. It was, after all, the site of a great miracle, echoing the one that accompanied the liberation of the Jews from Egypt. The waters of the Jordan opened when the ark of the Lord touched them and piled them up so the Israelites could pass through on dry ground, enabling them to go against Jericho where Joshua achieved his great victory (Josh 3:14–17). These waters loom in the background of John's book like the six stone jars standing at the celebration in Cana waiting for water and a miracle. John too wants to cross over to victory.

Water offers the way, which is why John relates three miracles of water not found in any other account of Jesus: changing water to wine at Cana (2:1–11), healing the lame man at the pool of Bethesda (5:1–9), and drawing a great catch of fish from the Sea of Tiberias (21:11). Immersing himself, John makes water essential to his book. It ripples through Jesus' colloquies with Nicodemus and the Samaritan woman. And it is central to his discourses on the water of life (7:37–39) and washing his disciples' feet (13:1–20).

Water is such a palpable presence that it becomes a character in John's book whom Jesus confronts, comes to terms with, and finally embraces. He makes clear from the outset in his conversations with

Nicodemus and the Samaritan woman that all must consort with water to enter life. Just as the spies, who returned from the Land of Canaan reported in Gerard Manly Hopkins' poem, "Slabs of water many a mile / Blaze for him all this while." This is literally true in John's land of birth as well as in his vision of the eternal land. Jesus adopts Ezekiel's name, "Son of Man," and with it the prophet's vision of the eternal city with waters flowing from all its corners.

WATER POWER

In water is power. The water flowing through John's book is charged with literal and literary power. It makes dry land fecund. It alone can satisfy one of the body's basic desires. The water of vision derives power from the precious water found in a parched land, that water imbued in turn with power derived from a vision made from our deepest desires. We yearn for the imagined streams of a New Jerusalem as well as the literal fountains of the Alhambra, which mirror the Islamic heaven. Life itself, water takes on a numinous force.

Jesus competes with water for power. From the outset, it gathers power from ceremony—John's practice of baptism and the custom of ritual purification with water as prelude to marriage—and must finally be confronted. His first miracle at Cana asserts his dominance over water. At will he changes water to wine. But this too is water. When Jesus finds rapprochement with water in the course of John's book, out of him comes living water and, as the "true vine" (15:1), presumably wine. Always the trickster, water can assume any form.

Jesus takes another tack at the pool of Bethesda. Rather than confront water head on with his magic, as at the marriage celebration in Cana, he sidesteps the power of water, independently asserting his own. When aroused by the water gods, which John calls "angels," the pool's water possesses a healing power equal to Jesus' own (5:4). He recognizes this and short circuits its power by healing the lame man apart from the potent water. Jesus clearly recognizes water as his rival. He collaborates with it, however, in healing the blind man, who can see only after he has washed in the pool of Siloam.

Struggling, Jesus oscillates between strategies of attempting to defeat or to appropriate its power. He knows "how impossible water is," as the poet Christopher Bursk exclaims. If his domination of water at Cana was called into question by Bethesda, he is more successful in a subsequent scene that John presents of the disciples' boat in a great wind on the sea. Like Nicodemus, Jesus comes to his disciples by night, but walking on the water (6:19).

Behind this struggle is, of course, God's against the "waters" of chaos in his creation of the world (Gen 1:2). Though triumphant at creation, he continues wrestling with Leviathan, the primeval sea monster (Isa 27:1), a symbol of chaos like the god Tiamat of ancient Babylonian epics. And Jesus, too, struggles against a pagan god. Dionysus was popularly associated with water and wine, the amorphous world of nature, as in Euripides' great play *The Bacchae*, written long before John's book. Creator and destroyer, Dionysus is nature giving and taking life. He is excessive, unpredictable. Central to his mission, Jesus redefines the Dionysian vocabulary of water, wine, and blood from an old tradition and makes it his own.

But this public struggle belies his private conflict, one that John identifies with completely. A part of Jesus strives to divide the world into the true and false, those who hear and those who do not. Another part refuses to judge. This internal tension is fundamental to Jesus' character. He embodies contraries, a love of the differentiated and undifferentiated, a commitment to the precise and imprecise. These contraries are reflected in his relationships. Jesus oscillates between keeping his followers at a distance, the lines of relationship clearly drawn, and inviting them to come close, the lines between master and servant, shepherd and sheep erased. In Jesus' character the Word struggles with the word, intellect and law against pleasure and compassion. And male struggles with female. John apprehends the two in one: Jesus the temple, its solidity outlined by his own light, versus the fluid, unpredictable Jesus of "living water" (7:38).

As sharp-edged light sword, Jesus illuminates and clarifies. At the same time he obscures; he postpones clarification and full revelation. Because he is order and chaos, clarity and muddiness wrestle in his language. He lives in radiant open spaces, sea and river his companions, as well as in the enclosed darkness of the cistern-like womb/tomb. Jesus cannot be confined to either space. As the water of life, a fountain overflowing, Jesus lives where edges waver and truth bubbles to the surface despite the will. Water is his element blurring outlines and erasing divisions in nature—at the wedding with the ceremonial jars of water (water versus wine)—and in society—at the well with an unclean woman (Jews versus Samaritans).

But Jesus initially resists taking the well as his wife. This metaphor from Proverbs (5:18), hovering in the back of John's mind, makes the association of women and water explicit. The male Jesus, who gravitates to cities, those sharply defined forms of imagination, grows into an identification with water, the undefined. At the beginning of the book in Cana, Jesus asserts his maleness, behaving rudely to his mother and dominating water (held within the womb-like space of a stone jar). By degrees he comes to recognize the female part of himself and, after a pivotal encounter with a woman at Jacob's well, accepts it fully. Now he can marvel, with the French poet Paul Valéry, that "I seem to refind myself and to reknow myself when I return to this universal water." Reconciled to water and women, Jesus himself receives the power to give birth. John who gives birth to his book about the one who gives birth to new creatures, radically insists on mother water, the womb of Jesus. For "out of his belly shall flow rivers of living water" (7:38).

SHAPE SHIFTER

In John's world of light and dark, believers versus unbelievers, why water? Shape shifter, chaos, the undifferentiated one, water is the world of Both/And, not Either/Or.

This is precisely why John needs water, and why Jesus comes to terms with water. Just as God ultimately does, whose "path" is in the "great waters," his "footsteps," as the poet King David says, "not known" (Ps 77:19). Jesus claims to be a shape shifter himself like Dionysus, becoming whatever he wants—a lamb or a vine, light or water. Subject and object merge in Jesus, the line between them dissolves. Such is his most persistent claim, as though taking into himself the paradoxes of water that Christopher Bursk identifies in his questions: "Why is water clear when we lift it out of itself? / Why does water dry into us and the light?" Where is the subject, where the object? Jesus loves water as the natural symbol of paradox: the world as his own body, all become subject; and the world as the other, an alien land of darkness in need of light, pure object.

The surface of John's book, consequently, undulates above deep waters. In the background, we are continually made aware of John the Baptist baptizing in the river Jordan. And in the foreground, after only two chapters, when Jesus says, "Except a man be born of water and of the Spirit, he cannot enter into the kingdom of God" (3:5), water has already taken on tremendous resonance. We're prepared for this (though

Nicodemus is not) by the river water ceremonially transformed (John the Baptist) and the miraculously transformed ceremonial water (Cana). In Nicodemus and water, John's imagination overpowers his didactic intentions.

Living in a desert climate, John is understandably obsessed with water. It is the occasion for celebration, purification and play, life itself. Unlike the Greek philosopher Thales of Miletus who lived some six centuries earlier, however, John does not make water the underlying principle of everything. Instead, he gives it a power and presence equal to other characters in his book. Nor is he tempted like the Qu'ran, written several centuries later, to make water the material from which Allah creates "every living creature." John must incorporate water, taking the lead of Jesus, both of them rooted in the same land and driven by the same thirst, but he does not make it the ground or origin so much as the force of life. It does not lie behind things but manifests itself in many forms, variously a troubled pool, stormy sea, or flowing stream.

As he identifies with its power, furthermore, it becomes manifest in Jesus himself. John gives us a Jesus who offers water and brings forth water not primarily because of the climate in Palestine but because of the climate within himself. Water lives within John's psyche as the mother. From her womb springs life, and within her depths life returns to non-life. His Jesus promises a second birth and is himself born twice, once from his mother's womb and once from the womb/tomb in the garden. Jesus can no more be nailed down than water itself. The well and the swell of the sea enclose this mystery. Immersion by baptism reenacts it.

WATER OF LIFE

This promise of living water out of the body of Jesus is nothing less than the promise of eternal life. John makes water his primary symbol of everlasting life, the subject of his book. It is necessary because water becomes invested with John's desire to be reborn, to again participate in the metamorphic power of the womb. Not to be reborn into life, however, but out of life.

John's hope in Jesus is the promise of a new birth out of the death-dealing life that we know into a transcendent death-proof life that we desire. This wish is Dionysian, the abolition of limits to life and of the boundary between life and death. Life, Jesus asserts by his own appearance and reappearance, is a fluid continuum of life and death. His is a liquid character—the male bringer of light and the female giver of birth to water. Hence the Spanish poet Miguel de Unamuno apostrophizes Jesus, "We bathe in You, Jordan of flesh."

Where boundaries are blurred change can occur. For those clinging to rigid categories, this is the very definition of chaos and death, but for Jesus, life and more life. Jesus inhabits a shape-shifting universe, where above and below merge, the human and the natural world flow into each other, worlds without limits where any transformation is possible.

The Book of Water is a book of transformation. This is the subject of Cana, scene of a transforming miracle and marriage. John places this event, the metamorphosis of the natural and human world, at the beginning of his book in order to establish the fluidity of substance and self. Materials like water and wine are not immutable; individuals merge one with another in the union of marriage. This establishes the liquid world in which the transformation that Jesus calls for in his conversation with Nicodemus can take place. Transformation assumes the fluidity of character and the world, as well as their distinct selves and parts.

The water from Cana and from the conversation by night flows into the scene with the Samaritan woman. Here Jesus makes explicit the meaning of transformed or living water as eternal life. John's book is an extended meditation on this possibility of transformation that we can pass from our present life into a new life, from our slowly (or quickly) decaying body to a new body.

It is also, of course, a call to transformation, a challenge to change ourselves, which is in John's design accomplished by adopting Jesus' new language of birth in "water" and "spirit." Marx and Freud were later to share this fervent belief that once the fluid world was established, the old boundaries washed away, a new language became possible and thus transcendence and a new being in the world.

THE WATERLINE

Transformation entails threshold. We experience a crossing over. We recognize and erase a boundary at the same time. Water is a powerful image for this. Paradoxically, it separates and unites. Water signifies the threshold as well as its dissolving. It has a shape and is shapeless. For Jesus knows that it is both bounding line and boundary breaching that accomplishes transformation. The people must cross over the Sea of Galilee to learn about the true bread from Jesus. Similarly, like the

Israelites at the Red Sea, Joshua at the Jordan must cross over to achieve victory. And breaking through they are liberated to a new life of freedom and strength.

At Cana Jesus separates from his mother (2:4) and crosses over into society. His action recapitulates our passage from the womb into the world. All of us cross the birth waters and separate ourselves from our mother. For John this is the model. We are to be born out of one world into another. He uses the marriage setting skillfully to reinforce this on more than one level. A marriage celebrates the breaching with parents and the binding with spouse. The disciples leaving their family and following Jesus, which John has shown us just prior to the Cana scene, is echoed here as well. Baptism like marriage ritually celebrates separation and union, the disciples leaving the world for Jesus. Similarly, Jesus' foot washing at the end of the book ritually celebrates his leaving the world for the sake of his disciples. Attachment dissolves and reappears, just as water is reborn as wine.

Water symbolizes for John the separation from an old life and initiation into a new one. It is an image of the experience of transformation as well as of its end—eternal life. Jesus, after binding his followers to him, bursts on the public scene at Cana and initiates himself as a prophet. The onlooker guests would, of course, think of Moses who in Exodus changed the water in the Egyptians' stone jars to blood (7:19). And, following the writer of Exodus, John also calls Jesus' action a "sign." By this act of power Jesus crosses the threshold into adulthood, separating from his mother, but more important to John's design, into "prophethood." By the same token, guests of Greek background would remember legends of Dionysus, a miracle-worker who also called himself God and took as his own the world of water and blood.

At the end of John's book Jesus crosses a threshold in the other direction. After taking leave of his disciples, he crosses over the "brook Cedron" (18:1) into the garden where he will give himself to the authorities and death. He returns to the garden of the womb, which will also be a tomb, for another birth. John brings us full circle, signaling closure in his image of crossing over the water. Accordingly, he changes pace. His narrative picks up and moves quickly. After the meditative, reflectively circling prayer of leave taking with its chant on the word "world," John plunges to the end. Jesus achieves rebirth as a new being whom we last see on the shores of Tiberias, John being compelled to return to water, as early on we saw him by the shores of Galilee.

To cross a boundary is to erase it. The threshold between the present world and the world to be dissolves in moving from one to the other. Jesus' rebirth from the tomb erases the boundary between life and death. This story flows from Jesus' character. The drama that fascinates John and us in turn, the wellspring of his stories of hope and promise, is the dissolving within the man Jesus of those seemingly clear lines between the cosmic Logos and the mundane body, between spirit and flesh.

Head music and blood music reverberate in Jesus' character. He speaks of spirit apart from flesh. Yet in the same breath the Word became flesh, and blood feeds the spirit. How to reconcile the cosmic Logos with the mundane body of ours driven by thirst for bread and water, sex and power.

The music of the head and of the blood are distinct sounds and, at the same time, the same sound. John dramatizes the conflict in Jesus between his desire to keep head and blood separate, spiritual and physical, while yearning to merge them. A powerful solvent within Jesus erases the line between them. Water, of course, is John's image for this solvent, which can be ours as well. "He that believes on me," as Jesus promises, "out of his belly shall flow rivers of living water" (7:38). In his conversation with Nicodemus early in the book, Jesus associates water and spirit. At the end, dying on the cross, water and blood come from his body (19:34). Water is the mediator between head and blood, spirit and flesh.

In this role, water makes more poignant two of John's complementary and most moving scenes: Jesus approaching Peter to wash his feet and Peter approaching Jesus from a boat near the shore of Tiberias at dawn. Significantly, in both John allows us to glimpse their nakedness. The former scene shows Jesus disrobing and wrapping a towel around his body before stooping to wash the disciples' feet. The latter glimpses Peter naked, who as a result is shy and quickly wraps a cloak around his body before plunging into the waters to go and greet Jesus. The head music of spirit is inseparable, John's dramatic scenes make clear, from the blood music of the body.

And scrambling from the boat Peter is all body. A great comic as well as poignant scene, underscored by John's drawing our attention to his wrapping himself with a cloak first, Peter is suddenly shy and addled. We laugh at his embarrassment and impetuousness. Completely understandable, it's the idiocy that affects any of us in the presence of greatness (or mere celebrity). The excited Peter will flounder in his eagerness but finally make it to shore and Jesus' side.

Peter is the figure of excess. Abundance of blood matched only by exuberance of spirit. And seeing Peter here at the end we recall an earlier scene as well. When he understands that Jesus insists on washing the disciples' feet, Peter asks him to wash not only his feet but his whole body as well. We laugh at Peter's sudden change of mind. His whole-hearted plunging into life once he has made a decision is comic. He revels in the physical because he intuits that it's the way to the spiritual. I think of Blake's advice, "Dip him in the river who loves water."

And this is why John clearly loves Peter, making him one of the most affecting and memorable characters in his book. He is nature itself beyond control. Like the women of John's book, he is unpredictable, capable at any moment of crossing the boundaries and cutting off an ear or even, we would not be surprised, of pouring perfume over someone's head.

Like John's women, Peter is strongly associated with water, symbol of the fluidity of life and transformation to a new life. It is the natural element of the excessive, whose exuberance of both head and heart overflows in comic excess. So the sound throughout John's book of flowing/living water is also the sound of laughter. Head music and blood music merge in this music of Peter's gestures toward Jesus. Laughter assumes a world of Both/And and brings it about. Laughter carries us across state lines to escape the tyranny of Either/Or.

No wonder John is so fond of Peter. "Exuberance is Beauty," as Blake says. Peter's impetuous, comic gestures erase the boundary between head and heart within, as well as between interior and exterior, private desire and public action.

BODY FOUNTAIN

The extravagance of Jesus' image, rivers of water, and his insistence on the physical, birthed from his belly (7:38), makes John uncomfortable. The drama of Jesus' character, as he tries to harmonize head and blood music, is heightened by John's squirming. Water pouring from the body is too much for John, and he pulls back, saying in an aside that this is not to be taken literally but metaphorically.

Jesus doesn't qualify his words. But John does, "this spoke he of the Spirit, which they that believe on him should receive: for the Holy Ghost was not yet given; because Jesus was not yet glorified." That is, Jesus' image of water from the body is metaphoric now but later it will be literal. Hardly convincing.

Jesus' listeners, of course, do not have the benefit of John's irritating editorial comment on his image. They would feel the literal force of the image in the here and now, precisely the power that Jesus wants to preserve because he experiences it himself. It must be powerful in order to dissolve the boundary between head and blood. Instead, John blunts the force of Jesus' metaphor, averring that he was really talking about the spirit.

Exactly this retreat is what Jesus wants to defeat: John's taking the Either/Or position. Jesus insists on Both/And. John avoids the literal force of the image in the present, preferring to put off its literal meaning to the future. But Jesus' listeners know better, and the irony, which John leverages, reinforces our sense of the mighty forces within Jesus that must be mediated, which are directly proportional to the power that John gives to water. John brings us closer to the words of Jesus, in short, by revealing his own struggle to assimilate these words.

∽

Jesus' image of water pouring from the body answers the question implied by, "If any man thirst, let him come unto me, and drink." He preserves the literal and metaphorical force of "thirst." Expanded by the context of the festival, the Feast of Tabernacles, on the last day of which Jesus makes this statement, the word takes on political force from the context of Isaiah's prophecy of the New Jerusalem where water and wine will be plentiful and free to all (Isa 55:1). It gathers magical force as well from the liturgical context of the festival that included prayers for rain. The metaphoric sense of thirst is carried by Isaiah's vision of the future that will fulfill the needs of the poor; its literal sense is carried in the magic of efficacious prayers that will produce water in a dry land. This image of desire is both literal and metaphoric in the same way that "We praise water's certainty on our palms," as Christopher Bursk observes, "our fingers' bewilderment afterward."

We feel the full resonance of "thirst," however, from an earlier scene, Jesus' meeting with the Samaritan woman at Jacob's well. John emphasizes the physical by framing Jesus' meditation on thirst and the water that satisfies with references to hunger. As the scene opens, the disciples have just gone into the city to buy food (4:8); as it closes, the disciples have returned and urge Jesus to eat the food they've brought (4:31). We are reminded that in Jesus' critical program of redefinition, bread/flesh is to hunger as water/blood is to thirst (6:35). Physical desire drives the scene. The woman not only thirsts for water, which is what brings her to the well, but perhaps for sex, so John seems to imply in pointing out that she has had many more than the socially acceptable number of husbands.

John has Jesus tenderly tease out the meaning of water, as the woman comes to realize that Jesus is not speaking of "flowing water" in answer to her question but of "living" or eternal water (the same phrase in Greek, as we've seen), a magically potent water that effects everlasting life. Jesus bluntly asserts that whoever drinks the water from the well that they sit beside shall thirst again, "But whosoever drinks of the water that I shall give him shall never thirst; but the water that I shall give him shall be in him a well of water springing up into everlasting life" (4:14).

The well, associated with women who are the traditional drawers of water, as well as with courting, Jacob of Rachel, becomes a womb from which the water of life springs forth. In Jesus' very redefining of water, John makes its association with birthing clear. We understand its force as an image of the process of a new birth as well as the result of that birth, eternal life. And the woman asks for the water, so "that I thirst not" but also "neither come here to draw" water again. The tension of the metaphoric, which is possible if we have only her first phrase, and the literal, which the second phrase forces, is palpable.

Ironically, at the end of John's book, after all things were "accomplished" according to the scripture, Jesus "says, I thirst" (19:28). A great stroke on John's part, we are prepared for this phrase and at the same time unprepared. It is the expected though surprising climax to John's Book of Water. That he pulls it off is marvelous. While achieving closure, he manages to preserve a tension that Emily Dickinson captures, perfectly intuiting the state of the woman at the well earlier. "We thirst at first—'tis Nature's Act— / And later—when we die. . . . It intimates the finer want—," John's most fervent desire, which we all share, "that Great Water in the West— / Termed Immortality—."

And John cannot resist coming full circle in his last image of "blood and water" (19:34) gushing out of the side of Jesus as he hangs on the cross, having been speared by the soldiers. John builds to this. He knows that he has charged the blood/water image with tremendous power over the course of his book. Part natural (we expect blood) and part invention (water does not flow from a wound), John calls our attention to this act. Blood and water, where a wound would only yield blood. The soldiers' act has overtones of a sexual assault, then, because water signifies a birth, and we're reminded of the waters earlier that flow from Jesus' belly. We're also taken back to the marriage in Cana, which resonated with Moses' changing water to blood. Now John achieves further resonance, for the soldiers striking Jesus parallels Moses striking the rock in the desert and bringing forth water. Jesus at the end is the beginning. The Book of Water is the book of the promise of eternal life.

The Mother and the Mary's

A great mind must be androgynous.

—S. T. Coleridge

WATER ALLOWS WOMEN INTO John's book. The Jewish apocalyptic books obsessed with the sons of light and sons of darkness admit no women. Mindful of origins, Jesus is light. Meditative on the present and future, he holds with women and water. The unequivocal Father becomes fluid mother. Giving in to death at his Father's insistence, Jesus gives birth to his children—believers.

IN THE BEGINNING THE MOTHER AND IN THE END

The mother frames John's story. Early on at Cana Jesus rejects his mother, and only later from the cross does Jesus accept her, recognizing her publicly and arranging for her care after his death.

The scene at the wedding in Cana makes her power clear. She takes charge in a crisis, demanding and then commanding the servants. Her appearance alone is dramatic because John introduces for the first time a woman among all the men of his book. That she remains nameless magnifies her power; we experience her more as a force than a personality. The skeptical and unpredictable Mary, Lazarus' sister, and the adventurous Mary Magdalene are memorable, and we would seek out their company as does Jesus. But the mother of Jesus is a presence. In his last scene with her, he does not ask the disciple "whom he loved" to take care of her, but simply declares: "Behold your mother!" (19:27). She does not need to be cared for, so much as he needs her and, therefore, takes her into his home. She is the source of life, a necessary force to be sheltered for his own sake. The implications are clear. This personage is both his mother and the Mother.

Nevertheless, the rudeness of Jesus to his mother is scandalous. How can he say to her, "what have I to do with you?" (2:4) Identifying with the light that is the Father, Jesus breaks with his mother at the wedding in Cana. At the outset of John's book, Jesus substitutes the Father in his head for the father that he grew up with in the home. This abstract and unequivocal Father, shining a hard light on the world, rules his exterior life, all that can be seen.

By contrast, Jesus' mother has the effect of bringing aspects of his inner life into the open. Only in reaction to his mother, understandably, do we find Jesus unguarded. We discover for the first time something of Jesus' emotional life. John's introducing her is a brilliant stroke. Thus far in his book Jesus has been referred to as "lamb" and "Rabbi," labels that do not reveal character. At the wedding in Cana, John grounds Jesus for us in a human, social context and shows us a different Jesus from the sage or charismatic.

Only after Jesus consorts with water, does he finally reunite with his mother. As the book progresses, the Mother of creation who appeared in the form of a dove above Jesus at the river Jordan, evoking for John's readers the "hovering" spirit that broods like a bird over the waters in the Genesis creation story, becomes increasingly important. This Mother, represented by women such as the Samaritan and the adulterer and Mary the sister of Lazarus, grounds Jesus in the world, a fluid and ambiguous reality. This grounding enables Jesus to transform himself in the course of John's book. Jesus grows into an identification with the female principle, the creative source, signaled by his acceptance in the end of his own mother.

Jesus shuns his mother in order to accept her. Jesus breaks off the relationship in order to assert his separate being, to claim the space necessary for making his adult self, neither son nor husband. Recapitulating Jonah's journey, he enters the watery world, disappears and reappears. At Jacob's well he reveals his true self to a strange woman, then finds himself in a womb/tomb from which he is reborn on the shore of a sea (Tiberias). Only by separating from his mother into the world, being forced to rely solely on his Father from the heavenly world of light, can Jesus come to understand that light is not sufficient. One must also be born of water from the interior which returns him to women and ultimately to his own mother.

Thus Jesus is aggressive at the start of the book, driving the moneychangers out of the temple, but passive before Pilate at the end. The macho Jesus gives way to the reflective. Exaltation of light and the ideal gives way to clouds of fragrance, as he succumbs to the pleasures of touch and rejects abstract notions, such as the "poor" (12:8). Jesus has passed over water into the garden of the end and the beginning, into a female space where he rejects the way of the sword that Peter offers.

JOHN & JESUS WHO LOVE WOMEN

Women are necessary, therefore, to Jesus' growth. John selects and arranges scenes to emphasize their importance. Or underscores the centrality of specific women, such as Mary and Martha, naming the town where Lazarus lived by reference to them (11:1). Women aid Jesus in creating his prophetic self, beginning and ending with the reaction to his mother. And within this frame John presents a series of encounters with women essential to Jesus' education, from the Samaritan and the adulteress to the two Mary's, Lazarus' sister and Magdalene.

Engaging in a sexually-charged conversation with the Samaritan women at Jacob's well, Jesus enters a circle of intimacy that brings him to confess, not only to her but to himself, that he is the Messiah. In a parallel conversation earlier with Nicodemus, he had taken the unyielding male posture of having the last word. Consequently, he made no new self. In contrast, here at Jacob's well, which resonates with John's readers as a place of courtship, Jesus leverages the role dictated by the prophetic writings and makes another self through the agency of a woman. His posture has relaxed. He will not again perform magic tricks at weddings or drive peddlers from their living. By the action of this alien woman, Jesus allows himself the discovery of a self he had not identified before. He has taken possession, with his self-bestowed title "Messiah," of a calm authority.

The woman taken in adultery is instrumental in deepening this assured self. Completely passive in the hands of the male religious authorities, she silences the voice of the Father in Jesus' head for a moment. She pushes him beyond words. And the self he creates as a result in this silent space is not judgmental, as we would have expected, but forgiving. From this point on, having been taught by these woman, Jesus exploits the creative tension of contraries—his brightly lit, sharply-defined Father self and his intimately amorphous Mother self—to progress in creating his own person.

∾

It is Mary, sister of Lazarus, and Mary Magdalene who aid Jesus at two pivotal points in his progress, both scenes of death/birth. John uses sister Mary to reveal to Jesus, who we know loves her (11:5), his connection with the world. He and his disciples separate from the world at the outset of the book, and he in turn separates from them on occasion into the solitude of a mountain. But in response to the actions of Mary and Martha Jesus moves in the opposite direction. The disciples are irrelevant, absent from the scene, and John shows us Jesus moving into the sisters' circle of domestic intimacy and more, with Mary moving into the vaguely erotic.

Taking Lazarus' place in the tomb, in the later and parallel scene, Jesus moves into the intimacy of mutual recognition. In the enclosed space of a garden, as previously in Mary and Martha's house, he discovers with Mary Magdalene's help a tenderness in his new life that was previously inaccessible to him. Clearly moved by Mary's reaction to the empty tomb, Jesus says, "Woman, why do you weep? Whom do you seek?" (20:15) In the stunning recognition scene that follows, she serves to reveal to Jesus what it means to be desired and to fulfill that desire. She wants him not to die, and he obliges. Simultaneously, Jesus recognizes what she desires, and she recognizes the object of her desire.

Like the woman at the well, Magdalene is Jesus' confessor. He appears to her before anyone else, as if knowing that a woman, who is by the very nature of her physical being closer to her body than a man is to his, would understand the intimate nature of his revelation. For his male disciples, Jesus' bodily appearance is purely a public revelation, but John knows better and lets us in on the secret.

Beyond this, the two Mary's allow Jesus to discover a sensual self. Sister Mary caresses and encloses Jesus with her perfume. As she pours oil over Jesus' feet, we can't miss the erotic overtones of this scene. Nor do John's readers, who would recall Ezekiel's description of the act as that of a husband to his bride (Ezek 16:9). John calls attention to its importance by announcing this act before it takes place, when he introduces Lazarus, saying, "It was that Mary which anointed the Lord with ointment, and wiped his feet with her hair, whose brother Lazarus was sick" (11:2). Significantly, Lazarus is defined by his sister, and she is defined by her action.

John focuses us again on the gesture after it has taken place by exaggerating the oil's expense, claiming that it was worth almost an entire year's wage (300 denarii, where one denarius was roughly equivalent to a day's wage). More important, John underscores the sensuousness of the act by pointedly noting that Mary used her hair to wipe Jesus' feet and, further, including the finely observed and wonderful detail, the only account of Jesus to do so, that the room was filled with the oil's fragrance.

Jesus composes his body in the act of allowing himself the pleasure of touch, as sister Mary rubs his feet with her hair; and in denying the same pleasure, as he shrinks from Mary Magdalene's touch. This seeking and fleeing from touch emphasizes the importance of the physical self, the body that Jesus is precipitated into and must assimilate. Both scenes assert the concrete and physical against abstract and otherworldly values. Jesus defends sister Mary against Judas, sensuous oil against abstract gain, even for a good cause. And he grants Mary Magdalene's wish for a physical rather than spiritual body. Both scenes demonstrate that there is more than appearance; the world has an interior where impulse and feeling live. And the progression of these parallel scenes, as the acceptance of touch prepares for and intensifies the rejection of touch, makes clear the importance of Jesus' acceptance of the physical.

The spirit body was given to Jesus by his Father from the beginning, as suddenly as light. But Jesus had to come to an awareness and gradual acceptance of his physical body as he progressed through the experience of Lazarus' death/birth to his own. Only with the aid of John's cast of women does Jesus come to accept his physical self. As palpable and elusive as water, the Mary's give Jesus his own body.

∽

Hence women have a special place in John's book. Throughout, the women understand Jesus better than his disciples do. In return, Jesus does not patronize them as he does his disciples. Neither does he tease, let alone skirt meanness as with Philip, nor does he accuse them of obtuseness.

He senses what John knows, that women understand him implicitly. They are not awed, as is Peter, or perplexed, like all the disciples. Sister Mary, unlike them, shares the disinterestedness of Nicodemus, being skeptical and hanging back while Martha runs out to meet Jesus immediately (11:20). Mary's distance is only overcome in "secret," probing conversations with her sister, when she finally yields to Jesus' spiritual and sexual radiance. But because the women maintain a more physical, combined with a more distanced perspective on Jesus than the disciples, they can take an active role with him, rather than being like the disciples merely passive recipients of the word.

Jesus chooses the disciples, almost as foils to his ever-expanding self that ultimately fills all space, while the women choose Jesus. The women simply put themselves in his hands and lead Jesus into knowledge.

The Samaritan woman at Jacob's well clearly pays closer attention than the disciples. They are concerned about getting lunch, while she cares about exploring the strange circumstances of living water. It is a great irony, humorous even, that the disciples who have gone to get food miss Jesus' key exposition on water that leads to his singular revelation of being the Messiah. John emphasizes this by how he frames the scene, having the disciples leave at its beginning to buy food in the city (4:8) and return just after Jesus' admission to the woman, astonished that he had been talking to her at all (4:27).

True worship, Jesus tells the woman, is to "worship the Father in spirit and in truth" (4:23). God is a "spirit" which are the words of his Father and echo the scene with Nicodemus. But the progress toward "truth" in this scene is bound up with its sexual and social charge. In the previous scene Jesus has the last word, as I've mentioned. In this scene Jesus engages in true conversation, his last word being a simple declaration in response to her statement. Jesus discovers his Messiah self here in the transgression of boundaries, in the presence of a woman, which scandalizes the disciples. He follows the Father into the world of the mother, "water and the spirit," to ultimately create his Messiah self.

For this reason, Mary Magdalene is the first to see Jesus' resurrected self. She so wants Jesus not to die, she conjures angels. But this is not enough. She insists on the physical presence of Jesus, as does John, as does Jesus in full realization of who he is. So John grants her the privilege of the physical Jesus, who appears to her before he does to any of his disciples, including his beloved disciple. Significantly, John gives her a full scene with Jesus, reporting their conversation (20:11–18), while Mark, the other writer to mention this appearance to Mary, reports only the fact (Mark 16:9). What Jesus learned in the garden from Mary Magdalene, he later teaches Thomas in the upper room. And Thomas touches him as would a man the woman who loves him—by penetration.

THE FEMALE JESUS

Only by interacting with the women in John's book and learning from them, does Jesus create and integrate his feminine self. John strategically includes women throughout as agents who feminize Jesus. Sister Mary touches Jesus as she would another woman or as a husband would touch his bride, which John emphasizes by focusing on her anointing the feet, just as Jesus washes the disciples' feet later with water, having learned from Mary. Actively choosing disciples and angrily clearing the temple at the outset, he passively accepts suffering and martyrdom in the end. Ironically, only as he comes to terms with women and engages his own female aspect can Jesus fulfill his Father's mission.

Jesus is not the warrior hero, a Roman Caesar Augustus or Jewish King David, who leads a conquering people, but the prophet hero like Hosea, who if necessary accepts the betrayal of his people and is conquered in order to become their salvation. Thus John undercuts the masculine Roman virtues. Jesus weeps in public. John makes known Jesus' pleasure in the company of women. Nor does Jesus conform to the Greek model. We can't imagine Socrates washing the feet of his followers. To establish Jesus' character in opposition to the Greek and Roman ideal and in line with the prophetic model, John asserts the physical, feminine interior against the abstract, masculine exterior. Women serve to surface an inner life in the hero that we have not seen before. In the Garden of the End, therefore, Jesus chooses the condign over the confrontational, the prophet's way over the warrior's, telling Peter to sheath his sword (18:11).

The female aspect of Jesus is deeply embedded in John's book. "When she kills with her glances, her speech restores to life, as though she, in giving life thereby, were Jesus," says the Sufi mystic Ibn Arabi of the Queen of Sheba, who came to symbolize the "infinitude" of women. This conceit that all women are Jesus is a profound intuition. Arabi grasps the female self of Jesus, which perhaps he found in John's book. For Jesus too stops us dead in our tracks with his radiance. And he restores us from our shock, reeling from his words that promise life beyond death. As evidence, he offers water from his belly/womb, life from the tomb/womb.

Regarding his body as a temple (21:21), an enclosed space open to ritual entry, Jesus often conceives of his body as a woman's. Accordingly, he views his body as the gate to a sheepfold, the passive entrance. A sheepfold, moreover, penetrated by the thief as in rape. John reinforces these metaphors even as Jesus hangs on the cross. Is the spear thrust in Jesus' side a sexual wound? Jesus is in the position of a woman being penetrated and, as John emphasizes by the water flowing forth, giving birth. Extending this imagery, John points out that Jesus is buried in a garden in a "new" cave, which is first discovered by a woman come in the dark, as he emerges from the womb/tomb.

John prepares us for this conclusion by using the imagery of birth throughout his book. The dove that accompanies Jesus at the beginning (1:32) is associated by the Romans with Venus, goddess of love. Just as this dove settles on Jesus at the beginning, so Jesus "breathes" on his disciples out of love at the end (20:22), giving them the holy Spirit. He passes on the power to give birth. Now, not only can they do Jesus' signs, performing miracles themselves, but forgive sins just as Jesus does and as God himself. Jesus speaks for the Father, but he acts on behalf of the Mother Dove and gives birth to his children the disciples, expecting them in the same manner to give birth.

Jesus identifies, then, with the female creative principle. An aspect of his character intuited by Herman Melville in calling him the "soft, curled, hermaphroditical" Son. More specifically, Jesus comes to overtly identify with a woman in travail (16:21). This does not surprise us because he has been saying all along, like a woman who anticipates giving birth, that his hour is not yet come.

Jesus is fond of this metaphor because it refers both to the birth of knowledge in his disciples, which Jesus effects, a part of John's deferred-understanding plot, and to his birth from death, the ultimate knowledge of life. Like Socrates, Jesus conceives of spiritual understanding as pregnancy—the hour of knowledge will come when understanding is given birth. By the same token, Jesus' self-understanding includes his own second birth and requires that he does not go, for example, to the Feast of Tabernacles because his time has not yet come (7:8); at the end of the Feast he speaks, giving birth to living water (7:37). When his hour does come on the cross, he is pierced and water comes forth as in birth, foreshadowing his emergence from the womb/tomb.

∽

After completing his apprenticeship with women, that is, Jesus gains the power to bring his female self into creative union with his male self. The role of prophet demands that these contraries be unified. To carry out his mission of prophetic martyrdom, Jesus must bring the judging sword-in-the-hand self, a confrontational warrior, Ezekiel setting his forehead like flint, into unity with the forgiving finger-in-the-dust self, an evasive picaresque capable of dissolving into a hostile crowd and disappearing.

Jesus accomplishes his mission because he succeeds in uniting the Father and Mother parts of his being. Identifying with the Mother, Jesus refers to his disciples as his little children (13:33). Yet Jesus also says that he and the Father are spiritually (10:30) and physically (14:9) one, and his Father's words are in him (17:8). The disciples are to remain in Jesus and his words in them; he gives birth to his words, which is to give birth to them, as they are in turn to give birth to his words. Just as Jesus is the gate to the sheepfold (10:7) and also the shepherd (10:11), paradoxically, Jesus is both mother and father.

More than this, he defines those that "believe in his name" as born of God, clearly a mother god. But God is also the Father (1:12–13). And Jesus says to Nicodemus that he must be born from "above" (1:3, 7), which is the light-world of the Father, while the water-world of women lies below. John does not shy away from suggesting that God is androgynous, being both Mother and Father. And as the Father who gives life (5:21), therefore, Jesus shares his/her androgyny. Astonishingly, Jesus is his own father (10:30), while being self-created by the Word, the mother of creation. This sexual ambiguity at the core of Jesus' incandescence both discomforts and draws people, a secret rock stars have known since Elvis and Mick Jagger.

And John comes. Jesus' successful formation, with a little help from his female friends, and integration of his sexual selves is powerfully appealing. John is in love with Jesus. John wants Jesus to be his mother and lover. And Jesus obliges, wanting to be a mother capable of giving birth to new men. At the same time that he calls himself shepherd, he wants John to be one of his children. His injunction to Peter, "feed my sheep," is the exhortation to be Jesus, both mother and father.

Wanting a mother, wanting to be reborn, is the same as wanting not to die, which is what John wants. The desire to re-enter the womb drives his book. It is so powerful and the radiance of Jesus so compelling that this imagined union is subtly eroticized. Early in his book, John invokes a bride and marriage (Cana). He quotes John the Baptist, a stand-in for John the writer whose words also herald Jesus' arrival, calling Jesus a bridegroom (3:29). If Jesus is the bridegroom, who is the bride? In the abstract, possibly believers. For the believers' relationship is the lovers' (made explicit in myriad cultic hymns). Specifically, in the world of women and water, the bride is John himself whose book among the gospels is, as the poet Miguel de Unamuno recognized, "the feminine gospel."

At the end of his book, John speaks of "the disciple whom Jesus loved" (21:20). If not John, and the writer John is deliciously coy in his reference, this disciple becomes a stand-in for John, the one yearning throughout his book to be specially loved by Jesus. Moreover, this disciple is the one of whom it was rumored that he "should not die" (21:23). The John who writes of the John "which testifies of these things, and wrote these things" (21:24) about Jesus, the same who "leaned on his breast at supper," plays the bride of Jesus. By this gambit, John makes himself the erotic center of Jesus' circle of followers.

At the same time, John must write as one ultimately thwarted. Whatever John wanted to make of Jesus, he ultimately gives himself to the Jesus he made. The center of his book remains Jesus—an obscure object of desire.

As "the disciple whom Jesus loved" or his alter ego, John gives an erotic charge to his book, but the central fact remains: Jesus is self contained. Always the object, never the groom, Jesus does not need a wife. For Jesus marries himself. This autoerotic nature is one reason why Jesus so powerfully draws so many to himself. All manner of people desire in the figure of Jesus protection and love because he is, as John gives him to us, both Mother and Father, bride and bridegroom.

Symmetry

THE FATHER WORLD OF light, the heavens and Heaven itself, versus the Mother world of water. Above versus below. John clearly loves the balance of these. Their satisfying opposition defines one dimension of his book's space. Within this theatre, established at the outset, Jesus plays his role, emphasizing later to his listeners that "You are from beneath; I am from above" (8:23). And paired with this vertical of John's theatre is the horizontal dimension that Jesus identifies stretching from Moses, who lifted up the serpent on his rod, to Jesus himself, who was lifted up on the cross (3:14).

These balanced pairs are inordinately satisfying, whether disjunctive, up/down, the ascending versus descending; or conjunctive, past & future, the lifting up in the past completed by its rhyme in the future. They have an air of definitiveness in their accounting for the world. More than pleasing, they are powerful because the beauty of balance carries a conviction of truth. Binaries combine the power of analysis with the pleasure of synthesis. John revels in seemingly self-evident categories of reality, as he presents Jesus analyzing the world into up versus down. John also delights in synthesis, ascending and descending brought into a unity as Jesus invokes Jacob's ladder (1:51), which bridges Heaven and earth.

BALANCING

Jesus' espousal of symmetry is the model for John's book. Or symmetry has a powerful attraction for John the artist. Either way, he selects and arranges his materials accordingly. Critical scenes, such as the conversations with Nicodemus and the Samaritan woman constitute, in effect, a balanced pair. By the same method he connects the dimensions of a character, as in Peter's threefold denial of Jesus in the courtyard and threefold acceptance on the beach. This balancing of scenes in parallel gives them an open quality that allows thematic echoes and verbal ripples.

In linking the conversations of Nicodemus and the Samaritan woman, John makes clear how central they are to his book and heightens the drama of authority they introduce. He presents Jesus as teacher in the former and as prophet in the latter. That John intends us to view these scenes as a pair is evident from his presenting Jesus alone in each, his interlocutor coming to him, and pointedly establishing at the outset the time of their conversation, night (3:2) and noon (4:6), respectively, both unusual times for a colloquy, rabbis not normally visiting by night, and women not normally drawing water in the heat of the day. Also, both conversations, which touch on water and the spirit, are based on a misunderstanding that Jesus attempts to clear up.

Astonishingly, however, while John increases the stakes as we move up the hierarchy from teacher to prophet, he denies us certainty about authority. Nothing is cleared up because Jesus' success in both roles is ambiguous. This irony allows us to more fully identify with the characters who visit Jesus and thus to feel the force of their questions. Echoing throughout the rest of John's book is Nicodemus' question "How can these things be?" and the Samaritan woman's "Could this possibly be the Messiah?" (4:29, trans., R.E. Brown) These questions establish the essential vectors of the book: the truth of what Jesus says and the claim that Jesus makes about himself.

Placing ourselves in the position of Nicodemus and the Samaritan woman, we are forced from the beginning to evaluate the hero of John's book and what he says. Unlike a polemicist, John doesn't present us with scenes that mechanically and thus unconvincingly illustrate the authority of Jesus as teacher and prophet. Knowing the truth to be more complex, John dramatizes rather than answers the questions that will drive his book.

Consequently, for very good reasons at this juncture, we're left in ambiguity. Nicodemus and the Samaritan woman, though sketched with just a few strokes, nonetheless stick in our imaginations. Both have encountered Jesus himself and yet have gone away in a state of mind that can neither be called belief nor unbelief, the former accepting Jesus as a "teacher come from God" and the latter suspecting he must be the Messiah because this is the only way to explain his knowledge of her intimate life. Their powerful questions, which are at the heart of the matter, ring in our ears, countering Jesus' powerful statements. John prepares us for this experience by making the conversations pivot on puns, respectively, "wind" (spirit) and "flowing" (living) water, that create the misunderstanding essential to John's drama and to its ambiguous outcome regarding belief.

The symmetry of these scenes enables John to put key aspects of Jesus' character in dramatic relief. This effect depends on the scenes' basic contrasts: male/female, night/day. More important, Nicodemus is a central and powerful figure in the community, while the Samaritan woman is marginal even in her own community, being a woman as well as immoral, Jesus implies, and hence powerless. John's drama gains an inclusiveness by these contrasts, but more significantly it admits a contrast of voices. As a teacher and prophet in these scenes, respectively, Jesus speaks with two distinct voices. Both are compelling, but their effect on Nicodemus and the Samaritan woman, aside from the men of her village, is unclear.

The voice we hear Jesus use with Nicodemus is formal. Jesus repeats the phrase, "Verily, verily . . ." at critical junctures to underline a point and signal the divisions of his argument. By contrast, his voice at the well is more conversational, intimate, even pleading, "If only you recognized . . . " (4:10). Rather than arguing, as with Nicodemus, Jesus simply declares to the Samaritan woman that "Everyone who drinks the water will be thirsty again, but whoever drinks. . . . "

Tellingly, Jesus' mild exasperation in both scenes takes different forms as Jesus switches roles from teacher to prophet. The edge in his voice is directed personally at Nicodemus, "If you do not believe when I tell you of heavenly things, how can you. . . ." Whereas, with the woman, its edge cuts indirectly, being aimed impersonally at a nation, "You people worship . . . " (4:22). Clearly, both Nicodemus and the woman come under the spell of Jesus' voice, and both are impressed by his signs, those prior to the meeting with Jesus that Nicodemus has observed and those during it that the woman experiences. Profoundly impressed, she admits after the conversation to having spoken with a man who "told me all things that ever I did."

Yet, despite their respect for him as teacher and prophet, neither affirms belief. And we more easily discern the ambiguity of the woman's question to the men of her town because we have previously heard Jesus' conversation with Nicodemus end in irresolution. John's symmetry forces us to understand these scenes as a pair. The first increasing our awareness of the irony in the second, they dramatize at the beginning not affirmation but the twofold question that will drive the whole of John's book: Are Jesus' teachings and the claims about himself true?

Jesus gives us affirmation only at the end of the book in another pair of scenes. In the first, Peter rejects Jesus and suffers remorse; in the second, Jesus forgives Peter and accepts his love. John increases their poignancy by overtly paralleling the two scenes. Peter's threefold rejection takes place by a charcoal fire just before dawn (18:18); Jesus extends his threefold forgiveness by a charcoal fire just after dawn (21:9). John mentions a charcoal fire only twice in his book, tightly linking this initial rejection and subsequent acceptance in order to highlight the metamorphosis that has occurred from before the crucifixion to after the resurrection.

∾

Deeper than event and character, the underlying structure of John's book balances one rhythm with another. Two series of ritual events move in parallel: Jesus' verbal rituals of redefinition and the Jewish liturgical rituals of reinforcement of definition. One series echoes the other like the hull of a ship its keel. This symmetrical method enables John to connect the major events of his book, such as the raising up of Lazarus and the crucifixion/resurrection, within a larger architecture. Organizing his book around the succession of holy days in the Jewish calendar, a grand ceremonial rhythm, ensures its formality and solidity. But he preserves an open-endedness by not slavishly following the liturgical calendar, avoiding a one-to-one correspondence between his Jesus events and the Jewish feasts.

Three Passovers punctuate and anchor John's book (2:13, 6:4, 11:55). Choosing this structural principle is brilliant because its theme of sacrificial blood and ultimate liberation, so exhaustively defined and interpreted by the liturgical tradition, is precisely what Jesus determines to redefine. John counterpoints a key event or events in Jesus' life with a Passover or intervening feast. It is no accident that the Feast of Dedication (Hanukkah or Lights, 10:22), for example, celebrating the re-consecration of the Temple, parallels the raising of Lazarus. For in the early section marked by the first Passover, John highlights Jesus' cleansing of the temple. And John connects this overtly with the last Passover of the book, which marks the passion sequence, by interpreting Jesus' reference to re-building the temple in three days as a metaphor for his own body (2:21). Equally significant, John arranges the events of Jesus' death, contradicting the other gospel writers, to coincide with this last Passover of the book.

∽

John also balances Jesus' monologue on the bread of life (6:32–59) against the intervening Passover. His ceremony of language overtly reinterprets the Jewish ceremonial meal. John brings these parallel events together in the most forceful way, for Jesus speaks his bread monologue inside a synagogue. Movement is answered by symmetrical countermovement, just as John creates counter heroes and as we'll see a counterplot.

John embraces this method as a powerful way of gaining control over his material. He juxtaposes the old and the new, connecting them forcefully, even violently in the eyes of his audience, thus bringing a number of passions to bear on the monologue. If the Jews invariably make Jesus' place of habitation uncomfortable, Jesus programmatically makes the Jews' ritual celebrations uncomfortable, finally replacing the traditional sacrificial lamb with himself. In short, John wants to arrest his listeners. And he succeeds. Jesus' ritual monologue strikes an arc with the Passover ritual, throwing off high-voltage sparks. We know this because both the Jews and the disciples "murmur" loudly at Jesus' outrageous interpretation of the traditional bread, and even "many of his disciples" desert him in disgust.

Jesus introduces his program of redefinition innocently enough by focusing not on the Passover bread before liberation but on the manna in the desert after. A bit coy, but this strategy is effective in not immediately arousing the ire of his audience. This also allows him to exploit the symmetry of above/below, transmuting this opposition into the movement of bread (manna), which is identified with Jesus himself, "down from heaven" by the same Father who will "raise him up at the last day."

After establishing the backdrop of his theater, he begins his ceremony of redefinition, its three movements formally marked by the phrase "Verily, verily, I say unto you" (6:32, 6:47, 6:53), each of which invokes the symmetry of up and down. The ceremony of reinterpretation moves by ritualized verbal repetition from literal bread in the desert to metaphoric bread, the "true bread" from the Father, which is Jesus himself. Then it returns full circle to the redefined literal bread, where Jesus bluntly says in the second movement of his monologue, "Your fathers did eat manna in the wilderness and are dead," and concludes in the last: "He that eats my flesh and drinks my blood dwells in me and I in him.... This is the bread which came down from heaven: not as your fathers did eat manna and are dead; he that eats of this bread shall live forever." This verbal ritual succeeds in substituting for the literal bread of the Passover ceremony the literal bread of Jesus' body, center of a redefined Passover that does not celebrate the past liberating event so much as dedicate its participants to their future liberation by sacrificial blood.

The strong reaction of his listeners, many of the curious dismissing him and many of his followers deserting, is proof of the effectiveness of Jesus' ceremony of language as a counter to the Passover. They are not prepared to accept the need for another liberation. John balances one ceremony, the traditional, with another, Jesus' new interpretation with which he bids for a new tradition. Against a backdrop of coming down and raising up, he metamorphoses bread to true bread, the bread of immortality.

Given more to formal arrangement with its echoes and reverberations than to any melodramatic plot, John is at heart a lyric rather than a narrative writer. Balancing one ceremony with another, John stops time. For it is within this expanded moment that we can examine or even undergo transformation. Accordingly, he is more enamored with the vertical intersection of time by an image or the sound of a voice, savoring like all lyric poets moments of feeling, than with the horizontal succession of events in time. This is why instead of exploiting the climactic possibilities of the crucifixion, he deliberately flattens its impact.

John uses symmetry to render his book strangely anticlimactic. He undermines the crucifixion event as a consequence of previous events, contrary to the way stories normally work, and thus heightens its impact as an event in itself that draws power from a previous and parallel event. Signs build cumulatively to Lazarus, and then John's story rushes to the ultimate sign of the crucifixion/resurrection. But at this point our mind eddies because it circles back to the earlier and parallel scene with Lazarus. As a result, we are forced to confront the singular grandeur of Jesus' metamorphosis.

The drama of the resurrection is further dampened by the breakfast scene on the beach and its circling back to the corresponding scene of Peter's denial just before the crucifixion. By framing the crucifixion/resurrection, leaving us with Jesus and Peter on the beach, John deflates the ostensible climax of the crucifixion and expected culmination of the resurrection. He levels what his book has been building to. Circling Jesus and Peter back is extremely important to John and the thrust of Jesus' program of redefinition. What matters is not the heroic climax of Greek romances but the ritual balancing of the crucifixion with another Passover and its new, substitute bread confirmed by Jesus' simple, movingly human ceremony on the beach.

MIRRORING

Symmetry in the general sense of balancing elements is clearly very important to John, but also in the more precise sense of mirroring. The bilateral symmetry of our body defines this mirroring. If we pass a line through our nose and navel, dividing the body in half, one side reflects the other across this line, which becomes the axis of reflection. The two halves balance, of course, but they also reverse each other, the points most distant from the central axis, like our outstretched hands, framing the whole. John's frames can be as simple as his having the disciples leave at the beginning of Jesus' conversation with the Samaritan woman and return at its end, or as sophisticated as having the crowd at the beginning of the scene clamor to stone the woman taken in adultery and at its end to stone Jesus.

Just as John connects elements of his book by simply balancing them, he intensifies language, scenes, and entire sections by subtle framing and mirroring. In contrast to the open-ended symmetry of parallel elements, mirroring entails closure. It affects us like a box lid shut with a satisfying click. John taps into our innate craving for pattern and as an artist exploits it, whether using open symmetry (balancing) to connect or closed symmetry (mirroring) to intensify.

Mirroring combines framing with reversal, ordering elements in an ABBA or ABCBA pattern (called "chiasmus" in the handbooks of rhetoric), a technique he could have learned from the poet King David (Psa 85, 92). For example, John places Jesus alone with the Samaritan woman at the outset of the scene and surrounds him with a crowd at the end, while in the subsequent scene with the woman taken in adultery John places him in a crowd at the beginning and alone with the woman at the end. This ABBA pattern, alone-crowd/crowd-alone, concentrates the action and intensifies the latter scene, as the former lingers in our memory. Jesus conjectures about the Samaritan woman's life and what's in her mind, dwelling on the substance below the surface (at a well, fittingly), while in the latter scene all is on the surface, pure public gesture. All the drama surrounding the adulterous woman is external, embodied in action, and John's careful mirroring of elements, combined with his subtle framing of the scene, contributes to its dramatic power.

Employing such closed symmetry, John achieves compression and increases the emotional heat of Jesus' language in his bread monologue, which he delivers in the charged atmosphere of a synagogue at Passover. John uses mirroring to place emphasis on Jesus' key statement, "For I came down from heaven" (6:38), where he equates himself with the manna in the wilderness. As the axis of John's verbal symmetry, this image takes on great significance. It becomes the pivot point, two terms preceding it (AB) mirrored by two following (BA). The frame is seeing-believing. The first terms point up the discontinuity between seeing and believing (6:37); the second set stresses the unity of seeing and believing, which brings "everlasting life" and the raising up (6:40). Enclosed within these terms, immediately flanking the pivot, are balanced references to the Father who gives the believers into Jesus' hands (6:37, 39).

John characteristically uses this technique of closed symmetry not only for verbal heightening but for dramatic effect. In the wonderful recognition scene with Mary Magdalene, he uses this to place emphasis on her gesture, a literal pivot point where "she turned herself back" (20:14) to see Jesus whom she did not yet recognize. John skillfully engages us with this movement, which encapsulates the entire scene, by flanking it and thus centering it structurally with Jesus' words, "Woman, why do you weep?" (20:13, 15). He flanks this in turn with balanced announcements of her name, poignantly shifting from impersonal to personal. The narrator John names "Mary" at the beginning of the scene (20:11), observing her from a distance; Jesus names her at the end (20:16), addressing her with exquisite tenderness. This shift to the direct address of Mary that brings us from outside to inside the scene heightens its emotional intensity. As a result, I find her easy recognition of Jesus, after having mistaken him for the gardener, immensely moving.

∼

Closed symmetry shapes John's language and key scenes, as we've seen, but it determines the architecture of important narrative sequences as well. In the crucial events that he selects leading up to the crucifixion, for example, John employs a complex mirroring (ABCDCBA). He uses its framing elements to establish the scene in Pilate's "hall of judgment" (A, A; 18:28, 19:13) and remind us that Passover is near (18:28, 19:14). John makes the scourging of Jesus the central axis (D) and thus the pivotal event of the scene between Pilate and Jesus (19:1–3). Immediately flanked by Pilate finding no fault in Jesus (C, C; 18:38–40, 19:4–8), the event is enclosed in turn by Pilate's dialogue with Jesus (B, B; 18:33–38, 19:9–11). And the whole is framed in turn (A, A) by the Jews demanding Jesus' death sentence (18:28–32) and finally obtaining it (19:12–16).

These nested frames, in effect, give the scourging great prominence. But it is strangely placed in John's book. All the other gospel writers place this event at the end of the trial, which is more logically understandable and historically plausible. Why does John move this scene from the end of the trial to the middle?

Symmetry. John is unable to resist the demands of symmetry. Aside from his highly wrought mirroring, John loves the dance of binaries in this trial scene. The setting oscillates with each successive mirroring between the inside, where Pilate interrogates, and the outside, where the Jews demand. And John delights in carefully balancing the give-and-take between Pilate and the Jews, and between Jesus and Pilate. It's a pretty scene, aesthetically satisfying; it's a tense scene, emotionally harrowing.

By employing closed symmetry, John focuses a burning glass on the scourging of Jesus and heightens its tension unbearably, as if his humiliation were more important to John than his sentence of death. In getting us to identify more fully with the hero Jesus at his lowest point, John is successful, but this can't be the whole answer because this sequence is so crucial to his story. And though one answer to why John arranged the events as he did is symmetry, which led him as an artist into a discovery of their true order, counter to what must certainly be their historical order, this truth at the same time goes beyond the aesthetic.

Looking further, we realize that John's emphasis on the scourging dampens the story's natural bent toward climax, as the Jews ultimately obtain the sentence they demand. This shifts our attention to the irony of the scene at the pivot of the encounter with Pilate. Jesus' humiliation may not be more important to John than his death sentence, but irony is.

Wearing a crown of thorns and a purple robe, Jesus is hailed as a mock king, while Pilate whips him and the soldiers beat him (19:1–3).

John emphasizes the violence done to Jesus by making this scene the pivot of the narrative sequence. It is a harrowing scene made more emotionally wrenching by its dramatic irony. But heightening the violence done to Jesus has the further ironic effect of pointing up Jesus' passive-aggressive actions in the two flanking scenes where he turns the tables and forces Pilate into questions (18:35, 19:10), and answers him with infuriating non-answers: "You say that I am king" (18:37) and "You could have no power . . . unless it were given you from above" (19:11). Pilate is driven to playing the role of good and bad cop.

Focusing on Jesus as the scourged, rather than condemned, ironically inflates his role in bringing about his own demise, while diminishing the role of Pilate and the Jews. He responds to Pilate just as Dionysus did to King Pentheus in Euripides's *The Bacchae* five centuries earlier, which also resulted in Dionysus's death. De-emphasizing the climax of the sequence by intensifying Jesus' pain and surfacing its irony enables John to underline Jesus' role in bringing about his own death. And John thereby redefines the heroic. This truth, discovered in the writing of his story, which is inseparable from its symmetrical arrangement, necessitated John's departing from the historical.

SYMMETRY LOVE

John loves symmetry more than fact. The actual order of events leading to the crucifixion is attested by the other gospel writers and confirmed by what is known of Roman judicial practice. To express the truth, John succumbs to the beauty of symmetry and, as an artist, allows it to lead him into discovery. His compulsion to follow where symmetry leads in shaping his story is analogous to Jesus' compulsion to follow where the prophet's stories lead him in shaping his life. Just as the prophetic writings possessed greater authority than the historical facts of Jesus' life, as John inherited them from the oral tradition, so his love of symmetry wins out over what we would consider the factual sequence of events.

For John and his contemporaries, the factual derived from both the traditional and the observable (as it still does, though we pretend to worship only the observable). Furthermore, if the prophets said the facts were thus and so, John was obliged to give this the edge over what he saw first hand (the reverse of our own weighting). A "fact" for John is more like a coat woven from many strands of experience than a stone found on the road. Along with his contemporaries, in short, he assumes that a fact is created from the word, the heard, and the observed.

Symmetry asserts the formal. John admits to a selection of facts and thus tacitly to arrangement, but his evident love of symmetry constitutes an overt admission of being the artist. And like all artists John understands that formal, aesthetic values often force an arrangement of material counter to conscious purpose or any preconceived doctrine. The formal demands of design undercut the polemicist's design on his audience.

Symmetry is evidence of John's desire to shape, a compulsion of the artist which ultimately reshapes the pamphleteer's intent. John uses all the rhetorical methods at his disposal to persuade, but at the same time finds himself wanting to make a shapely, beautiful book. In the formal elegance of its symmetry, John asserts against the beliefful world, in which we must take either the right or the wrong way, the aesthetic world in which we can be still. In this garden of forking paths, we can be receptively observant, savoring both ways as equally possible. Like Nicodemus we can take pleasure apart from any itching after judgment.

The artist's formal stance, as opposed to the moral, is not alien to Jesus himself, who often takes a formal attitude toward the materials of this world, including its people. Like the artist he is engaged and disengaged. Jesus adopts a formal stance when he treats his disciples and friends as objects. Though moved by his friend Lazarus, for example, he also casts him in a drama, a carefully scripted event, as John constructs the scene. Strangers, likewise, can be merely means to display Jesus' glory and further his ends in the Theatre of the Way, which he freely admits in healing the blind man (9:3). Excusable? Indifference to suffering is no more excusable in Jesus than in the artist, but it is understandable.

∽

The world defined by the exigencies of the formal, which both John and Jesus accept, is one of control that makes possible the achievement of lasting works. Jesus assumes control over his materials, including those of his own life; John strives for control. And he succeeds, for as the writer he achieves control over our conception of his hero Jesus. Whatever the facts of his historical existence, Jesus is a construct of John's artistry. Furthermore, Jesus' power over subsequent readers is owing to John's.

In this sense, as Fernando Pessoa declares, "The Gods are contingent on style." We cannot escape the obvious fact that the Jesus presented by John's book is John's invented Jesus. He has been constructed, as we've seen, by careful selection and arrangement of his acts and words, as well as by artful shaping of fact.

We're ultimately forced to come to terms with only two things in John's book: the feeling body and "formal feeling" in Dickinson's phrase. Where the former confronts us, the latter "after great pain" comforts us. And these intersect in symmetry. By insisting on the body of Jesus, his literal blood and flesh, John confronts us with the interior—immediacy, engagement, the visceral and emotional. By insisting on the formal, John comforts us with the exterior—distance, the edifice of a life or formally pleasing thing made, such as his book. John the writer knows that he can accept the "way" without being an artist, but he cannot construct the book of the way, a gospel, making it a satisfying and puissant creation in the mind, and the hero of the way a haunting figure that will not let go of the imagination, without being an artist.

So John marries art. Its formal character is not only joy but conviction of something lasting. This is, of course, rooted in John's ecstatic encounter with the incandescent Jesus and in his ironic contemplation of this encounter that necessarily comes with thinking and writing about it. Apart from its origins in ecstasy, creating a formal permanence, a work of art, is itself a method of attaining immortality of a sort. John is committed to following "the way" to eternal life, certainly. But he is equally committed to building the book of the way, to following his writer's path even when it leads into unknown terrain.

The Book of Unknowing

*It is the unknown element that confers infinite value
on objects, living or otherwise.*

—Paul Valéry

What I do you know not now; but you shall know hereafter.

—Jesus

JESUS OFFERS UNDERSTANDING WITH one hand and holds it out of reach with the other. He continually promises clarification but delivers obfuscation. A fundamental aspect of John's ecstatic encounter, this must be central to his work. Consequently, two meanings wrestle in perfect symmetry throughout John's book: tragic knowing and comic unknowing. The tragic life of Jesus is a trajectory of certainty, the new lamb must replace the old lamb on the altar. And with it a new vocabulary shoulders aside the old. At the same time, the words of Jesus, who is himself the Word (*logos*), tease and perplex his listeners in a comic cycle of uncertainty.

John's book is about the certain and the uncertain. And they are the same. What John insists is certain, the answers that Jesus promises his disciples, are uncertain because Jesus postpones answering to the very end, even beyond the book itself. And what John initially presents as uncertain, the questions of Nicodemus and the Samaritan woman, prove to be certain. Their questions about Jesus and his claims, in fact, drive John's book. Hence the disinterested Nicodemus turns up at the most unexpected times. The only way to certain knowing, John knows, is by unknowing.

Contraries, both are necessary for the truth to be told. Thus in constructing the tragic plot of Jesus' determination to die, John carefully builds certainty. Jesus does die and we know why. Just as carefully, however, John dismantles certainty in Jesus' on-going comic story of postponement, his hour not yet come and the time when all will be plain still in the future. That is, John systematically unknots what he has so tidily knotted.

PLOTTING AGAINST THE PLOT

Master of character and counter character, John is also master of plot and counterplot. Jesus, of course, is the hero of both. In the tragic plot of his book, John's hero progressively clarifies the nature of his sacrificial mission, even as he pursues that mission, and ultimately succeeds in carrying it out. In the parallel and comic counterplot, the hero progressively obfuscates his mission, perplexing disciples and enemies alike. John oscillates between these plots throughout his book. He can only proceed in this way because, in fact, the beautiful and absurd Jesus cannot be wholly understood.

Yet the symmetrical tension of John's declared plot and undeclared counterplot drives his book and keeps us coming back to his hero. Its presence is a mark of John's integrity as a writer. Scrupulously honest about the complexity of Jesus' life and words, he knows that his book requires the counter hero, such as Caiaphas, as well as the counterplot of unknowing, which lead down paths counter to his avowed intent.

John's declared plot is the story of knowledge proffered in the present. It is the sequence of signs that builds to a climax with Lazarus and dissolves in Jesus. Signs are immediate and undeniable. Jesus pulls no punches. He even refrains from interpreting some of them, confident that they carry their own clear message. John's undeclared counterplot is the contrary story of knowledge deferred to the future. In contrast to the aggressive display of signs, Jesus backs off in this story, teasing and withholding.

The plot of immediate knowledge is carried on the wind that blows from Jesus' dialogue with Nicodemus through the rest of John's book. While the counterplot of deferred knowledge flows with the water Jesus alludes to. It is various, unpredictable. The wind sounds a single voice of authority; the water has many voices. The one voice of certainty caught up in a babble of antagonistic (the Jews), disinterested (Nicodemus), incredulous (disciples), and interpretive (John) voices.

THE ANXIETY OF MEANING

John wants his plot of certainty, the curve of signs from Cana through the crucifixion and resurrection, to be clear and unequivocal. Clarity is necessary to understanding, and understanding to belief. Simple in purpose, we know, but complex in practice. The writer John, who must present the truth of his experience in language, is hence compelled to include evidence of Jesus' obfuscation. The disciples complain, "What is this that he says unto us, a little while, . . ." (16:17), for example, and some even turn away. And the signs themselves that constitute the tragic plot of knowing are apparently not obvious; for John scrupulously includes with them Jesus' own interpretations (except for the signs at Cana), often in extended discourses. Nonetheless, clarity is the very point of the signs, the backbone of John's plot. What is seen with the eye cannot be denied, so it is assumed by many, and trumps the ear.

But John wavers. He has reservations about the eye gate, sharing Jesus' ambivalence about the efficacy of signs. Also, he has great anxiety about the ear gate. So intent is he on keeping his declared plot on track and ensuring clarity that he attempts to compensate for the possibly misleading implications of Jesus' statements. His anxiety that we won't understand overcomes him and in a characteristic move, instead of simply saying, "Jesus therefore, . . . went forth, and said unto them, 'Whom seek you?'" to the soldiers approaching him in the Garden of the End, John says, "Jesus therefore, knowing all things that should come upon him, went forth. . . . " (18:4). He interjects his opinion because he can't bear the implication that Jesus asked the question out of true ignorance, as the question without John's qualification would imply.

John pushes the limits of compensating for his hero, being so bold on occasion as to elaborate on Jesus' statements. "But there are some of you that believe not," Jesus says to his disciples straightforwardly (6:64). John, however, in a fit of anxiety, lest we not fully understand, glosses Jesus' statement immediately, "For Jesus knew from the beginning who they were that believed not, and who should betray him."

Nor is John shy about reading Jesus' mind in order to make sure that we, unlike the disciples, don't misunderstand. Jesus says to them, for example, that Lazarus "sleeps." Taking Jesus literally, they respond, "Lord, if he sleep, he shall do well." And right on the heels of their statement, John makes clear what he believes to be the true interpretation: "Jesus spoke of his death: but they thought that he had spoken of taking of rest in sleep" (11:13). What the disciples understood literally, John understood Jesus to intend figuratively. Though he calls our attention to an alternative meaning, he goes out of his way to make the meaning of "sleep" unequivocal. Along with his tendency to compensate, then, John desperately tries to confine meaning here to a single sense. But it becomes clear that Jesus intended both meanings because he does wake Lazarus up. From the perspective of Jesus' power and action, Lazarus was in fact not dead. There is an exquisite tension in this moment with the disciples, as John corrects them, and with Jesus, as he over-interprets him. More than Jesus, the anxious John is a shepherd of meanings; when one strays off the path, he is quick to corral it.

ESCAPED MEANINGS

For this reason, unlike the other gospel writers, John prefers discourse to parable. He bathes us in Jesus' language, extended speeches that wash over us in waves. At the same time, these monologues and dialogues pivot on puns and misunderstandings. Hoping to corral meaning, John is careful to follow the one parable he includes in his book immediately with Jesus' own commentary. At the same time, Jesus does not provide a single interpretation with an unequivocal meaning, but rather two interpretations that spawn multiple meanings.

The parable, which we've seen before, focuses on a shepherd, his voice, and the sheep's response to that voice. "Verily, verily," Jesus says:

> He that enters not by the door into the sheepfold, but climbs up some other way, the same is a thief and a robber. But he that enters in by the door is the shepherd of the sheep. To him the porter opens; and the sheep hear his voice: and he calls his own sheep by name, and leads them out. And when he puts forth his own sheep, he goes before them, and the sheep follow him: for they know his voice. And a stranger will they not follow, but will flee from him: for they know not the voice of strangers (10:1–5).

John's fears are immediately realized, for Jesus' listeners don't understand (10:6). So Jesus ostensibly comes clean in his first interpretation: "I am the door of the sheepfold" (10:7, 9). But as we've seen, this swerves from the parable's focus on the shepherd. As if aware of this, Jesus immediately offers a second interpretation: "I am the good shepherd" (10:11, 14). As if the thieves and robbers of his first weren't red herrings enough, however, he now introduces an additional character (the hired hand)

and theme (sacrifice), declaring three times, "I lay down my life . . . " (10:15, 17–18).

Is Jesus the "door" of the sheepfold or the "shepherd" who enters through the door? John knows as well as we do that these claims are contradictory. As much as he wants to resolve the paradox, he also knows he must include both interpretations to be true to the complexity of his hero. To further complicate meaning, Jesus returns almost perversely in his second interpretation to the "voice" at the heart of the parable. He makes this the center of the relationship between sheep and shepherd, but only to launch into the notion of "one fold" and "one shepherd" that the original parable does not include at all.

An exquisite riddling, this concept provides no grounds for construing his statement, "I lay down my life, that I might take it again." Bold and opaque at the same time, this declaration possesses a wonderful strangeness, as if it were part of some mystery which neither Jew nor disciple is privy to.

The outcome, which John honestly reports, is not surprising. Half the crowd concludes that Jesus is mad; the other half, who likewise fails to understand, retreats from the voice to the eye, arguing that it is the signs that count (10:20–21). John leaves the interpretation of his one parable in Jesus' hands, but instead of narrowing its meaning Jesus complicates and expands. Jesus himself, then, undermines the certainty that John the believer craves, who nonetheless keeps faith by including both these acts of interpretation.

∽

If Jesus' listeners have a difficult time, John's readers are equally at a loss. Without establishing any grounds for a shift from the imagery of light to sheep, Jesus launches into his parable immediately after the sign involving the blind man whom he has healed. Within the space of two sentences Jesus completely changes direction (9:41 to 10:1), causing a sharp discontinuity between scenes. The urbane atmosphere of the sign-of-healing suddenly gives way to the mundane parable-telling scene. Having ended on a note of abstraction and paradox (9:31, 41), Jesus launches without warning into a story. We're not prepared to understand the parable, having just come from the argument of the miracle scene and its lively drama involving the blind man, the Jews, and Jesus. Where the blind man was the center, now Jesus is the center. John shifts us abruptly from eye to ear, from seeing the light to listening for voices, and Jesus' emphasis shifts from others to self, judgment to sacrifice.

Radical discontinuity of scene and language disorients us. And here it leaves the parable floating free, thus more liable to bind with unintended meanings. However important to Jesus' program of redefining sacrifice, his parable lacks context and thus incurs the risk of misunderstanding.

Paradoxically, given his anxieties, instead of closing down possibilities, John opens them up. This lays the groundwork not for a single meaning but for multiple meanings. Some, of course, escape and gather in John's undeclared plot of uncertainty. Just as Jesus' interpretation of the parable leads to his cryptic statement about sacrificing in order that he might end sacrifice, allowing the parable to blossom with meanings, so his interpretation of the sign that involved healing the blind man led Jesus to another bold and opaque declaration: "I am come into this world, that they which see not might see; and that they which see might be made blind" (9:39). Jesus uses language not to narrow meaning to a single interpretation, but in both instances—sign and parable—to open up and multiply meaning. And the discontinuity in John's telling fertilizes this garden of meaning.

Despite himself, then, John follows Jesus' lead and complicates rather than simplifies meaning. Whether at the level of plot or language, John cannot keep his book on the single track of knowing, the clear presentation of certain knowledge. Failure to adhere to his declared plot is not owing to lack of skill, for John amply demonstrates his astonishing powers as a writer throughout, but is in fact due to his skill. He wants to simplify, but in the face of complexity he is the artist refusing to yield to temptation.

∼

John explicitly declares that he constructs his book for one purpose only, to induce belief, yet he includes not only the parties of disbelief, such as Jesus' brothers, but ample evidence to deduce his Inverse Law of Belief: the farther from Jesus, the more likely one is to be a believer. He builds toward certainty but uses uncertain materials with some curious results. The disciples believe but don't understand; the Pharisees understand (and are appalled by the implications) but don't believe. Then there's Nicodemus, full of curiosity and affection, who keeps turning up but no doubt does not come to accept Jesus as the "way," or we would have heard because John would be most eager to report such a fact.

Additionally, this ground base of uncertainty includes the writer. John is his own counter party, for he contradicts himself. John states unequivocally, for example, that Jesus baptized (3:22, 26), as did John the Baptist, but later notes rather punctiliously that Jesus, in fact, did not baptize (4:2). Uncertain materials indeed.

Embracing discontinuity and tolerating contradiction, it is clear that John realizes the "importance of unknowing oneself in order to conceive and to play against the I," in the French poet Paul Valéry's sly conclusion. This instability of the "I" is characteristic of the artist, who must try on masks, inhabiting many selves in order to conceive the truth of the self, one's own and that of others. John's playing against himself, calling his own stance into question, is projected into his playing the parties of disbelief against the central characters who come to belief. John's unknowing, his playing off self against the self and thus getting distance from himself, enables him to handle his anxiety about misunderstanding and the impossibility of limiting language to a single meaning. Playing allows contraries, nothing less than the fullness of meaning, and necessarily results in counter character and counterplot.

More significant, John demonstrates this same unknowing in Jesus, which inevitably mystifies the disciples who expect Jesus' self to be stable. We see Jesus trying on various identities—shepherd, lamb, even the sheepfold gate—and playing other roles like prophet (4:44) or king (12:15) in order to create his own self. In this way Jesus succeeds in creating the sacrificial lamb-self necessary to his mission, the focus of John's declared plot of knowledge, thus concluding, "I lay down my life, that I might take it again." This creation requires Jesus to play self against self.

Hence John gives us, like himself, the self-contradictory Jesus who, for example, comes to judge and not to judge, saying, "I judge: and my judgment is just" (5:30). Only in the same breath to contradict himself, saying, "you judge after the flesh; I judge no man" (8:15); "And if any man hear my words, and believe not, I judge him not: for I came not to judge the world, but to save the world" (12:47). Judge Jesus who refuses to judge is the spirit that informs John's counterplot, for meaning expands to include the possibility of disbelief, which is accepted by Jesus himself. Those who do not believe miss salvation and its promised reward of eternal life but are not judged. Jesus, therefore, opens up the way of Nicodemus who concludes that Jesus is neither madman nor Messiah.

COUNTERPLOT

John brings us face to face with the shadow of unknowing, the possibility in the end of not knowing at all, by presenting the impenetrable Jesus who uses language on occasion not to clarify but to cloud. Obfuscation, discontinuity, contradiction, and perversely opaque language emitting its earthy smell of strangeness, all serve to expand meaning. The wordy, disjointed, and repetitive become values even as they cause anxiety. We're reminded of Virgil's description just a few decades earlier of the Sibyl of Cumae who "Chanted fearful equivocal words and made the cave echo / With sayings where clear truths and mysteries / Were inextricably twined."

It is a similar kind of extreme speech that John gives us, incomprehensible to the point where many of Jesus' listeners conclude, as we've seen, that he is mad. Or give up on his language and seek refuge in his signs, which even Jesus doesn't completely trust. And we're left with mystery, the shadow stretching toward infinity, hence powerfully attractive.

John reveals to himself, in short, that because it must be achieved in language, his clear and unequivocal objective cannot be achieved by clear and unequivocal means. There are those, even some of Jesus' listeners, who will never see his signs. Thus language is unavoidable, a fact weighing heavily on John the writer. Ironically, Jesus' language itself demands that certainty travel hand in hand with uncertainty. The tragic plot ending in knowledge demands its contrary counterplot, a comedy of confusion ending only in further questions. Yet the deferral of clarity and ultimately of understanding, an ever-receding knowledge, becomes in itself a counter knowledge.

Thus John tells two symmetrical and contrary stories simultaneously. His understanding-and-certain-knowledge plot climaxes within the book—crucifixion/resurrection. His uncertainty-and-knowledge-deferred plot extends beyond the book into the future—a promised teacher. The plot of knowing, signs progressing inexorably to the ultimate sign on the cross, is essentially tragic, even with its resurrection reversal because the hero still leaves the world that the disciples inhabit. John's counterplot, on the other hand, continually defers clarity and knowledge to the future, and is thus essentially comic. Not so much humorous, though the disciples' puppy-like persistence and patience despite Jesus' relentless teasing can make us smile, as it is evasive and ironic.

Only by including this counter to knowing can John remain true to the complexity of the character he portrays. As John develops this plot, he dwells at length on deferral (13:31–14:31; 16:4–33) and milks the suspense that arises from the promise of knowledge. We fully expect, as do the disciples, that by the end of John's book we will be given the long-promised key to the mystery. Yet it is not to be; the "Spirit of Truth" who will "teach you everything" (14:17, 26) hovers just beyond reach. Finally, knowledge is deferred once again, to be found only outside his book.

The tension of John's two plots in motion and counter motion commands our attention. We know and yet do not know what's coming next. John seduces us with these rhythms. We delight in the rhythm of fate, an inevitable unfolding of successive events that end in death, playing against the rhythm of hope, a promise glittering on the horizon. The revealing of events in the present is countered by a great concealing—the promise of life-giving events veiled in postponement.

∽

From the outset, expectation echoes like the blast of a ram's horn. Postponement is the foyer of John's book. The Baptist's going before prefigures all to come, the understanding and ultimate knowledge promised to the disciples. From the very beginning reality exists in the future. John intensifies this in his scene with the Samaritan woman. Ostensibly a revelation scene, the knowledge revealed about "true worship" and "spirit" lies in the future. Even Jesus' identity as Messiah remains unrealized, for the woman goes away convinced only that he is a prophet. So the scene that appears to reveal proves elusive, which launches the plot of unknowing.

John builds suspense from here by returning again and again to the disciples' lack of understanding. He develops his counterplot, building tension through the middle of the book, by quoting Jesus in what almost becomes a refrain, "my hour is not yet come" (7:30, 8:20) and showing his disciples' increasing confusion. Jesus' irony alone, of course, is bewildering. He explicitly identifies with a woman in travail, yet his "hour" is that of death (17:1) not birth. In conversation with his disciples as he washes their feet, the suspense becomes unbearable. John keeps his focus on the act, a moving gesture so precisely imagined that we feel their very presence, but modulates with a sure hand to his theme of knowledge postponed.

The plot of unknowing thickens when Jesus raises the stakes, telling his disciples that he would give them full knowledge in the present, but they are not able to handle such knowledge (16:12), and introduces the "Spirit of truth" who will give them this knowledge in the future. Following on the heels of this promise, as the hour is "now come," John reaches the denouement of his tragic plot and its climax in Jesus' crucifixion and resurrection. But the plot of unknowing brings anticlimax, where Jesus offers yet another deferral of knowledge, having earlier promised that the "Holy spirit" of truth will come. Though John says that Jesus "breathed" on his disciples, giving them this spirit (20:22), it is only to do future things, not to inherit present knowledge. Now equal with Jesus himself, they have the power to forgive sins (20:23), yet it is power postponed. We know that they do not exercise it before Jesus goes and John's book closes.

～

We are reminded that John's book works by epicycles of interpretation and reinterpretation, the gyring of deferred clarification held in tension with the arrow of understanding. Cycles of misunderstanding spiral upward to ever greater inclusiveness but are ultimately inconclusive. The plot of knowing appears to hit its predicted target—crucifixion and resurrection come to pass—while that of unknowing moves the target ever farther and farther beyond range.

Jesus states his reason for deferral plainly, "Now I tell you before it come, that, when it is come to pass, you may believe that I am he" (13:19). His disciples, nevertheless, don't understand in the present what John makes his reader aware of, an irony he relishes. Jesus speaks here specifically of Judas betraying him, but its relationship with foot washing is left purposely vague, which expands its meaning. We're visited and opened up by a great power that the scene gathers from the force of John's images of water. The future knowledge Jesus promises is ostensibly that of knowing the betrayer's identity, a simple fact, but more than this is implied at the climax of the washing when he says, "What I do you know not now; but you shall know hereafter" (13:7).

Our suspicions are confirmed as Jesus expands this context beyond betrayal, saying to his disciples, "yet a little while I am with you. You shall seek me: and . . . where I go, you cannot come" (13:33). Ever alert, Peter blurts out, "Lord, to where do you go?" John maintains the suspense of his deferred-knowledge counterplot by having Jesus answer rather coyly, "Where I go, you cannot follow me now; but you shall follow me afterwards." John develops very skillfully the elusive nature of Jesus' knowledge and the disciples' struggle to understand. Just when the disciples believe that they're closing in on knowledge in the present, Jesus puts them off and defers it with a promise. This time postponed beyond the revelation of his betrayer's identity and into an indefinite future. Elaborating on the dialog between Jesus and Peter, while at the same time making clear that the disciples still don't grasp his meaning, John maintains the tension of his counterplot.

But Peter persists, "Lord, why cannot I follow you now? I will lay down my life for your sake." Jesus' tone now changes abruptly. He meets Peter's touching, almost childlike earnestness with withering sarcasm. From addressing his disciples with tenderness as "little children" and proceeding evasively but respectfully, he shifts tonal gears to mockery, bringing Peter up short, "Will you lay down your life for my sake?" It's a rhetorical question, of course, implying that the answer is "no." Jesus then downshifts to contempt, made more painful by his portentous preface, "Verily, verily, I say unto you," in order to deliver his sting: "The cock shall not crow, till you have denied me three times."

Peter slams up against unknowing at its most intractable. Not only does Jesus refuse to answer Peter but takes the offensive. He is left wounded and mystified. This emotional exchange is a crisis point in both John's plots. They intersect here, and John uses the pivot to wonderful advantage, furthering both simultaneously. Jesus not only defers knowledge in his refusal to answer, developing the counterplot, but builds suspense by his prediction of Peter's future act of cowardice, which comes to pass, thus also furthering the plot of knowledge.

∼

In developing the counterplot of unknowing, John leverages this crisis in Jesus and Peter's relationship, subtly calling into question the plot of knowledge. He does this by expanding the notion of betrayal and deflating the crucifixion/resurrection event. Betrayal is no longer a simple matter of revealing the identity of a person, providing certain knowledge, but a complicated matter of character and the uncertain interaction of friends forgiving each other, yet fully aware of the inevitable small betrayals that attend. Pointedly, Jesus no longer calls his disciples servants or children but "friends" (15:15). And "Friendship cannot exist without Forgiveness of Sins continually," as Blake says, embedded in the mystery of love and thus ultimately unknowable.

Furthermore, the very act of denial in the courtyard and its parallel act on the beach, we remember, frame the crucifixion/resurrection, the climax of John's plot of knowledge. Because this flattens the plot's climax, deflating its putative significance, John makes us realize that these events do not, in fact, fulfill the promise of knowledge. For Peter's question still hangs in the air unanswered: "Lord, to where do you go?"

As his plot and counterplot thicken, John teases us into expecting an answer, even when we suspect that it will not be forthcoming. Our hopes that the denouement is close are raised, as John shrewdly gives and takes, having Jesus assert, "all things . . . I have made known unto you" (15:15), when the disciples know better. They are still in the dark (the reader, if not the dark, in the shadows). Jesus reinforces this with what must fall on the ears of the disciples as an evasion when he asserts that they had nothing to do with this journey they've been on, for they did not choose to follow him; he chose them (15:16). This undercuts the will that Peter displays, the drive to obtain a promised knowledge, and lays the groundwork for a new evasion.

Jesus doesn't ignore the disciple's question, but now takes another tack. A familiar tease, he announces, "I have yet many things to say unto you," then delivers the punch line, "but you cannot bear them now" (16:12). He still doesn't answer Peter's question, that is, not out of contempt but out of concern for his disciples who he maintains cannot handle the knowledge he has promised. But this can only seem specious to them. So Jesus attempts to soften the blow by saying that when "the Spirit of truth is come, he will guide you into all truth." Promises, promises.

And his follow up impresses them as outright gibberish; they will see him and not see him. "A little while," he says, "and you shall not see me: and again, a little while, and you shall see me, because I go to the Father" (16:16), which he repeats like a litany. They pick up on the rhythm of this evasion, as if returning his earlier mockery of them,

"What is this that he says unto us, A little while, and you shall not see me: and again, a little while, and you shall see me." What Jesus is saying is not too hard to bear, then, but impossible to make any sense of, even at this late juncture in the disciples' relationship (and the reader is with the disciples here). Concern about his sanity no doubt rises again.

∽

Another crisis point in both John's plots has been reached. On the one hand, knowledge alluded to in the future, the now-you-don't-see-me, now-you-do riddle, materializes—the crucifixion/resurrection event. On the other, knowledge is postponed indefinitely to the future when the promised "Spirit of truth" will come at last. Time to level with the disciples again.

Turning his attention to language, thereby diverting them from the actual knowledge he promises, Jesus admits frankly that "These things have I spoken unto you in proverbs: but the time comes, when I shall no more speak unto you in proverbs, but I shall show you plainly of the Father" (16:25). A typical move because every time Jesus has been challenged by his disciples to be clear, he claims to speak plainly but turns finally to figurative language. Now he's more brazen, promising that language itself will like the Marxist state fall away completely in the future. Speaking rendered unnecessary by showing, the word replaced by the Word on the tree (the cross) and walking among the trees with Mary Magdalene.

Thus Jesus fleetingly indulges John's fantasy that knowledge can be delivered outside of time and apart from language. But in fact, Jesus never ceases speaking in proverbs, "For the Father himself loves you, because you have loved me, and have believed that I came out from God. I came forth from the Father, and am come into the world: again, I leave the world, and go to the Father" (16:27–28). Resistant to a single meaning, this father/son story is, in short, another "proverb," figurative rather than the "plain" language promised. Moreover, Jesus has once again deferred the disciples' understanding to the future when he will "go to the Father."

Desire reaching fever pitch, John can hold off no longer on the climax to his plot of knowledge. He has Jesus declare: "Behold, the hour comes, yea, is now come, that you shall be scattered, every man to his own, and shall leave me alone: and yet I am not alone, because the Father is with me" (16:32). Yet "now" extends again into a promise to be fulfilled in the future when the paradox of Jesus being simultaneously alone and not alone will be resolved. Even so John's story of present knowledge picks up speed from here and finds its mark—the crucifixion/resurrection. Short-term misunderstandings, such as the identity of Jesus' betrayer, are now clarified, yet the greater knowledge promised, such as the nature of the "Spirit of truth," remains to be revealed.

Accordingly, John hints that this long-awaited climax, where all the promises of knowledge are fulfilled and understanding given in the present with a single flash of illumination, is in fact not a climax. For Jesus tells Mary Magdalene in the garden not to touch him and explains, "I am not yet ascended to my Father" (20:17). In effect, he makes another promise. He will ascend not now but in the future at which time he will become touchable. Cunningly, to heighten the drama of his counterplot, John unlike other gospel writers does not show the ascension. Thus the plot of unknowing carries us still, flowing slowly at times through wide and shallow beds, at other times swiftly down deep gorges toward the end of John's book.

CONCLUSION IN WHICH NOTHING IS CONCLUDED

Jesus confirms this open-ended counterplot in his last conversation with Peter. His language of contingency and promise reasserts its power at the end of John's book to resist reduction to a single meaning. Right after their exchange in which Jesus' forgiveness and Peter's love are renewed, Jesus addresses him, "When you were a young man, you used to fasten your own belt and set off for wherever you wished. But when you grow old, you will stretch out your hands, and another will fasten your belt around you and take you where you do not wish to go" (21:18; trans., R.E. Brown). We are left looking to the future in this strange and poignant story, outside the book to the time of Peter's old age, and puzzling over what it holds for him.

The story's proverbial message of inevitable dependency in old age includes a mysterious twist, dark hints of something untoward in Peter's future. So John anxiously intrudes with an interpretation, explaining that Jesus was "signifying by what death" Peter "should glorify God" (21:19). We're struck by John's phrase here, which echoes earlier interpretations that refer to the death of Jesus. Twice before he glosses Jesus' statements, saying, "This he said, signifying what death he should die"

(12:33, 18:32). Because this memorable phrase, still reverberating in our heads, is so strongly associated with Jesus' death, it wrenches our attention away from Peter and from the future.

Directing our gaze back to the climax of his tragic plot that relates the straightforward story of Jesus' life ending in death and glory, John's interpretation employs the language of inevitability. He is narrowly specific, as a result, saying that Jesus predicts a bad end for Peter, whereas Jesus himself is resolutely mysterious about Peter's future. In fact, Jesus' own interpretation of his story about old age, which consists of a simple admonition to Peter, "Follow me" (21:19), refuses to limit its meaning.

John, of course, anxious interpreter and self-conscious writer (21:24), orchestrates this fine tension between interpretations. While John's is a non sequitur, its perfunctory tone revealing an attempt to salvage what he knows is an anti-anticlimax, Jesus' interpretation is elegantly satisfying. Having just forgiven Peter, his simple words are charged with tenderness and promise. And maintaining his gaze toward the future, a time when Peter will "stretch out" his hands (21:18) in some unexplained need, Jesus furthers his comic counterplot of deferred knowledge. He hints darkly and promises ambiguously.

~

After two false cadences, where it seemed that he would bring his book to a close following the physical exchange with Thomas or the verbal exchange with Peter, John now modulates to a distant key full of color and dissonance, depth and complexity. He opens up language, that is, in a way necessary to comprehend the character of Jesus. Extending the ambiguity of the story about dependency that Jesus told Peter, John confirms Jesus' open-ended interpretation over his own. He shrewdly introduces this irony in order to expand the meaning of the conclusion to his book that does not conclude.

Alluding to a rumor that one of the disciples, possibly the writer John himself, had been granted the boon that he "should not die" (21:23), he reports Jesus' response, "He shall not die; but if I will that he tarry till I come, what is that to you?" An exhilarating move, as John at the end of his book flings wide the gates of meaning. Not only is the identity of the disciple ambiguous, but in a superbly economical move John proceeds to render the writer's self, the "disciple which testified of these things, and wrote these things" (21:24), ambiguous as well.

More important, having arrived at the end of the book, Jesus leaves the future open. Implicit in "till I come" is another promise. An opaque promise never to be clarified, John knows full well. In his concluding scene, John offers equivocal certainty. The best that can be said is that Peter's question is conclusively left unanswered. "Lord, to where do you go?" echoing yet.

The counterplot of unknowing, then, flows on beyond the book, beyond Jesus' living and dying, beyond its listeners and readers. To the end John keeps us attuned to his rhythm of hope, even as we hear the constant drumming of fate. He chooses not the pamphleteer's rousing exhortation as finale to his book but the artist's flippant non-conclusion, which playfully continues to proffer promises of understanding in a future day when his listeners and readers no longer "tarry." For John makes one last move before succumbing to writer's melancholy—"the world itself could not contain the books that should be written" about the "things which Jesus did" (21:25)—and plunging into the abyss of silence. He teases us with a question, the five last words of Jesus: "What is that to you?"

Silence

Like the mound, my silence sprouts
Grass, a green bleeding.

—Yehuda Amichai

A Jesus who defers knowledge is a silent Jesus. Paradoxically, the man called the Word, the man who adopts the prophet's speaking-out life, cherishes silence. It is the oxygen of mystery that feeds his incandescence.

Following suit, John makes a paradoxical work. To comprehend his encounter with radiance, the work must comprehend opposites, balancing the determinant Book of Light, a book of knowledge glittering with certainty, against an undetermined babbling Book of Water. The former book establishes the ground base on which John harmonizes the latter. Both ultimately become the Book of Unknowing. Yet even as it depends on language for its very life, the Book of Unknowing witnesses the incommunicable. It is made of words devoted to a silent, ever-expanding cosmos of Jesus, a body that exists before and after words like the gestures that he and Thomas make with their hands.

The power of silence, as Jesus demonstrates before Pilate, rivals the power of the word. No one is more aware of this than John. Like the atom, made largely of space, John's book is composed of silence. The unspoken informs its speaking. John is, as Philip Levine says of a great jazz horn player, a man who "stared for years / into the breathy, unknowable voice / of silence and captured the music." John found the music of Jesus' voice, the words and acts woven into his book, but first and last he had to stare hard at Jesus' silence, making a companion of it like a painted image. In doing so, he became intimately acquainted with silence and its power. And we're still smarting, acutely aware that withholding the words of Lazarus is an act of power.

As a writer, he knows the importance of this strategy in controlling his reader. Placing Jesus in a space of silence enhances his mystery. The hinted at but unspoken convinces us that we understand more than we know. The unspoken, then, enables John to forestall objections and establish belief and, once established, acceptance of miraculous signs and all manner of claims follows.

Publicly, of course, John turns this inside out, claiming that the signs establish belief. But this is a conclusion after the fact, not the method his book demonstrates. By using specific strategies of speech and silence, he establishes his authority as a writer, and all else follows. He well knows that skillfully woven words create the belief that establishes authority that yields followers. Hero and counter hero, plot and counterplot, all informed by a disarming irony are John's principal ways of gaining our confidence in his speaking Jesus' speaking.

∼

John's complementary strategy of silence, ironic in the company of speech, begs to be understood in pictorial terms. A part of John relies on signs, after all, entering through the eye gate. And for all its babble, his is a book of scenes: Jesus walking on water; Jesus washing his disciples' feet; Jesus surrounded by lanterns and torches in the Garden of the End (18:3); Jesus hoisted on the cross, a sign above his head. And then he "showed" himself (20:20, 21:1). It's a movie. John the director, obsessed with light and dark (1:5, 8:12, 9:4–5, 12:35–36), closing on a figure who emerges from night (Nicodemus) or tracking on one who goes out into the night (Judas). The painter Paul Klee reminds us that "The eye travels along the paths cut out for it in the work." And just as we've seen John at work in the daylight of understanding and in the dark wood of unknowing, constructing plot and counterplot, so he blazes silent paths that we are to follow into the uncanny heart of his book.

Accordingly, he makes two of his most critical scenes pivot on silence. Jesus characteristically condenses silence, consolidating its power like a single energizing dot of color on a painting, as he does when he falls into the hands of Pilate; or Jesus extends silence, multiplying its point of energy like a line curving to infinity, as he does when he gives himself into the anointing hands of Mary.

The complement to this concentration and extension of silence, its energy reverberating, is absence. John makes us conscious of what he does not talk about—keeping topics at bay that clamor to get into his book or dropping us into chasms that he opens within it. Like a painter or sculptor, John uses negative space skillfully. He implicitly demonstrates how what he does not talk about supports the edifice of his book, as when he leaves us in silence on Lazarus' return.

And in the end, John uses silence to point beyond speech, giving power to words on the other side of silence. Like all writers, he knows his "book leans on the void." Words emerge, after all, from a matrix of silence. His book is in a double sense "an act of silence directed against silence, the first positive act of death against death." Taking advantage of the obvious, he expands the reach of words, pointing our way through silence as explicitly as an arrow.

DOT/LINE

But Jesus gave him no answer.

—JOHN

The Silence of the Lamb

When the adulterous woman is brought to him and questions are first posed, Jesus does not answer the Scribes and Pharisees at all, immediately stooping down "as though he heard them not" (8:6). John draws our attention to the strategic silence that Jesus creates in this instant. He carves out a silence filled with foreboding, for they want to sacrifice the woman. Nothing could settle dread on us more forcefully than this silence charged with murderous intent. And, by the same token, nothing could fill us with awe more completely than this brief eternal moment, the collective breath suspended. Jesus' strategy works, it's clear, because the murderous storm is quelled. We are witness to power.

Later Jesus uses precisely this same strategy on his own behalf. At a pivotal point in the interrogation with Pilate, John tells us that in the face of his persistent questions, "Jesus gave him no answer" (19:9). On this moment of silence rests the tip of Pilate's sword. Will he condemn Jesus and drive it home or will he put up his sword? Jesus knows his very life is at stake. And again his strategy succeeds; Pilate seeks to free him in a temporary stay against execution.

Both these scenes of silence are instants of incipient blood sacrifice. The first does not result in sacrifice, while the second ultimately does. The first scene is an isolate point. All blood lust brought to a single moment of emptiness, a singularity at the intersection of the mob and the lone man, in which the woman takes on all the world's hatred and compassion. She is the lens focusing the world into the single mark that Jesus makes on the ground with his finger. The second scene is one point on a curve of sacrifice moving inexorably from the beginning of the book to its climax. The silence of Jesus before Pilate participates in the events that led to this scene and in the events precipitated by it, all of Jesus' own making. Jesus dwells in a silent moment of fullness, as if removed from and about to partake of his own body, suspended on a quantum of life's trajectory to be completed in blood.

The Seam of Silence

Jesus' strategy in these scenes of imminent sacrifice is to concentrate silence, almost unbearably, achieving a still point of power. A complementary strategy is to tear the fabric of silence, where the presence of sacrifice is felt but lies outside the scene either in the past, having already been accomplished, or in the future. The power of silence is used not to deflect sacrifice but to reflect its meaning. In this strategy silence is rent and opened up to language. "What a seam of silence to be unsewn!" the poet exclaims. This appears to be by nature its fate, "the place where a writer offers his voice up to silence."

Without a word soldiers thrust a spear into the side of Jesus. Silently, blood and water flow out. Our attention is arrested by this strange, purely visual event, seemingly superfluous in its following Jesus' sacrifice. What could this silent scene mean? John makes clear that Jesus is rent in order that the voice of the prophets can be heard (19:35–37). This silent piercing of Jesus opens in his side the mouth of a prophet, ironically, his "other / mouth being locked," as Miguel de Unamuno remarks.

As the mouth that Jesus has used thus far is silenced by his sacrifice, another mouth appears in his side. Here the ancient prophet opens his mouth to bear present witness. The onlookers, that is, recall the words of the prophet Zachariah fulfilled in this scene: "They shall look on him whom they pierced" (12:10). It is first a silent speaking, which John emphasizes, saying, "he that saw it bore record, and his record is true: and he knows that he says true." Seeing in silence comes first, then hearing what the prophet says. Silence is torn in order to release the voice that is "true." The power of silence thus flows into the true word.

Conversely, the false word carries us back to the truth of silence. Silence rent only to take on greater power. When sister Mary took a pound of spikenard ointment and "anointed the feet of Jesus, and wiped his feet with her hair," an act in which we are intended to feel the imminence of sacrifice, John notes explicitly that the house was "filled with the odor of the ointment" (12:3). All is silent. He prepares us for this, teasing us not only with Lazarus' silence at the supper table about his experience in the grave where he "stinks" (11:39), but with his sisters' annoying silence as well, their not asking a single question. The ointment banishes the stink of death, and by its perfume, silence is extended throughout the whole house. In pausing to allow us to smell it, John purposely expands this moment of silence. The scent lets us luxuriate in silence.

Lulled by the extended moment, we are shocked by Judas' rude question, "Why was not this ointment sold for three hundred denarii, and given to the poor?" Suddenly, he rends both the tender spirit of the scene and its silence. We are jolted out of a dream of the senses. But John has accomplished his purpose; we are carried back into the space of silence now informed by the nightmare of sacrifice. Responding to Judas, Jesus makes this clear as he links Mary's act to the "day" of his "burying." Torn open by Judas, then, the perfumed silence gains power.

NEGATIVE SPACE

Silence' oblation to the Ear supersedes sound.

—Emily Dickinson

What John Talks About When He Doesn't Talk About It

If one strategy of silence is power, another is mystery. As incandescent figure, Jesus deals in power and mystery. As a writer who must convey more than he says in convincing us of Jesus' incandescence, John too deals in power and mystery. Mystery, he knows, can be conveyed by silence. It allows us to see, like the space between the dots and lines of a picture, the nothing that is. As in a Matisse drawing, what John leaves out of his book is as crucial as what he includes.

Jesus is not born. At least John leaves this fact out of his book. Jesus simply is. Nor do we see him grow up, get circumcised, learn a trade, marry. Yet we have a powerful need to know this, witness the numerous and popular books to follow John's providing details of Jesus' childhood, such as his making clay sparrows, recorded in *The Infancy Gospel of Thomas*, which when he clapped his hands, flew off chirping. John heightens Jesus' mystery by fighting off the impulse to give him a family history or even any physical characteristics. How tall? What color eyes? John knows that the answer to these questions would limit our imagination of his hero and thus reduce his mysterious power. He knows, in short, how potent the subject avoided is as a subject.

Likewise, the power of absence hollowed out of a subject embraced. When John does not have Jesus interpret either of the Cana miracles, for example, though he follows each of his other signs with a discourse, we find ourselves revisiting the metamorphosis of water at the wedding and the healing of the nobleman's son. At close range and at a distance, respectively, these are feats of magic without props, incantations, or gestures. Pure acts, they are beyond language. Their very accomplishment—great power demonstrated in so casual a manner—hollows out space around them. And the absence of explanation in their wake, as if words would break their spell, renders them uncanny. To borrow a sentence from Paul Valéry, the "ear expands, grows more and more awake in these empty spaces." Our senses brought to a pitch, we find ourselves in the presence of great mystery.

∽

More than hollowed out space, John on occasion creates a veritable chasm in his text. More than an inchoate sense of the uncanny, absence in this case is charged with meaning. After the lively dialog with the Pharisees that follows Jesus' healing of the blind man, John cashes in on the set up, saying that "some of the Pharisees which were with him heard these words, and said unto him, Are we blind also?" (9:40) That is, John has them voice the very interpretation that Jesus wants to give the actions we've just witnessed. Though a bit unsatisfying because it seems somewhat contrived following on the heels of the blind man's dialog, which was totally convincing in its psychological portrait of a man caught in verbal and social crossfire, Jesus' cryptic follow up has a strangely satisfying air of finality. He answers them, "If you were blind, you would have no sin: but now you say, We see; therefore your sin remains" (9:41).

Then John drops us into a great chasm of silence. From this realistic scene in a realistic setting, from psychological complexity and verbal play (blind/see), John takes us suddenly to parable, simplicity, and seriousness. For Jesus' very next statement, using a completely different tone, is "Verily, Verily, I say unto you, he that enters not by the door into the sheepfold, but climbs up some other way, the same is a thief and a robber." John offers no logical bridge or even associational link from one scene to the other. Between these disparate worlds of reality and fiction (chapters 9 and 10), therefore, lies a great emptiness.

The gap here disrupts continuity and thus meaning itself, which creates another meaning. The gap between breaking off and starting again tells us that stories by their very nature in their confident unfolding are suspect. Here lies the motive of John's counterplot. Yet he embodies his true "record" (19:35) in a story. Disruption of its plot forces us to shift our point of view, forces a change in context, which necessarily entails further interpretation. We extrapolate the flight of his story, but our expectations are thwarted as its trajectory is broken off.

The negative space that lies between the blind man and the shepherd, as a result, not only creates meaning but carries meaning in itself. We're confronted with the writer John. Our complacency in looking through John to Jesus is shaken. The window between us and the "record" becomes apparent. We become acutely aware of John's opaqueness; he is working the stage machinery, directing our attention, guiding us down a path, hiding and revealing. In this space, then, we see the means of our progression which changes where we've been and where we're going. John's disruption by silence forces us to take another angle on his story and so bends its meaning, as we move abruptly from one scene to the other, just as at the interface of air and water, light is refracted.

Dumb Show

Excluding subjects altogether and withholding from subjects included in his book adds to the mysterious aura of Jesus while demystifying John himself. There is an appealing coyness about this method, as when he withholds the name of Jesus' mother or brings Nicodemus back at the end of his book but not to be heard.

Nonetheless, this coyness can be calculated. John's leaving out demonstrates just how deliberately he proceeds as a writer. He knows Lazarus, of course, but does not use his name after Jesus brings him back from the dead. A curious silence. Instead, John says, "he that was dead came forth, bound hand and foot with grave clothes: and his face was bound" (11:44). Here is coyness with an edge. John's withholding the name contributes to the force of this spectacle on the audience of Jews. He emphasizes that in the context this is not so much Jesus' good friend Lazarus as it is a man playing his role in a coming-forth-from-the-dead pageant. We are meant to see and experience the spectacle, not identify with a specific individual. John wants to maintain awe. Hence he shows us the grave clothes, his camera panning the hands and then the feet, finally the face, but does not let Lazarus speak.

Even in confession is coyness, a sly withholding that leaves his book mysteriously open ended. In its final sentences the writer intrudes, admitting: "This is the disciple which testifies of these things, and wrote these things: and we know that his testimony is true. And there are also many other things which Jesus did, the which, if they should be written every one, I suppose that even the world itself could not contain the books that should be written. Amen" (21:24–25). John implies that his "testimony" is a single self-contained "true" story and in the same breath states that it is multiple, consisting of as many stories as "books" that could be written. That is, John's story of Jesus in his last days is only one of a multitude of possible stories. All presumably true. John finds this unsettling, as evidenced by his switch from the coy reference to himself in the third person, "his testimony," to the disarmingly casual first person, "I suppose." John himself becomes the show as he experiences a moment of vertigo in his vision of an endless proliferation of true testimonies. In pointing to this horizon, John reminds us of the vast silence surrounding the single story we've just been given. We will never hear all the other stories in all the books that John did not write.

ARROW

Blank, the first and last page of the book.

—Edmund Jabès

The Ceramic Bible

The Japanese potter Takako Araki's *Ceramic Bible* is a haunting sculpture. A black Bible, which seems to be the extension of its solid base, lies open to a gospel text. Its pages are charred, their edges flaking like weathered shale. The details are so realistic, separate leaves and legible text, that we can scarcely believe it is sculpted from clay. The book appears to have just been rescued from a fire.

Stone and paper, it is a paradoxical object. Its leaves are a crystalline form of the soot-black base, and they are the lettered petals of its bloom. Its strangeness clings to us, daring us to turn the page that we know will crumble in our hand at the merest touch, promising words that we know will not reach our ears. The sculpture appears in one moment to be a thing from outside our human world, as if we had found a meteorite; in another it appears to be a highly crafted object, something lovingly made. Caught at the intersection of the permanent and impermanent, mute and voiced, found and made, we're confronted in this sculpture by a silent parable.

The *Ceramic Bible* images John's consciousness that his book is both given to him and constructed by him. A sign as well, it is a physical parable of his exalting the word while reckoning with silence. For him the word is to silence as the wing of the bird to air. The word must bear us through silence. By contrast, an eastern tradition exalts silence above the word. Silence is the state of enlightenment. Rumi, the thirteenth-century Sufi poet, draws on this tradition when he exclaims that though everyone is tempted by speech, "I am the slave of / the master of silence."

No slave, John leaves us at the end of his book in his "testimony" with an image of the endless possibility of books wrested from silence. He must speak. Like Camus in our own age, John is painfully aware of the "confrontation between the human need and the unreasonable silence of the world." His testimony like an arrow points the way through silence. He calls out to the world for more life and from its silence wrests everlasting life.

∼

Like the *Ceramic Bible*, John's book also suspends us between the conviction that it is an object unrelated to John, a gift from beyond, and one that is deliberately made by John the writer. But John himself is suspended between the same poles, conscious on the one hand that the words of the incandescent Jesus are spoken through him, rather than by him, given to John from somewhere else, such as the realm of the Father; and on the other, that the words must be selected and arranged, even corrected and annotated, and that Jesus himself takes many of his words from other writers, the prophets, which he freely revises. John realizes that Jesus derives his authority more from old writings than from his Father. To make himself into a prophet, he interprets previous prophets, their way of acting and speaking. He knows that "The words of a dead man / Are modified in the guts of the living." He is, in fact, both called and self-created. Likewise, John shares the writer's profound sense of simultaneously building his book and discovering it.

We can feel this double sense of "authoring" in his portrait of Jesus. On the one hand, John desperately wants Jesus to be an absolute character, having a consistent self; on the other, he knows this to be false. Striving for a single meaning as a preacher to deliver the Truth, a message discovered, John creates many meanings as a poet in making his book. Consequently, John gives us a Jesus who does not assume he is the last prophet, having the last word. On the contrary, Jesus assumes that his disciples (listeners/readers) by appropriating his acts and words will come to possess the same truth and power (16:13, 23) as himself. In short, he expects his disciples to use his method of constructing a life.

While John gives "true" testimonies of the character of Jesus, he also makes clear that they are provisional. He introduces us to a Jesus named "Light," for example, which we take to be the truth, only to find that he's also "Vine" and "Door." His way is to continually re-name himself. His names, instead of pointing to a given fixed character, build a self as he goes. Yet we experience one called "Jesus." We know his voice. The power of John's language convinces us that there exists a self behind and prior to Jesus' constructed selves, such as "temple" and "shepherd," behind the "resurrection and the life," called the "Word."

The danger of powerful language, as well as its achievement, is that his book seems to transcend the writer John. It is the "most beautiful poem one can make from blood," to borrow a sentence from Federico Garcia Lorca about a friend's painting. Part of us wants to believe that his book was washed up on the shore at our feet, a pure message from beyond. Given the transcendent power of the work, seemingly beyond human possibilities, we have difficulty keeping John and his work together, just as we do Shakespeare and his *Hamlet*.

At the same time, another part of us knows the danger of separating the work from its creator. After separation triumphs, veneration follows and finally oppression. When a book comes to be perceived as an object from a realm outside the human imagination, and thus unassailable, rather than something made by a human writer with designs on us, the inevitable response is to bow before it in silence. Like any idol it demands worship. The closing of imaginative possibilities results.

The great lyric life that John makes is so powerful in its figuration—the Word, the lamb, the empty tomb—and its configuration—plot and counterplot—that it is dangerous. Double-edged, his book opens the mind to endless possibilities; it also inspires a single-minded possessiveness of one of these possibilities as the Truth. Separated from the maker of the book, the whole is reduced to a single meaning. Political structures, church and state, are then constructed to preserve this meaning become dogma. And when meaning is institutionalized, writings canonized, countless voices are thereafter silenced.

A poem made by a true poet is true in many ways, John well knows, and so out of it flows many voices. John's Jesus also knows this. He wants to silence his audience, charging some who do not accept the one way with being of the devil, a coercive strategy; at the same time, he refuses to silence any voice, charging his disciples with the "Spirit" of truth. John the writer is too much in love with the sound of water, too much in love with characters like Nicodemus, Peter, and Mary Magdalene to silence them. They must be heard along with the voice of Jesus as necessary to the telling of a "true" testimony. Though sharing the fantasy of all writers, who would like their words to be the final interpretation after which only silence and awe, John simply identifies too much with their restless, befuddled questioning as an integral part of his true story to silence them.

The Unmade Bed

Mary Magdalene sees two angels dressed in white, one at the head and one at the feet, marking the place "where the body of Jesus had lain" (20:12). John intends us to see the empty place. Its very emptiness, which he intensifies by carefully framing it with Angels, points as plain as an arrow to the meaning of the entire scene. Absence is presence. John's book pivots on this notion. Jesus talks throughout about a leaving that makes his arriving meaningful. He postpones understanding and knowledge, which opens up space in the story, a silent space of mystery. He discusses his absence in the future as presence within the disciples.

John's book is an "unmade bed of absence" to borrow Edmond Jabès's phrase. It is the ghostly figure left in the mold. Suggestive rather than definitive, the book is in this sense not the vase but the space occupied by the vase. All attempts to evade this fact, to get outside or go beyond the book and escape its concrete complexity, are futile.

John precludes such a move by giving his book a mysterious derivation. "In the beginning was the Word," one of the world's great opening sentences. It is also one of its cleverest ploys. This move gives his book a privileged origin and no origin; it places his book within time, the beginning of time itself, and outside of time. John has it both ways. Where then does the book originate? In the acts of Jesus or in the acts of the writer? Is the source of his book in the book itself, its rhetorical moves and symmetry as it so often seems, or outside the book, in the observed acts and shared stories about the acts of Jesus? All-of-the-above is John's answer or the truth of testimony evaporates.

For that matter, where is the author of this book? We feel John's presence as writer throughout, yet he is coy at the end, as if he were hostage to the real author, perhaps a writer-editor disciple of his. And rather than being intended for those who do not yet believe, is his book intended instead for believers whom he wants to ensure "continue believing" (20:31; trans., R.E. Brown)? Is the author Jesus himself? His monologues, his interpretations, after all, are the book regardless of their metamorphosis. And the stories about him, his stories. Yet Jesus is himself authored; he experiences his own life as a story written by the prophets before him. In the final analysis, we're left with a book whose author is absent.

If the origins of John's book are obscure and its author elusive, the words themselves also seem to shift, and we're left gazing not at the text but at the place where the text "had lain." Where it seems to declare straightforwardly, we often find ourselves in an ironic context. Where the text purports to be "plain," it pivots on puns. And where it promises continuity, it delivers disruption. Like Mary Magdalene, we're often left with the sense that we are looking not at the thing itself but its imprint. What we see is a clear impress in the clay, but like a strange tongue it is radically unfamiliar. Its clarity is not that of bas-relief, figures emerging from their matrix into light, but of cuneiform, indentations cupping their angular shadows.

We see dots and lines, palpable voids, and even arrows pointing the way if we allow ourselves. There are points and their curved extension in spacetime before there are words and gaps in words. But with arrows we enter the human world of desire and so language, "And the Word was made flesh."

To John silence is in love with the word. His book answers the Greek hymns to Silence as the God-who-has-hidden-himself. Like an arrow, silence in John always points beyond itself. "The father of the arrow is the thought: how do I expand my reach?" as Paul Klee observes. A deeply embedded wish fulfillment, the pathos of John's book is his reaching beyond life for more life, while fully aware of our human state. "Half-winged—half imprisoned, this is man!" Klee sums up; "the broader the magnitude of his reach, the more painful man's tragic limitation." But the grandeur and breathtaking foolishness of John's book is its refusal to recognize limitation. Its arrow passes clean through tragedy to comedy.

∽

For in the moment of rising from the waters of his book, which ends with resurrection and reunion, I feel not half but fully winged. Yet what is left after I finish listening to John's voice mingled with the voices of Jesus and Nicodemus and Mary Magdalene, and with the lapping and flowing waters, is silence. Meditating in this silence on what John has wrought, bearing the marks of his creative fires, I ask, Why do I want to re-read this book, listening again, and inhabit once more the charged silence after its voices have fallen away on the shore of Tiberias?

What is it about this book that matters to me? The boldness of John's sketching Jesus—incandescent figure of our desire for immortality—follows me like the sun. The honesty of the writer John who enlists the most unlikely characters, such as Nicodemus and Peter, in his work of testimony is with me still. The love that John shows equally for Jesus and Peter is moving; the understanding of both Caiaphas and Jesus is astonishing; the identification with Jesus and Nicodemus, engaged and disinterested at the same time, exhilarating. More important, they bring me back to his book again and again because by these commitments is the complexity of his obsessive desire for everlasting life infused with a sense of its being a "true" testimony.

Now my speaking about John's telling the story of Jesus speaking ceases. At the same time, arriving at the end of John's book, as with any true work of art, the realization strikes us that our boat has struck something very large in the depths. "And nothing happens," to borrow the words of Juan Ramón Jiménez, "silence. . . .

> Or has everything happened,
> and are we now, quietly, in the new life?"

My Unnamed Sources Here Named

With Montaigne, I happily own up to the fact that my book is "built up" of the "spoils" from other books. A great pleasure it is to acknowledge my profound debt to their authors, as I've explored the tricky terrain of John's book. I reserve all errors in fact or judgment, of course, for myself. In the end, it's "all mine and none mine," as Robert Burton says of his *Anatomy*, quoting Macrobius.

Particularly difficult to name are the influences that flow like underground streams beneath my text, bubbling up throughout. These nurture and sustain a life, not just a book. Harold Bloom's "Introduction" and "Commentary" to *The Book of J* gave me courage not only to approach the "sacred" text as I would any of the great literary texts of our culture, but to trust the power of appreciative criticism; and Charles Olson's slender volume of great tensile strength, *Call Me Ishmael*, gave me a model of variety, rhythm and clarity. Each of these passionate essays returned me to its original, the Hebrew Bible and *Moby-Dick*, respectively, with awe and gratitude, which is my hope for the slim book you hold in your hands.

More profoundly, William Blake gave me a way of reading and a loom for weaving books like the Gospel of John into my life. I continue weaving and unweaving, believing "Exuberance is Beauty," as Blake exclaims, and that "Praise is the Practise of Art." So "I should have liked this book, which is the child of my brain," let me readily admit with Cervantes, "to be the fairest, the sprightliest, and the cleverest that could be imagined; but I have not been able to contravene the law of nature which would have it that like begets like."

I indicate below some of the general influences bubbling to the surface of each chapter. All specific sources follow in the Notes, cited by page number and quotation.

BEFOREHAND

I'm grateful to the late Richard Rorty for the liberating metaphor of weaving and unweaving the fabric of our beliefs, the self-making project that is our life, which he develops in his essay, "Inquiry as Recontextualization" (*Objectivity, Relativism, and Truth*). The Polish poet, Adam Zagajewski, in *Two Cities* suggests the necessary dialectic of ecstasy and irony.

HANDS

Frank Kermode calls attention to similar details that "fracture" the surface of the Gospel of Mark. Particulars, such as a hand rising from John's text, are not only arresting but mysterious. Narrative always "entails a measure of opacity," as Kermode observes in *The Genesis of Secrecy*. My poet's gaze across the landscape of the Gospel of John is caught by the minute particulars that break through the surface and prevent reducing John's book to a false coherence, a deceptive clarity. It's worth remembering, Kermode reminds us, that "we find it hardest to think about what we have most completely taken for granted." It's the strange particulars that force thought, our facing head-on the "mystery" of the text, which cannot be "reduced to other and more intelligible forms." And in the end, as "something irreducible," it is "therefore perpetually to be interpreted."

THE TREMBLING WOMAN

The title of this chapter is from William Blake, *The Everlasting Gospel*. Believing that the Bible is the "Great Code of Art," as he states in the *Laocoön*, Blake taught me to read it, as he did Northrop Frye and Harold Bloom before me.

THE SCARLET EXPERIMENT

After reading the poet and Classicist Anne Carson's astonishing nonfiction book, *Eros the Bittersweet*, I could not look at the body in the same way as before, which is evident here and in the "Body" chapter below.

BODY

The poet Diane Ackerman's *A Natural History of the Senses*, from which I've borrowed the phrase, "extreme of touch," hovers in the background. The wide open spaces of America impressed the poet Charles Olson,

Call Me Ishmael. The body/word that encompasses the world—animal, vegetable, and mineral—is brilliantly elaborated by Northrop Frye in his *Anatomy of Criticism*.

THE LAMB

The philosopher Richard Rorty doesn't claim to be a poet, modestly accepting a role as "auxiliary to the poet" in his essay, "The Contingency of Language" (*Contingency, Irony, and Solidarity*). But as a poet, I identify strongly with his philosopher's commitment to metaphor and contingency (inherited from Nietzsche). His contention that poets in the broadest sense invent a new vocabulary, as did Yeats and Galileo, for example, that wins our hearts not because it is more true than the old entrenched vocabulary but because given our needs, it is more compelling than the old, bubbles to the surface throughout my book.

This new way of speaking that arises from the clash of vocabularies in a given culture constitutes the "revolutionary" achievements in the arts and sciences, including the creation of new religions. And a new vocabulary is a tool for doing something that couldn't be envisioned earlier. In short, this is how novelty enters the world. "What is now proved was once," as Blake reminds us in *The Marriage of Heaven and Hell*, "only imagin'd." Our reality, then, is discourse answering discourse. Change in belief is a change in vocabulary. And accepting the new is a project of redefinition, something Blake did for me, as all great teachers do for their students. That Jesus teaches John to speak a "new language" of the lamb and bread became evident to me on reading Rorty's essay. The initial incomprehensibility of truly novel language and the significance of adopting a new way of speaking, a new vocabulary that "promises great things," informs many of my meditations, "Voices," "Jesus," "John," and "You," as well as "The House of the Interpreters" and "The Book of Unknowing."

WIND

Anne Carson attends to the significance of edges, breathing, and crossing thresholds in *Eros the Bittersweet*, especially her chapter, "Archilochos at the Edge."

NICODEMUS

Rereading my short book, I must acknowledge Nicodemus who gave me a place to stand both outside and inside the arena of John and Jesus, a place of freedom where any question can be smuggled in by night, an answer revealed by moonlight.

JESUS

On Socrates (sections XV, XVI), I follow Plato in the *Apology* and *Crito*, of course, but my view is shaped by I.F. Stone, *Socrates' Trial*. Similarly, my view of Don Quixote (sections XVIII, XIX) is influenced by Ortega y Gasset, *Meditations*, and Miguel de Unamuno, *The Tragic Sense of Life*, but especially by a brief, extraordinary book by Richard L. Predmore, *The World of Don Quixote*.

ONE BIG WORD

William Carlos Williams' poetic account of writing in his *The Great American Novel* brings John's struggle to mind. We become aware in reading John's book that he must also break words, those "indivisible crystals," as Williams puts it at the end of chapter II, and at the same time drink words, which are milk, in order to get from word to word to the Word. Wrestling to make each word "clean" and "new for himself so that at last it was new, free from the world for himself" is what constructing a new vocabulary entails.

SIGNS

Raymond Brown confines "signs" to the first twelve chapters of John, which he calls the "Book of Signs." A slippery category, I extend it and include Jesus himself.

HOUSE OF THE INTERPRETERS

As a student, I was thrilled by Dominic Crossan comparing the parables of Jesus and Borges in his *Raid on the Articulate*, and vestiges of his approach flit through this section.

THE BOOK OF WATER

Many readers will recognize Camille Paglia's *Sexual Personae* hovering in the background throughout this chapter. From reminding me that, as happened to John in his Gospel and Spenser in his *Faerie Queene*, "a poet is not always master of his own poem, for imagination can overwhelm moral intention," to pointing out the "Dionysian liquid nature" in Shakespeare's plays, she speaks directly to me, encouraging and aiding me throughout this chapter. Declaring that "female experience is submerged in the world of fluids" and claiming outrageously that "male tumescence is an assertion of the separateness of objects"; pointing to the opposition of thresholds and fluidity, father light and mother water, the central and the peripheral, such observations in her lively and richly imagined Book of Sex allowed me to penetrate more deeply into what moved me in John's "Book of Water." For my portrait of Dionysus, however, I rely mainly on Walter Otto.

Notes

ALL REFERENCES ARE TO THE BIBLIOGRAPHY FOLLOWING.

BEFOREHAND

Page xiii—"enter and spread through the whole body": Pesikta Rabbati, 3.2.

—"objections, digressions, gay mistrust, the delights of mockery . . . pathology": Nietzsche, aphorism #154.

ACKNOWLEDGEMENTS

Page xv—"True Shandeism": Sterne, 264.

EPIGRAPHS

Page xvii—"In the deepest convictions reaching into the very depths . . . against us": Milosz, 9.

—"I believe in the immortal origin . . . my soul": Unamuno, *The Tragic Sense of Life*, 48.

—"We are narcissists, we want to live forever": Landau ("Meditations" #2), 17.

HANDS

Page 1—"The Father loves the Son, and has given all things into his hand": All references to the Gospel of John are to the KJV (chapter and verse in parentheses), as are all Bible references, unless otherwise noted. I've taken the liberty throughout, however, to substitute "you" for "ye" and change "eth" endings to "s," to eliminate an unnecessary distraction for the modern reader.

THE TREMBLING WOMAN

Page 4—"Good & Evil": Blake ("The Everlasting Gospel"), 512.

THE SCARLETEXPERIMENT

Page 5—"Split the Lark": Dickinson, *Poems*, #861.

THE LAMB

Page 12—"None of the other arouse all sides of my being to cry 'Crucify Him'": Auden, *Prose*, 197.

Page 13—"I never kept sheep . . . My soul is like a shepherd": Pessoa, *Keeper*, 3.

BREAD &

Page 16—"Our desire is appeased only by feeding . . . immortality": Unamuno, *The Christ*, "The Eucharist," Part One, XXXII.

Page 18—"You want to knock on all the doors . . . on the cross!": Vallejo, *The Black Heralds*, 119.

Page 22—"rouzes the faculties to act": Blake (letter to Dr. Trusler, 23 August 1799), 676.

VOICES

Page 29—"given a name to everything": Jiménez, 91.

Page 30—"Nature has no Outline, but Imagination has": Blake, 268.

—"A word that breathes distinctly / Has not the power to die": Dickinson, *Poems*, #1651.

WIND

Page 31—"wind-addled and wind-sprung": Wright, 148.

—"organs of mind": Carson, 48.

—"Windblown we come" . . . "All that we look on is windfall. / . . . wind": Wright ("The Southern Cross"), 54.

Page 32—"memories and yearning" . . . "You've never listened to the wind. . . . part of you": Pessoa, *The Keeper*, 37.

Notes   195

NICODEMUS

Page 33—"The self forms at the edge of desire": Carson, 39.

Page 34—"in landlessness alone . . . indefinite as God": Melville ("The Lee Shore"), 97.

LIGHT

Page 45—"Light is time thinking about itself": Paz, 575.

—"He eats light and his droppings are copper": Davenport ("Au Tombeau de Charles Fourier," XXVII), 103.

—"Where is the light of a god propped against nothing?": Juarroz ("Eighth. 1"), 3.

Page 46—"where tenderness would be so high . . . sway with the fruit of light": Ammons, 226.

Page 47—"living light": Dante, *Paradiso*, XXX.61.

Page 48—"living name" . . . "making love an immortality": Shelley ("Letter to Maria Gisborne"), 176.

JESUS

Page 49—"The exceeding luster and the pure / Intense irradiation of a mind": Shelley ("Letter to Maria Gisborne"), 181–182.

—"Jesus & his Apostles & Disciples were all Artists." . . . "The Eternal Body of Man is The Imagination, . . . Divine Body, Jesus": Blake, 271.

Page 50—"radiance among men": Dante, *Inferno*, XV.81.

—"These two activities, falling in love . . . feel genuinely alive": Carson, 70.

Page 51—"I do not know how to describe the emotion . . . thousands as one": Langer, 102.

—"The meaning of the sight . . . obliterated meaning itself": Dillard, 94.

Page 52—"There is only one positively beautiful person, . . . an infinite miracle in itself": Dostoevsky, letter to Sophia Ivanova, January 13, 1868.

Page 53—"atom-cracking" . . . "impious": Burke ("Dictionary of Pivotal Terms"), 94.

Page 54—"impulse" . . . "not from rules": Blake, 42.

Page 58—"The lamb slaughtered": Frye, 141.

Page 59—"friends in Eternity" . . . "immediate dictation" . . . "even against my Will": Blake (letter to Thomas Butts, 25 April 1803), 697.

Page 62—"internal oracle": Plato, *Apology*, 23b.

—"to fulfill the will of God": Plato, *Crito*.

Page 63—"He who has realized that in respect of wisdom he is really worthless": Plato, *Apology*, 23b.

Page 64—"If Morality was Christianity" . . . "Socrates was the Savior": Blake, 272.

Page 66—"numberless Amadises, of that multitude of famous knights": Cervantes, I.49.

—"stands for everything that is gentle, . . . and gallant": Nabokov, 7.

Page 68—"I tried to compel them to live, so they compelled me to die": Lawrence, 32.

Page 69—"To be singular under plural circumstances, is a becoming heroism": Dickinson, *Poems*, #625.

ONE BIG WORD

Page 71—"The stopped the sun with a word . . . cities to the ground": Gumilev, 107.

Page 72—"something radically new": Saint Augustine, VII, 9.

Page 73—"Like this consent of Language / The Loved Philology": Dickinson, *Poems*, #1651.

—"If I make a word, I make myself into a word": Williams, 113.

SIGNS

Page 78—"common squalid stuff" . . . "I open to the writer in the sand": Abrahams, 135.

Page 80—"Jesus could not do miracles where unbelief hinderd": Blake, 606.

JOHN

Page 85—"The stutter is the plot": Olson, 104.

—"Counter thought thought out": Howe ("Scattering as Behavior Toward Risk"), 65.

—"over-conscious world . . . only the greatest": H.D., 49.

Page 86—"the grapes that hung against the sun-lit walls": H.D., 52.

—"He was the gulls screaming at low tide . . . among the knotted weeds": H.D., 53.

—"we are figure-oriented, we are narcissists, we want to live forever": Landau, 17.

Page 87—"Serene last evening, . . . / I want to be eternal": Jiménez, 2.

—"we will be software, . . . sufficiently careful to make frequent backups": Kurzweil, 129.

Page 88—"to present a positively beautiful man. . . . the task is so infinite": Dostoevsky, Letter to Sophia Ivanova, January 13, 1868.

—"beautiful only because he is ridiculous. . . . achieved his immortality": Unamuno, *The Tragic Sense of Life*, 306.

Page 90—"For me alone Don Quixote was born and I for him; . . . two are one": Cervantes, 1170.

Page 100—"futile to ask of records . . . that they be true": Blake, 607.

YOU

Page 108—"Every thing possible to be believ'd is an Image of Truth": Blake, 36.

—"The true is the name of whatever . . . good in the way of belief": James, 520.

HOUSE OF THE INTERPRETERS

Page 110—"overthrowing the authority . . . books of chivalry enjoy in the world": Cervantes, 16.

Page 113—"Both [of us] read the Bible . . . where I read white": Blake, 516.

Page 122—"tell it slant": Dickinson, *Poems*, #1129.

THE BOOK OF WATER

Page 123—"Meditation and water are wedded forever": Melville ("Loomings"), 13.

Page 124—"Slabs of water many a mile /. . . all this while": Hopkins, 15.

—"how impossible water is": Bursk, 31.

Page 126—"I seem to refind myself . . . this universal water": Valéry, 179.

—"Why is water clear when we lift it out of itself? / . . . and the light?": Bursk, 31.

198 Notes

Page 127—"every living creature": The Qur'an (Surah XXIV), 45.

Page 128—"We bathe in You, Jordan of flesh": Unamuno, *The Christ* ("XIV. Stream—Fountain," trans. mine), 431.

Page 131—"Dip him in the river who loves water": Blake, 35.
  —"Exuberance is Beauty": Blake, 37.

Page 132—"We praise water's certainty ... bewilderment afterward": Bursk, 31.

Page 133—"We thirst at first—/... Termed Immortality—": Dickinson, *Poems*, #726.

THE MOTHER AND THE MARY'S

Page 135—"A great mind must be androgynous": S. T. Coleridge, *Table Talk*, September 1, 1832.

Page 141—"When she kills with her glances," ... "infinitude": Glassé, 88, 100.

Page 142—"soft, curled, hermaphroditical": Melville ("The Tail"), 315.

Page 144—"the feminine gospel": Unamuno, *The Agony*, 51.

SYMMETRY

Page 153—"John employs a complex mirroring (ABCDCBA)": R.E. Brown notes this complex chiasmus, II(29a), 859.

Page 156—"The Gods are contingent on style": Pessoa, *The Book of Disquiet*, #87.
  —"formal feeling": Dickinson, *Poems*, #341.

THE BOOK OF UNKNOWING

Page 156—"It is the *unknown* element ... living or otherwise": Valéry ("Amor," IV), 42.

Page 163—"importance of unknowing oneself ... to play against the I": Valéry, 146.

Page 164—"Chanted fearful equivocal words ... / Were inextricably twined": Heaney ("The Golden Bough," translation of *Aeneid* VI, 99–101), 3.

Page 168—"Friendship cannot exist without Forgiveness of Sins continually": Blake, 199.

SILENCE

Page 173—"Like the mound, my silence sprouts / Grass, a green bleeding": Amichai, "At Right Angles: Hebrew Quatrains," #10, *A Life*.

—"stared for years / into the breathy, . . . and captured the music": Levine ("The Unknowable"), 37.

Page 174—"The eye travels along the paths cut out for it in the work": Klee, I.13.

Page 175—"book leans on the void": Jabès, 157.

—"an act of silence directed against silence, . . . death": Jabès, 183.

Page 176—"What a seam of silence to be unsewn!": Valéry, 166.

—"the place where a writer offers his voice up to silence": Jabès, 122.

—"other / mouth being locked": Unamuno, *The Christ* ("The Wound in His Side"), 107.

Page 177—"'Silence' oblation to the Ear supersedes sound": Dickinson, *Letters*, #458.

Page 178—"making clay sparrows that when he clapped his hands, flew off chirping": *The Infancy Gospel of Thomas*, 399.

—"ear expands, grows more and more awake in these empty spaces": Valéry, 47.

Page 181—"Blank, the first and last page of the book": Jabès ("The Line of the Horizon"), *From the Book*, 203.

—"*Ceramic Bible*": Araki, 289.

—"I am the slave of / the master of silence": Rumi.

—"confrontation between the human need . . . silence of the world": Camus, 28.

Page 182—"The words of a dead man / . . . guts of the living": Auden, *Collected Shorter Poems* ("In Memory of W.B. Yeats"), 141.

Page 183—"most beautiful poem one can make from blood": Stainton, 167.

Page 184—"unmade bed of absence": Jabès, xvi.

Page 185—"Half-winged—half imprisoned," . . . "man's tragic limitation": Klee, III. 37.

Page 186—"And nothing happens . . . in the new life": Jiménez ("Oceans"), 63.

MY UNNAMED SOURCES HERE NAMED

Page 187—"built up . . . spoils": Montaigne ("Defense of Seneca and Plutarch"), II, 32.

—"all mine and none mine": Burton ("Democritus to the Reader"), 19.

—"Exuberance is Beauty": Blake, 37.

—"Praise is the Practise of Art": Blake, 272.

—"I should have liked this book . . . to be the fairest, . . . begets like": Cervantes ("Prologue"), 11.

Bibliography

Abrahams, Lionel. "The Writer in Sand." In *Ten South African Poets*, edited by Adam Schwartzman. Manchester: Carcanet, 1999.
Ackerman, Diane. *A Natural History of the Senses*. New York: Random House, 1990.
Amichai, Yehuda. *A Life of Poetry, 1948–1994*. New York: Harper, 1995.
Ammons, A.R. *Brink Road*. New York: Norton, 1996.
Araki, Takako. *Ceramic Bible*. In *The Art of East Asia*, vol. 2, edited by Gabriele Fahr-Becker. Cologne, Germany: Könemann, 1998.
Auden, W.H. *Collected Shorter Poems: 1927–1957*. New York: Random House, 1966.
———. "Purely Subjective." In *The Complete Works of W.H. Auden: Prose: Volume II. 1939–1948*, edited by Edward Mendelson, 184–197. Princeton, NJ: Princeton U.P., 2002.
Blake, William. *The Poetry and Prose of William Blake*. Edited by David V. Erdman. New York: Doubleday, 1970.
Bloom, Harold, and David Rosenberg. *The Book of J*. New York: Grove, 1990.
Brown, Raymond E. *The Gospel According to John*. 2 vols. The Anchor Bible 29 and 29a. New York: Doubleday, 1966.
Burke, Kenneth. *Perspectives by Incongruity*. Edited by Stanley Edgar Hyman. Bloomington, IN: Indiana U.P., 1964.
Bursk, Christopher. "Questions At the Back of the Chapter." *American Poetry Review* 11:3 (May/June 1982), 31.
Burton, Richard. *The Anatomy of Melancholy*. Edited by Floyd Dell and Paul Jordan-Smith. New York: Tudor, 1948.
Camus, Albert. *The Myth of Sisyphus: And Other Essays*. New York: Vintage, 1991.
Carson, Anne. *Eros the Bittersweet*. Princeton, NJ: Princeton U.P., 1986.
Cervantes, Miguel. *Don Quixote*. Translated by Samuel Putnam. New York: Modern Library, 1998.
Coleridge, Samuel Taylor. *Table Talk of Samuel Taylor Coleridge*. New York: Kessinger, 2010 [1884].
Crossan, Dominic. *Raid on the Articulate: Comic Eschatology in Jesus and Borges*. New York: Harper, 1976.
Culpepper, R. Alan. *Anatomy of the Fourth Gospel*. Philadelphia: Fortress, 1983.
Dante, Alighieri. *Divine Comedy*. 3 vols. Translated by John Ciardi. New York: Mentor, 1954.
Davenport, Guy. *Da Vinci's Bicycle*. Baltimore, MD: The Johns Hopkins U.P., 1979.

Dickinson, Emily. *The Complete Poems of Emily Dickinson*. Edited by Thomas H. Johnson. Boston: Little, Brown, 1960.

———. *The Letters of Emily Dickinson*. Edited by Thomas H. Johnson. 3 vols. Cambridge: Harvard U.P., 1955.

Dillard, Annie. *Teaching a Stone to Talk: Expeditions and Encounters*. New York: Harper, 1982.

Dostoevsky, Fiodor. *Letters and Reminiscences*. New York: Kessinger, 2007.

Euripides. *The Bacchae*. Translated by Geoffrey S. Kirk. Englewood Cliffs, NJ: Prentice-Hall, 1970.

Frye, Northrop. *Anatomy of Criticism: Four Essays*. Princeton, NJ: Princeton U.P., 1957.

Glassé, Cyril, and Huston Smith, eds. *The New Encyclopedia of Islam*. Walnut Creek, CA: Rowman & Littlefield, 1989.

Gumilev, Nikolai S. *Selected Works of Nikolai S. Gumilev*. Translated by Burton Raffel & Alla Burago. Albany, NY: State University of New York, 1972.

H.D. (Hilda Dolittle). *Notes on Thought and Vision & The Wise Sappho*. San Francisco: City Lights Books, 1982.

Heaney, Seamus. *Seeing Things*. New York: Farrar Straus Giroux, 1991.

Herrstrom, David Sten. "Letters of Nicodemus (I)." *Mars Hill* Review, No. 19.

———. "The Nicodemus Glyph." *New River: Journal of Digital Writing and Art* (Fall 2006). No pages. Online: http://www.cddc.vt.edu/journals/newriver/herrstrom/nicodemusintroduction.html.

Hopkins, Gerard Manley. *The Poems of Gerard Manley Hopkins*. Edited by W.H. Gardner and N.H. MacKenzie. New York: Oxford U.P., 1970.

Howe, Susan. *Singularities*. Hanover, NH: Wesleyan U.P., 1990.

Jabès, Edmond. *From the Book to the Book: An Edmond Jabès Reader*. Translated by Rosmarie Waldrop. Hanover, NH: Wesleyan U.P., 1991.

James, William. *William James: Writings 1902-1910*. New York: The Library of America, 1987.

Jiménez, Juan Ramón. *Selected Poems: Lorca and Jiménez*. Translated by Robert Bly. Boston: Beacon Press, 1973.

Juarroz, Roberto. *Vertical Poetry: Recent Poems*. Translated by Mary Crow. Fredonia, NY: White Pine Press, 1992.

Kermode, Frank. *The Genesis of Secrecy: On the Interpretation of Narrative*. Cambridge: Harvard U. P., 1979.

Klee, Paul. *Pedagogical Sketchbook*. New York: Praeger, 1967.

Kurzweil, Ray. *The Age of Spiritual Machines: When Computers Exceed Human Intelligence*. New York: Penguin, 1999.

Landau, Jacob. "Meditations." In *Jacob Landau: The Graphic Work, Catalogue Raisonné*. Trenton, NJ: The New Jersey State Museum, 1982.

Langer, Lawrence L. "Satan's Biographers." *The Atlantic Monthly*, 283:2 (February 1999), 99–104.

Lawrence, D. H. *The Man Who Died*. Hopewell, NJ: The Ecco Press, 1994.

Levine, Philip. *The Mercy*. New York: Knopf, 2000.

Melville, Herman. *Moby-Dick*. Edited by Harrison Hayford and Hershel Parker. New York: Norton, 1967.

Milosz, Czeslaw. *Milosz's ABC's*. Translated by Madeline G. Levine. New York: Farrar, Straus and Giroux, 2001.

Montaigne, Michel de. *The Complete Essays of Montaigne.* Translated by Donald M. Frame. Stanford, CA: Stanford U. P., 1958.
Nabokov, Vladimir. *Lectures on Don Quixote.* Edited by Fredson Bowers. San Diego: Harcourt Brace Jovanovich, 1983.
Nietzsche. *Basic Writings of Nietzsche.* Translated and edited by Walter Kaufmann. New York: The Modern Library, 1992.
Olson, Charles. *Call Me Ishmael.* New York: Reynal & Hitchcock, 1947.
Ortega y Gasset, José. *Meditations on Quixote.* New York: Norton, 1963.
Otto, Walter F. *Dionysos.* Bloomington, Indiana: Indiana U.P., 1965.
Paglia, Camille. *Sexual Personae: Art and Decadence from Nefertiti to Emily Dickinson.* New York: Vintage, 1991.
Paz, Octavio. *The Collected Poems of Octavio Paz, 1957–1987.* Translated by Eliot Weinberger. New York: New Directions, 1990.
Pesikta rabbati; discourses for feasts, fasts, and special Sabbaths. Volume 1. Translated by William Gordon Braude. New Haven, CT: Yale University Press, 1968.
Pessoa, Fernando. *The Book of Disquiet.* Translated by Richard Zenith. New York: Penguin, 2003.
———. *The Keeper of Sheep.* Translated by Edwin Honig and Susan M. Brown. New York: The Sheep Meadow Press, 1985.
Plato. *The Collected Dialogues.* Edited by Edith Hamilton and Huntington Cairns. Bollingen Series LXXI. Princeton, NJ: Princeton U.P., 1973.
Predmore, Richard L. *The World of Don Quixote.* Cambridge, MA: Harvard U. P., 1968.
Rorty, Richard. *Contingency, Irony, and Solidarity.* Cambridge: Cambridge U.P., 1989.
———. *Objectivity, Relativisim, and Truth.* Philosophical Papers Volume 1. Cambridge: Cambridge U.P., 1991.
Rumi. Online: http://oceanofmind.tumblr.com/post/1126743152/everyone-is-tempted-by-the-eloquence-of-speech [accessed 15 November 2010].
Saint Augustine. *Confessions.* Translated by Henry Chadwick. New York: Oxford U.P., 2009.
Shelley, P.B. *Selected Poetry and Prose.* Edited by Kenneth Cameron. New York: Holt, Rinehart and Winston, 1967.
Stainton, Leslie. *Lorca: A Dream of Life.* New York: Farrar, Straus, Giroux, 1999.
Staley, Jeffrey L. *Reading with a Passion.* New York: Continuum, 1995.
Sterne, Laurence. *The Life and Opinions of Tristam Shandy Gentleman.* New York: Fawcett, 1962.
Stone, I.F. *The Trial Socrates.* Boston: Little, Brown, 1988.
The Holy Bible Containing the Old and New Testaments . . . Authorized King James Version. New York: Oxford U.P., [n.d.].
The Infancy Gospel of Thomas. In *The Other Bible*, edited by Willis Barnstone, 399–403. New York: Harper, 1984.
The Qur'an. Translated by M. A. S. Abdel Haleem. New York: Oxford U.P., 2008.
The War of the Sons of Light with the Sons of Darkness (Dead Sea Scrolls). In *The Other Bible*, edited by Willis Barnstone, 237–242. New York: Harper, 1984.
Unamuno, Miguel de. *The Agony of Christianity.* Translated by Anthony Kerrigan. Selected Works of Miguel de Unamuno, volume 5. Princeton, NJ: Princeton U.P., 1974.
———. *The Christ of Velásquez (El Cristo de Velazquez).* Obras Completas, VI: Poesia. Madrid: Escelicer, 1969.

———. *The Tragic Sense of Life*. Translated by J. E. Crawford Flitch. New York: Dover, 1954.

Valéry, Paul. *The Collected Works of Paul Valéry: Poems in the Rough*. Vol. 2. Translated by Hilary Corke. Princeton, NJ: Princeton U.P., 1969.

Vallejo, César. *The Black Heralds*. Translated by Richard Schaaf & Kathleen Ross. Pittsburgh, PA: Latin America Literary Review Press, 1990.

Williams, William Carlos. *The William Carlos Williams Reader*. Edited by M.L. Rosenthal. New York: New Directions, 1966.

Wright, Charles. *The World of the Ten Thousand Things: Poems 1980–1990*. New York: Farrar, Straus and Giroux, 1990.

Zagajewski, Adam. *Two Cities: On Exile, History, and the Imagination*. New York: Farrar, Straus and Giroux, 1995.

Scripture Index

Genesis

1:2	125
1:26	18
2:7	79

Exodus

12:13	13
12:46	111

Leviticus

16:8	12

Numbers

9:12	111

2 Samuel

22:14	61

2 Kings

42	17

Ezra

7:21	1

Psalms

22:15	66
22:18	78
77:18	61
77:19	126
82:6	112
85	151
92	151

Isaiah

5	66
7:11–25	66
8:18	78
17:8–11	14
27:1	125
42:7	66
55:1	132

Ezekiel

4:4–6	74
16:9	138
17:6–9	120
34	66, 118

Zechariah

9:9	66
14:21	66

Mark

16:9	140

John

1:1–2	25, 71
1:3	25, 41, 71, 143
1:4	25, 45–46
1:5	25, 46, 174
1:6	25
1:7	25, 45, 143
1:8	25, 45
1:9	26, 70
1:10	26
1:12–13	143
1:14	9, 72, 111
1:19	73
1:19–26	113
1:21	76
1:28	100
1:29	11
1:32	142
1:36	11
1:45	60
1:48–50	104, 114
1:51	19, 145
2:1–11	83, 123
2:4	129, 136
2:13	148
2:15	76
2:18	66
2:21	13, 110, 149
2:22	77
2:25	67
3:1	36
3:1–21	33
3:2	36–37, 88, 146
3:3	36, 38
3:4	36, 113
3:5	37–38, 126
3:6	37
3:8	13, 32, 115
3:9	32
3:10	37
3:10–21	114
3:11	31, 38
3:12	39
3:14	39, 145
3:14–17	123
3:17	40
3:18	39
3:19–21	40, 46
3:22	163
3:26	163
3:29	24, 143
3:35	1
4	83
4:2	163
4:3	75
4:5–6	68
4:6	146
4:8	133, 140
4:10	115, 147
4:11–15	116
4:14	133
4:22	147
4:23	140
4:27	140
4:29	146
4:31	133
4:39	97
4:44	97, 163
4:48	81
4:50	97
5:1–9	83
5:17	61
5:18	126
5:21	61, 143
5:25	26
5:30	59, 163
5:35	45
5:37	60
6	68, 83
6:4	148
6:6	52, 69, 88, 110
6:10	17
6:14	76
6:15	17
6:19	125
6:26	20, 80
6:28–30	105

Scripture Index   207

6:30	80	7:46	33, 72
6:31	17	7:47–49	33
6:32	19, 149	7:50	33, 88
6:32–59	114, 149	7:51	33, 34
6:35	18, 133	7:52	33
6:36	18, 75	8:2	34
6:37–38	18, 152	8:6	175
6:39	18, 59, 62, 152	8:7	3
6:40	18–19, 152	8:9	3
6:41	18	8:10	4
6:42	18, 20, 60	8:12	34, 70, 79, 174
6:43	18	8:14	99
6:44	18–19, 105	8:15	163
6:45–46	18	8:18	59, 69
6:47	18–19, 149	8:20	165
6:50	17, 19	8:23	145
6:51	18, 20	8:31–43	106
6:52	18, 20–21	8:41	52
6:53	5, 9, 18, 20, 22, 149	8:43	52
6:54	17	8:44	52, 106
6:54–56	18, 22	8:46–47	107
6:56	8, 16	8:48	111
6:57	18	8:48–57	67
6:58	17–18, 20	8:58	52, 67, 68, 105
6:60	55	8:59	67
6:61	21, 56	9	83, 179
6:61–65	114	9:3	58, 82, 155
6:64	22–23, 58, 105, 159	9:4–5	174
6:65	22	9:5	45, 79
6:66	21, 54, 75, 97, 106, 111, 114	9:6	48, 79
		9:7	66
6:67	52	9:14	48
7:5	21, 75, 96, 111	9:31	161
7:8	142	9:32	79
7:12	96	9:39	162
7:15	69	9:40	178
7:18	69	9:41	161, 179
7:19	129	9:41–10:1	117, 161
7:24	69	10	179
7:30	165	10:1	13
7:37	142	10:1–5	118, 160
7:37–39	123	10:2	13
7:38	114, 125, 126, 130–131	10:3	13, 27
7:45	33	10:4	13

John – continued

10:6	160	11:41	26, 55
10:7	53, 118, 143, 160	11:42	26, 55, 61
10:9	160	11:43	26
10:11	11, 13, 66, 118, 143, 160	11:44	180
10:14	160	11:45	58
10:15	161	11:49–50	12
10:17	59, 122	11:51	89
10:17–18	161	11:53	12
10:18–19	119	11:55	148
10:20	108, 118	12:3	177
10:20–21	161	12:7	53
10:21	118	12:8	53, 137
10:22	148	12:9	101
10:24	121	12:10	101, 176
10:24–27	108	12:14	66
10:25–26	105	12:15	163
10:27	117, 121	12:23–24	14
10:28	1, 61	12:25	14, 64
10:29	1	12:27–28	62
10:30	70, 112, 143	12:29	27, 60
10:31	119	12:32	48
10:32–34	112	12:33	48, 75, 110, 171
10:35	105	12:35	46, 48
10:35–38	113	12:35–36	174
10:38	61, 108	12:36	46
11:1	137	12:37	75
11:2	138	12:42	97
11:4	83	12:46	70
11:5	138	12:47	163
11:6	58	12:50	60
11:10	47–48	13–17	55
11:11	121	13:1–20	123
11:11–12	116	13:2	58
11:13	160	13:3	1
11:14	121	13:5	54
11:15	55, 58	13:7	166
11:20	58, 139	13:9	2
11:24	32, 68	13:12	58
11:25	32, 68, 83	13:15	58
11:38	55, 90	13:18	23, 54
11:39	177	13:19	166
11:40	55	13:21	54, 58
		13:30	40
		13:31–14:31	165

Scripture Index   209

Reference	Pages
13:33	143, 167
13:34	28
14:2	119
14:5	113, 119
14:6	112, 119
14:8	117, 122
14:9	28, 61, 143
14:10	61, 75
14:11–12	104
14:16–17	115, 119
14:17	165
14:22	113, 119
14:26	165
14:27	119
14:30	27
15:1	20, 27, 66, 124
15:2–6	117, 119
15:4	124
15:5–8	27
15:9–12	28
15:15–16	168
15:26	61
16	110
16:4–33	165
16:12	55, 166, 168
16:13	56
16:16	120, 168
16:17	121, 159
16:17–18	113
16:18	120
16:21	56, 142
16:25	13, 120, 169
16:27–28	169
16:28–29	121
16:30	122
16:32	170
16:33	182
17:1	28, 56, 59, 61, 165
17:2	122
17:4	61
17:5–6	28, 61
17:7	28
17:8	28, 122, 143
17:9	28, 61
17:10	61
17:11	29, 61
17:12	29
17:13	29, 56, 61
17:14	29, 56, 61, 62
17:15–18	61–62
17:21–22	61
17:23	61–62, 182
17:24–26	61
18:1	62, 129
18:3	101, 174
18:4	101, 159
18:5	56
18:10	1, 100
18:11	141
18:14	93
18:17	93
18:18	1, 93, 148
18:19–23	93
18:26–27	94
18:28	94, 153
18:28–32	153
18:32	171
18:33–38	153
18:35	154
18:37	27, 154
18:38–40	153
19:1–3	113, 153–154
19:3	1
19:4–8	153
19:9	175
19:9–11	153
19:10–11	154
19:12–16	153
19:23	77
19:27	135
19:28	66, 133
19:34	130, 133
19:35	98, 100, 179
19:35–37	176
19:36	66, 111
19:38	35, 41
19:38–42	33
19:39	35, 41, 88

John – continued

19:40–42	41
20:11	152
20:11–18	140
20:12	184
20:13–14	152
20:15	138, 152
20:16	24, 152
20:17	170
20:20	174
20:22	31, 142, 166
20:23	166
20:25	5
20:26	6, 53
20:27	5
20:28–29	81
20:30	13, 81, 113
20:31	98, 103, 114, 184
21:1	174
21:9	1, 73, 148
21:11	123
21:12	23
21:18	1, 170–171
21:19	75, 170–171
21:20	144
21:21	141
21:23	144, 171
21:24	98, 144, 171, 180
21:25	113, 171, 180

Subject/Name Index

A

Abrahams, Lionel (1928–2004), 78
abstraction. *See under* Jesus
Allah, 127
ambiguity. *See under* language
Amichai, Yehuda (1924–2000), 173
Ammons, A. R. (1926–2001), 46
androgyny, 142–143
anointing (of Jesus by Mary), 27, 53, 138, 141, 174, 177
Araki, Takako (1921–2004), 181
Auden, W.H. (1917–1973), 12
Augustine, Saint (354–430), 72
authority, 2–3, 110–111, 158. *See also under* Jesus; John
Authorized Version, xii
Aztecs, 5

B

balancing, 53, 75, 112, 145, 148–153, 173
belief, 6–8, 12, 31, 97, 112, 155
    act of, xvii, 10, 19, 21–22, 25, 28, 46, 80, 90, 98, 103–105, 107–108, 112, 183
    barriers to, 6, 18, 97
    of the disciples, 36, 77, 80–81, 104, 122, 162
    Inverse Law of, 97, 162
    and irony, 101, 105
    in Jesus, 19, 39, 63, 83, 90–91, 104, 130, 143
    of Jesus, 60, 62, 95, 163, 166
    of Jews, 106
    of John, 42–43, 73, 89, 90
    as madness, 106
    means to, 55, 58, 74, 76–77, 80, 82, 83, 97, 104–105, 159, 174, 189
    of Nicodemus, 146–147, 162
    as outcome, xiii, 63, 79, 81, 83, 89, 99, 104–105, 112, 147, 159
    as relationship, 45, 90, 96, 105–9
    of the Samaritan woman, 146–147
    as self-authenticating, 106
    and signs, 76, 77, 79, 80, 104, 174
    and Spirit, 114, 131
    and truth, 37, 108
    versus knowledge, 33, 35, 41, 63
    See also believers; knowledge; truth; unbelief
believe. *See* belief
believers, xii, 12, 19, 35, 65, 96, 99, 102, 106–108, 118, 120, 126, 135, 144, 152, 184
    See also unbelievers
birth, 37, 63, 82
    and Jesus, 37–39, 58, 124, 126–131, 133–135, 138–139, 142–143, 165
    of knowledge, 63, 65
    redefinition of, 38–39, 63, 111
    See also death
Blake, William (1757–1827), x, 22, 30, 64, 108, 168, 194, 196
    as aid to reading John's Gospel, xiii, 3, 131, 187
    The Everlasting Gospel, 188, 194
    House of the Interpreter, 49
    as incandescent, 49–50
    on Jesus, 49, 54, 80, 100
    Laocoön, 188
    The Marriage of Heaven and Hell, ix, 189

212 Subject/Name Index

Blake, William – continued
    as poet, 85, 99
    as secretary of "friends in Eternity," 59
blood. *See* body
Bloom, Harold, 187
body, x, xiii, 2, 5–6, 8–9, 14, 43, 49, 76, 141
    blood, 2, 5–8, 14, 16, 18, 20–22, 43, 65, 125, 129–134, 148, 150, 156, 176, 183
    as bread, 16, 19, 23, 67, 150
    eating of, 5, 8, 9, 12, 21, 22–23, 150, 176
    as immortal, 9, 17, 80, 122, 127, 184
    of Jesus, xiii, 5, 8, 9, 12, 16, 19, 22–23, 35, 36, 41, 45, 47, 49, 54, 59, 70, 72, 76–77, 111, 119–120, 126, 130–131, 139, 141, 150, 173, 176
    of John, xiii, 8, 73, 87
    John's obsession with, xiii, 8, 11, 16, 87
    as mortal, 11, 12, 36, 56, 58, 184
    new, 8, 9, 12, 73, 111, 128
    of Peter, 130, 131
    as physical, 5, 6, 8, 11, 24, 43, 131, 139, 156
    politic, 2, 3, 6, 95
    redefinition of, 9, 17
    as sacrifice, 15, 16, 17, 150
    as sensuous, 14, 53, 139, 177
    and spirit, 6, 130, 131, 139
    as temple, 141, 149
    transformation of, 17, 87, 128
    as ultimate category, 7, 156
    and water, 131–132
    as Word, 72, 111, 119–120, 122
    as world, 9, 126
    See also birth; death
The Book of Unknowing, xii–xiii, 173
bread, xi, 9, 16, 18, 20, 114
    as flesh of Jesus, 10, 16, 18–20, 23, 43, 67, 133
    from heaven, 19, 80, 150
    of immortality (Unamuno), 16, 150
    language of, 17, 20, 21, 68, 152, 189
    of life, 18, 20, 149
    as literal, 17, 20, 21, 80, 149–150
    as metaphor, 20, 80, 149
    miraculous,17, 75, 80
    new, 17, 18–19, 22
    Passover, 149, 150–151
    as political, 17, 18
    redefinition of, 9, 15, 18–20, 23, 149–150, 189
    true, 19, 23, 128, 149–150
    See also under body
bride, 138, 141, 143–144
Brown, Raymond E. (1928–1998), xiii, 190, 198
    translation of John's Gospel, 5, 104, 146, 170, 184
Burke, Kenneth (1897–1993), 53
Bursk, Christopher, 124, 126, 132

C

Caiaphas, 12, 89, 94, 186
    as counter hero, 92–93, 95, 158
Camus, Albert (1913–1960), 181
Cana, marriage at, 14, 16, 52, 58, 61, 75, 80, 123–124, 126–129, 134, 135–136, 143, 159, 178
Carson, Anne, 31–33, 50, 188–189
categories (defined, dissolved, new), 21, 30, 32, 34, 37–41, 45, 47, 52–54, 67, 76, 94, 128, 145, 190
center (versus circumference, periphery, marginal), x, 8, 14, 33, 44, 35–36, 51, 54, 59, 64, 73–74, 82, 86, 89, 144, 147, 150, 152, 161–162
Cervantes, Miguel de (1547–1616), 88, 90, 103, 110, 187
Christ. *See under* Jesus
circumference. *See* center
clarity. *See under* language
comic scene, 6, 89, 97, 130–131, 140, 157–158, 165, 171
contradiction. *See under* Jesus; John
contraries, 125, 137, 142, 157–158, 163–164

Subject/Name Index   213

counter characters, 73, 158
counter hero, 91–93, 95–96, 98–99, 101, 149, 158, 174
counter interpretation, 114
counter party, 163
counter thought, 85, 94–96
countermovement, 149, 165
counterplot (of unknowing, deferred knowledge). *See under* plot
counterpoint (of scenes, groups, events), 94, 96, 148
Crossan, Dominic, 190
crucifixion, 22, 58, 77, 148, 150–151, 153–154, 159, 164, 166–170

D

Dante, Alighieri (1265–1321), 47, 49–51, 85, 89
darkness. *See under* light
Davenport, Guy, 45
David, King, 118, 126, 141, 151
death, 33, 67–68, 76, 86, 88, 101, 109, 111–112, 121, 128, 153–154, 177
  and Jesus, 11–12, 14, 26, 48, 54–56, 58, 59, 62, 64–66, 75, 81, 86, 90–91, 112, 116, 119, 122, 129–130, 135, 138–139, 142, 165
  and John, 8, 11, 23, 46, 85, 110, 111, 127, 149, 153, 170–171, 175
  scripts, 59, 65–66, 112
  and Socrates, 49
  trajectory of, 12, 58, 87, 90, 111, 120, 129, 135, 165
  See also birth
Dickinson, Emily (1830–1886), xiii, 5–6, 30, 69, 72–73, 122, 133, 156, 177
Dillard, Annie, 51
Dionysus, 125–127, 129, 154, 191
disbelief. *See* unbelief
disciples, xi, 2, 6–7, 9, 12–13, 18, 21–23, 27–29, 31–32, 35, 46–49, 52–56, 58, 60–63, 67, 70, 81, 82, 90–91, 93, 96, 98, 101–102, 114–115, 117, 123, 125, 130–131, 133, 135, 138–143, 151, 157–158, 161, 164–169, 171, 174, 180, 182–184
  and belief, 41, 80, 111, 120, 129, 162, 167
  beloved disciple, 135, 140, 144
  incomprehension of, 55–57, 60, 68, 77, 110, 113–114, 118–119, 120–122, 139–140, 160, 162–163, 165–168
  secret disciple (Joseph of Arimathea), 35
  and unbelief, 22, 75, 97, 106, 149, 158–159
doctrine, xii, 93, 107–108, 117, 155
drama. *See under* Gospel of John
Dostoevsky, Fyodor (1821–1881), 52, 55, 66, 88, 100
dove, 136, 142

E

eating. *See* body
Einstein, Albert (1879–1955), 50–51
energy, 36, 51, 55, 67
Essene, 46
Eternal Life. *See* immortality
Euripides (ca. 480 – 406 BCE), 125
everlasting life. *See* immortality
experiment, 5–8

F

fact, 17, 38, 48, 50, 58, 67, 71, 83, 87, 101, 108, 117, 121, 123, 140, 144, 154–156, 160, 163–164, 166, 178, 184
father, 59, 141
  of Jesus, 19, 22, 26–29, 56, 61–62, 65, 69–70, 97–98, 104–106, 112–113, 117, 119–121, 135–136, 139–140, 142–143, 149, 152, 168–170, 182
  of the Jews, 116, 150
  as light, 136, 143, 145, 191

214   Subject/Name Index

father – continued
  as trope, 121, 169
  voice of, 59–62, 65, 68, 137
  See also under Jesus
feasts (Jewish), 14, 22, 132, 142, 148.
    See also Passover
figurative language. See under language
flesh. See body
forgiveness. See under Jesus
Freud, Sigmund (1856–1939), 69, 128
Frye, Northrop (1912–1991), 189

G

gestures, xi, 24, 43, 52, 139, 178
  of Ezekiel, 78
  of Jesus, 2–3, 23, 26, 29, 31, 45, 47,
    56–57, 58, 78, 166, 173, 178
  of Mary Magdalene, 152
  of Nicodemus, 35–36
  of Peter, 1, 131
  of Socrates, 64
  of Thomas, 2, 5–7, 31, 173
  See also anointing; washing
Ghandi, Mohandas (1869–1948), 50, 65
God, ix, xi, 3–5, 19, 25–26, 30, 34,
    36–37, 39, 40, 42, 45, 49, 58, 62,
    64, 67, 68–69, 71, 73, 81, 82, 88,
    98, 102, 104–107, 111–113, 115,
    117, 124–126, 129, 140, 142,
    143, 156, 169–170, 185
Gospel of John, ix–xiv, 14, 22, 30,
    89–90, 99, 126, 156, 162, 175,
    183, 187
  drama of, 20, 24, 26, 27, 34, 36, 38,
    40, 47, 53, 58, 79, 88, 91–96, 99,
    101–105, 107–108, 112–113,
    115–116, 130–131, 135, 146–
    148, 150, 152, 154–155, 161,
    165, 170
  as "feminine gospel" (Unamuno),
    144
  irony at core, 58
  as narrative, x–xi, 29, 59, 89–91, 92,
    95–98, 99–103, 111–112, 129,
    135, 150, 153–154, 158, 164,
    170, 179, 180, 183–184, 186
  reader of, ix, xiii, 10, 16–17, 28–29,
    48, 55–56, 66, 71, 77, 80–81,
    83, 85, 87, 91, 100–101, 103,
    110–112, 114, 136, 138, 155,
    161, 166, 168–169, 172, 174,
    182, 191, 193
  stories in, 2, 6, 17, 34, 70, 80, 83,
    108, 117–118, 120, 130, 150,
    161, 169–171, 184
  strangeness of, ix, xii, 1, 3, 13, 22,
    100, 111, 117, 120, 150, 153,
    161, 164, 170, 181, 185, 188
  subject of, 6, 9, 99
  symmetry of, 145–157, 184
  tension of, 7, 14, 19, 57–58, 82, 94,
    112, 125, 133, 137, 153, 158,
    160, 165–167, 171
  uniqueness of, 94, 117, 149, 153,
    154, 160, 170
  See also John; plot
Gumilev, Nikolai (1886–1921), 71, 73

H

Hamlet, 89, 183
H.D. (Hilda Doolittle) (1886–1961),
    85–86
Heraclitus (c. 535 – c. 475 BCE), 71–72
hero. See under Jesus
Hopkins, Gerard Manley (1844–1889),
    124
House of the Interpreter. See under
    Blake, William
Howe, Susan, 85
humor. See comic scene

I

Ibn Arabi (1165–1240), 141
Iliad, 13
image. See under language
imagination, xii, 3, 24, 29–31, 33, 49,
    73, 84–85, 96, 123–124, 126–

Subject/Name Index 215

127, 143, 146, 156, 166, 178,
   183, 187, 189, 191
immortality, xvii, 1, 8, 16, 19, 23, 44, 48,
   50, 85–88, 105, 133, 150, 156
incandescence
   definition of, 49–51
   experience of, 50, 88, 173
   power of, 50–51, 87
   See also under Jesus
   See also light
incomprehension. *See under* disciples
interpretation, 110–122
   clash of, 113–114, 122, 171
   by disciples, 96, 113
   epicycles of, 166
   by the Father, 59
   house of, xiii, 21, 120
   by Jesus, 111
   Midrash, xii
   new language (versus old), 18,
      20–22, 38, 111–113, 121, 162
   by Nicodemus, 32
   of signs, 83, 96, 162
   See also under Jesus; John;
   See also misinterpretation; naming
      and renaming
Inverse Law of Belief. *See under* belief
irony, 36, 63, 81–83, 105, 148, 188. *See
   also under* belief; Gospel of
   John; John; Jesus

J

Jabès, Edmond (1912–1991), 181, 184
Jacob's ladder, xii–xiii, 19, 39, 145
Jagger, Michael Philip ("Mick"), 143
James, William (1842–1910), 108
Jerusalem, 66, 74
Jesus
   and abstraction, xii, 8, 40, 51–53,
      82, 84, 107, 136–137, 139, 141,
      144, 161
   as androgynous, 135, 143
   as artist, 155, 182, 184

authority of, 53, 61, 69–70, 76, 90,
   98–99, 100, 106, 110, 137, 146,
   182
belief of, 60, 62, 95
body of, xiii, 5, 8, 9, 11–12, 19, 35,
   36, 41, 45, 47, 49, 54, 59, 70,
   72, 75–77, 111, 119–120, 126,
   130–131, 139, 141, 173, 176
character of, xi, 22–23, 29, 31,
   36–38, 46, 52–58, 60–61, 63–64,
   68–70, 76–77, 81–82, 90–91,
   110, 119, 125, 137, 139, 142–
   143, 147, 158, 164, 167–168
as Christ, 52, 98, 108, 115
and contradiction, 54, 57, 164
and counter hero, 92, 95
and Don Quixote, 59, 65–68, 70, 88,
   90, 103, 110, 190
as father, 63, 143–144
and the Father's voice, 27–28,
   59–62, 64–65, 68, 72, 137
and forgiveness, xi, 3, 36, 52, 57–58,
   64–66, 70, 94, 137, 142–143,
   148, 166, 168, 170, 171
as hero, x– xii, 1, 30, 65–66, 68–69,
   86, 88–89, 91, 93–101, 111–112,
   122, 141, 146, 153, 155–156,
   158–159, 161, 164
incandescence of, xi, 29, 44–46, 48,
   57–58, 70, 73, 85, 87, 89, 140–
   141, 143, 156, 177, 182, 185
and interpretation, xii, 17, 23,
   42, 59, 80, 83, 96, 111–114,
   117–118, 120, 122, 149–150,
   159–162, 171, 178, 182, 184
and irony, 27, 37–39, 41, 58, 63–64,
   101–102, 114, 119, 132, 140,165
and judgment, x, xi, 3, 34, 45, 55,
   57, 64, 69, 86, 125, 137, 143,
   155, 162–164
as lamb, 7, 9, 11, 13–15, 22–23, 53,
   58–59, 111, 126, 136, 149, 157,
   163, 183
as light, 25–26, 45, 47–48, 61, 67,
   70, 72, 79, 83, 125, 128, 135–
   136, 182
and the Mary's, 135–144

Jesus – continued
   as Messiah, 59, 65, 76,140
   monologues of, 18–20, 27, 37–40, 42, 68, 75, 149–150, 152
   as mother, 63, 126, 142–144
   and the political, 2–3, 6, 12–13, 17–18, 20, 27, 53, 65, 70, 78, 89, 93, 95, 132, 183
   power of, 1, 11, 13, 24–28, 29–31, 34, 36–39, 47–52, 54–58, 61–62, 65, 68–76, 78–83, 102–105, 110, 116–117, 119, 122, 124, 126, 129, 132, 142–144, 155, 160,166, 170, 173–178, 182
   as provocateur, 12, 50, 53, 68, 89, 101
   purpose (mission, program) of, 8, 12, 14–15, 38–39, 48, 58–60, 62, 65–67, 75, 82, 88, 96, 110–116, 121, 125, 133, 141, 143, 149, 151, 158, 162–163
   as sacrifice, 8–9, 11–16, 53, 58, 62–63, 111–112, 122, 161–162, 175–177
   as scapegoat, 12–13, 93, 95
   as shepherd, 11, 13–14, 27, 32, 55, 66, 108, 118, 122, 125, 143, 160–161, 163, 179
   and Socrates, 12, 48–50, 59, 62–64, 68, 70, 110, 141–142, 190
   and Son of man, 14, 20, 39, 43, 86, 104, 124
   strategies of, 9, 37–38, 53, 58, 63, 110, 114, 116, 118–119, 124, 149, 169, 176
   as vine, 14, 16, 20, 27–28, 59, 66, 86, 117, 119–120, 122, 124, 126, 182
   voice of, 6, 24, 26–28, 29–30, 42–44, 56, 64, 72, 80, 108, 117–118, 137, 147, 158, 173, 182–183, 185
   See also under birth; body; bread; death; father; gestures; language; signs; silence; spirit; word

Jews, xii, 9, 12–13, 15, 18–22, 30, 33–37, 42, 50, 52, 54–55, 57–59, 60, 65, 68–72, 75–79, 89, 92, 96–97, 99, 101–102, 106–108, 110–121, 123, 125, 135, 141, 148, 149, 153–154, 158, 161, 180

Jiménez, Juan Ramón (1881–1958), 29, 87, 186

John
   anxiety of, 8, 16, 88, 91, 97–98, 100–101, 159, 163–164
   audience of ("you"), 102–109
   authority of, 98–99, 111, 146, 154, 174
   and belief, 73, 87, 89, 96, 98, 101, 105–106, 108, 114, 161
   body of, xiii, 8, 11, 73, 87
   character of, xi, xiii–xiv, 73, 89, 91, 96, 127, 144
   and contradiction, 73, 163
   counter thought of, 92, 94–96
   as eagle, ix, xi, xiv, 2
   and ecstasy, ix, x, xi, xiv, 73, 156
   as follower, ix, xi, xiv
   and interpretation, xii, 48, 78, 96, 111, 113–114, 159–160, 170–171, 179, 182–183
   and irony, ix, x, xi, xiv, 6, 12, 23, 40, 53, 58, 90–91, 94, 101, 105, 140, 146, 153–154, 166, 171, 174
   obsessions of, xiii, 8, 11, 16, 87
   and paradox, xiii, xiv
   purpose (desire, hope) of, 1, 30, 74, 87, 91, 98–99, 101, 103–104, 108, 110, 114, 143, 155, 158–159, 162, 177
   as rooster, ix, xi, xiv
   strategies of, xiii, 1, 7, 12, 20, 23–24, 30, 35, 37, 71, 74–75, 78, 80, 91, 96, 98, 101, 103, 106, 110, 136, 146, 148–150, 153, 158, 161–162, 164–165, 167, 171–173, 174
   voice of, 25, 29, 159
   as writer/poet, ix, x, xi, xiii, xiv, 1, 7, 13, 25–26, 29–30, 35–38, 57, 71–73, 82–84, 86, 89, 91, 96–99,

Subject/Name Index   217

105, 108, 127, 132, 134, 137,
    140, 145, 148–152, 154–156,
    160, 162–163, 165, 167, 171,
    175, 177, 179–180, 182–183,
    191
  See also under body; Gospel of
    John; language; signs; silence;
    word
John the Baptist, 11, 24, 45, 47, 73, 111,
    113, 126–127, 143, 163, 165
Jonah, 123
Jordan, 123, 126, 128–129, 136
Joseph of Arimathea, 35–36
Juarroz, Roberto (1925–1995), 45
Judas, 23, 40, 47, 53–54, 58, 91, 101–
    102, 139, 166, 174, 177
judgment. *See under* Jesus

K

Kafka, Franz (1883–1924), 99
Kermode, Frank (1919–2010), 188
King, Martin Luther, Jr. (1929–1968),
    65
Klee, Paul (1879–1940), 174, 185
knower. *See* Nicodemus
knowing. *See* knowledge
knowledge, 50, 65, 74, 87, 92, 96, 157,
    159
  deferred, 58, 63, 90, 101, 158, 164–
    171, 173, 184
  of Jesus, 46, 51, 63, 140, 142, 146,
    167
  and Nicodemus, 33, 35–37, 41
  plot of, 158, 162–164, 166–168, 170
  of Socrates, 63, 110, 142
  See also belief; plot; truth;
    unknowing
Kurzweil, Ray, 87

L

lamb. *See under* Jesus
Landau, Jacob (1917–2001), xvii, 86
language, xiv, 2, 4, 71, 178

ambiguity, 12, 32, 35, 38, 47, 76,
    147, 171
  clarity of, 121, 125, 159, 164, 169,
    185, 188
  "consent of" (Dickinson), 73
  figurative use of, 7, 13, 17, 31–32,
    41, 43, 48, 55–56, 68, 109, 115,
    120–121, 131–133, 142, 149,
    160, 169
  image (imagery), xiii, 1, 5, 13–14,
    30, 32, 37–38, 48–49, 68, 72,
    88, 108, 117, 120, 128–133, 142,
    150, 152, 161, 166, 173, 181
  of Jesus, 8, 13–16, 18–22, 37–42, 53,
    55–56, 63–64, 68, 75, 87, 103,
    109–117, 120–122, 125, 128,
    132–133, 142, 149–150, 152,
    160, 162, 164, 169–170
  of John, xii, 22–24, 73, 104–105,
    109–110, 131–132, 151,
    153, 159, 160, 163–164, 171,
    182–183
  literal use of, 7–8, 11, 13–17, 20–23,
    31–32, 41, 43, 48, 68, 131–133,
    149–150, 156, 159–160
  new, 9, 12–13, 14–15, 19–21, 27,
    29–30, 40–41, 53, 63–64, 87,
    110–122, 128, 189
  of Nicodemus, 36–37, 41
  obfuscation, 18, 77, 110, 121, 125,
    157–159, 164–165, 169, 179
  parable, 13–14, 28, 55, 108–109,
    115, 117–120, 122, 160–162,
    179, 181, 190
  paradox, xiii–xiv, 13–15, 55, 76,
    84–85, 101, 105, 126, 128, 143,
    161–162, 164, 173, 181
  pun, 13, 115–118, 121–122, 147,
    160, 185
  rhetoric, 4, 37, 39, 94, 97, 102, 151,
    155, 167, 184
  symbol, xi, xiii, 1, 40, 46–47, 81, 83,
    100, 125–127, 129, 131, 141
  See also categories; naming and
    renaming; word
laughter, vi, xiv, 7, 24, 131

law, 3–4, 6, 27–28, 34, 39, 53, 69–72, 78–79, 85, 97, 112, 125, 162, 187
Lawrence, D. H. (1885–1930), 68
Lazarus, xi, 15, 26–27, 32, 43, 48, 55, 58, 75, 83, 86, 101, 116, 121, 135–139, 148, 150, 155, 158–160, 173, 177, 180
Leviathan, 125
Levine, Philip, 173
light, 38, 40, 45–48
  Book of, 173
  and darkness, 25, 38–41, 45–47, 51, 63, 125–126, 135
  John's obsession with, xiii, 38, 46–47
  as lover, 40, 45
  as symbol, 40, 46, 161
  world of, 143, 145
  See also under Jesus
  See also incandescence
literal language. *See under* language
Lorca, Federico García (1898–1936), 183
love, ix–xi, xiii, 1–2, 14–15, 26, 28, 33, 40–42, 45–48, 50–51, 57–59, 64, 69, 73, 75, 83, 85–87, 89–91, 101, 105–107, 125–126, 131, 135, 137–138, 140, 142–144, 148, 154–155, 168–170, 183, 185–186
lover, 40–41, 45–46, 90, 96, 105, 107, 144

M

Mandela, Nelson, 65
Martha (sister of Lazarus), 15, 55, 68, 137–139
Mary Magdalene, 24, 26–27, 36, 52, 54, 70, 135, 138–140, 152, 169–170, 183–185
Mary, mother of Jesus, 52, 61, 90–91, 126, 129, 135–137, 180
Mary, sister of Lazarus, xi, 14, 27, 32, 35, 53, 58, 102, 135–139, 141, 174, 177

Matisse, Henri (1869–1954), 178
meaning, 3–4, 17–23, 51, 55, 59, 64, 80, 82–83, 89–90, 95, 99, 107, 110–111, 113, 115–117, 120–122, 128, 132–133, 159–163, 166–167, 169–171, 176, 179, 182–184. *See also* categories
Melville, Herman (1819–1891), 34, 123, 142
Messiah, 78, 99. *See also under* Jesus
metaphoric language. *See* language
Midrash, xii, xiii
Milosz, Czeslaw (1911–2004), xvii
miracle, 16–17, 20, 23, 36, 52, 58, 76–83, 105, 123–124, 128–129, 142, 161, 178. *See also* signs
mirroring, 124, 151–153
misinterpretation, 113–114, 117. *See also* interpretation
Mollenkott, Virginia Ramey, xv
moneychangers (driven from temple), xii, 49, 54, 69, 76, 136, 141, 148
monologues. *See under* Jesus
Moses, 39, 74, 129, 134, 145
Mother, 36, 126–127, 136, 140, 145, 191
mystery, 91, 114, 127, 161, 164–165, 168, 173–174, 177–178, 184, 188

N

Nabokov, Vladimir (1899–1977), 66
naming and renaming (redefining)
  act of, 29–30, 32–33, 39, 100, 118, 124, 137, 143, 152, 160
  of birth, 38
  of body, 9–10
  of bread, 9, 15–18, 20, 23, 150
  of flesh, 38
  of the heroic, 154
  of law, 3
  of light and darkness, 40, 46
  power of, 24, 26–30, 39–40, 55, 91, 98
  project (program, mission) of, 4, 9–10, 13–16, 20, 29–30, 38, 108,

117, 125, 133, 148–149, 151, 162, 182, 189
  of sacrifice, 13, 53, 111, 122, 162
  of spirit, 38
  of water, 9, 115–116, 125, 133
  of wind, 9, 116
  withheld, 135, 180
  See also categories; language
narrative. *See under* Gospel of John
Nathanael, 104, 107–108
New Jerusalem, 124, 132
Nicodemus, ix, xi, xiii, 33–41, 66, 114
  belief nor unbelief of, 146–147
  fictive letters (to John) of, 42–44
  as ironic counter hero, 91, 96
  as knower (versus believer), 35
  "To Nicodemus" (poem), vi
Nietzsche, Friedrich (1844–1900), xiii
Noah, 123

O

obfuscation. *See under* language
Olson, Charles (1910–1970), 85, 187–188

P

painting, xiv
Paglia, Camille, 191
parable. *See under* language
paradox. *See under* language
Passover, 11, 13, 22, 94, 111, 148–153
Paz, Octavio (1914–1998), 45, 48
periphery. *See* center
Pessoa, Fernando (1888–1935), 13, 32, 156
Peter
  character of, 1–2, 35, 70, 90, 92, 93–94, 100, 130–131, 139, 141, 167–168
  denial of Jesus, x, 77, 93–95, 145, 148, 151
  eating with Jesus, 23, 57

  loved by Jesus, x, 11, 15, 45, 54, 57–58, 70, 86, 91, 130, 143, 148, 170–172
  loved by John, x, xiii, 1, 131, 183, 186
  and water, 131, 151
Pharisees, 36, 99, 100–101, 106, 112, 162, 175, 178
Philip, 28, 52, 69, 104, 110, 117, 122, 139
Pilate, 27, 34, 35, 37, 57, 77, 93, 113, 136, 153–154, 173–176
Plato (ca. 423–347 BCE), 12, 49, 51, 62, 64, 190
plot
  counterplot of unknowing, comic (deferred knowledge), 92, 98, 149, 158, 163–167, 170–172, 174, 179, 183
  of knowing, tragic (immediate knowledge), 157–159, 164, 166–167, 171, 183
  See also Gospel of John
Plutarch (ca. 46–120), 89
power. *See under* incandescence; Jesus; naming and renaming; silence; voice; word
Predmore, Richard L., 190
Presley, Elvis (1935–1977), 143
prophet, 14, 17, 42, 59, 61, 65–70, 72, 74–79, 82, 85, 96, 99–100, 104–105, 110, 124, 129, 137, 141–143, 146–147, 154, 163, 165, 173, 176–177, 182, 184
pun. *See under* language

Q

questioner. *See* Nicodemus
Qu'ran, 127
Quetzalcoatl, 5
Quixote, Don. *See under* Jesus

R

radiance. *See* incandescence

redefinition. *See* naming and renaming
resurrection, 23, 31, 41, 54, 90, 148, 150–151, 159, 164, 166–170, 182, 185
rhetoric. *See under* language
Rorty, Richard (1931–2007), 188–189
Rumi (Jalāl ad-Dīn Muhammad Balkhī) (1207–1273), 181
Rushdie, Salman, 113

S

sacrifice. *See under* Jesus
Samaritan woman, 27, 146, 147
scapegoat. *See under* Jesus
Scrimgeour, Andrew D., xv
scripts. *See under* death
sex, 6, 94, 130, 133–134, 137–138, 140, 142–144, 191
Shandeism, xv
Shelley, Percy Bysshe (1792–1822), 47–49
shepherd. *See under* Jesus
signs, xiii, 74–84, 142
    body of Jesus, 4, 55, 56, 75–76, 81, 83, 150, 164
    book (John's) as, 99, 109, 181
    Book of (R.E. Brown), 190
    changing water to wine, 66, 75, 129, 159, 178
    complications of, 76–77, 83
    feeding the multitude, 83, 114
    healing the blind man, 75, 161–162
    healing the cripple, 75
    healing the nobleman's son, 75, 81
    nature of, 79–83, 99, 105, 115, 129, 158–159, 164, 178
    of the prophets, 74–75, 78–79
    propositions about, 76, 80–82
    raising Lazarus, 75, 83
    selection and ordering of (John's), 74–76, 81, 83, 96, 150, 158–159, 164
    spitting on the ground (Jesus'), 79
    as tragic plot, 159, 164
    use of, 52, 66, 75–77, 79–80, 82–83, 87, 90–91, 99, 104, 118, 129, 147, 159, 161, 164, 174
    walking on water (Jesus'), 75
    writing on the ground (Jesus'), 78
silence, 173–186
    of Jesus, 43, 137, 173–176, 184
    of John, xiii, 172–173, 175, 179–181, 185
    of Lazarus, 175, 177, 180
    of Lazarus' sisters, 177
    and Nicodemus, 34–36, 38, 40–41, 57, 102
    power of, 173–174, 176–177, 186
    scenes of, 176–177
    use of, 174–177, 183
    and woman taken in adultery, 2–3, 70, 102
Socrates. *See under* Jesus
Son of man. *See under* Jesus
spirit, xii, xv, 6, 21–22, 31, 37, 43, 73, 86–87, 131, 136, 145, 163, 177
    and Jesus, 32, 38–39, 54, 61, 86, 111, 114–115, 122, 126, 128, 130, 132, 139–140, 146–147
    the Spirit (Holy, of Truth), 32, 37, 56, 114, 126, 131, 142, 165–166, 168–170, 183
Stone, I. F., (1907–1989), 190
story. *See under* Gospel of John
strangeness. *See under* Gospel of John
strategies. *See under* Jesus; John
symbol. *See under* language
symmetry, 16, 18–19, 23, 91. *See also under* Gospel of John

T

temple, xii, 9, 11, 33–34, 50, 54, 57–59, 66, 68, 76–77, 79, 89, 108, 125, 136, 141, 148–149, 182
testimony, 69, 180–184, 186
Thales of Miletus (ca. 624–546 BCE), 127
Thomas, 2–3, 5–9, 31–32, 36, 43, 73, 81, 90, 96, 108, 140, 171, 173, 178

Subject/Name Index   221

Tiberias, Sea of, 23, 57, 123, 129–130, 136, 185
tomb, 80, 125, 127, 129, 130, 136, 138, 141–142
Torah, xiii, 71
truth, 34, 37, 51, 65, 106–109, 140
    and art, 1, 73, 107–108, 122, 125, 145–14, 153–154, 159, 163, 177, 182–183
    and belief, 37, 107
    of Caiaphas, 93, 95
    deferred, 63, 168, 182–183
    of experience, xiv, 159, 184
    and hearing, 26–27
    of Nicodemus, 91
    and paradox, 105, 164
    prerequisites of, 96, 157
    project of, 38, 40, 63, 98, 140, 153–154, 159, 182–183
    as relationship, 109
    Spirit of, 56, 165–166, 168–170, 184
    the Truth, 28, 30, 71 , 146, 168, 182–183
    and the Word, 72–73
    See also knowledge

U

Unamuno, Miguel de (1864–1936), xvii, 16, 66–67, 88, 128, 144, 176, 190
unbelief, xi, 6–7, 43, 101, 163
    of the disciples, 22, 75, 159
    impossibility of (known from the beginning), 105, 159, 163
    of Jesus' enemies, 75
    of Jesus' family and friends, 21, 75, 96, 97
    of the Jews, 107, 120
    and miracles, 80
    of Nicodemus, 40, 146,147
    party of (disbelief), 96, 98, 162–163
    of Samaritan woman, 146, 147
    See also belief
unbelievers, 80, 99, 102, 108, 118, 126, 184
unknowing, 163

definition, xiii
    of Jesus, 158, 163–164
    of John, 158, 163, 174
    plot/counterplot of, 157–158, 165–167, 170, 172
    See also knowledge

V

Valéry, Paul (1871–1945), 126, 157, 178
Venus, 142
violence, xvii, 3, 94, 154
vision (visionary), x, xiv–xv, 19, 27, 30, 47, 49, 51–52, 59, 65, 74, 79, 85, 88, 104, 108, 110, 124–125, 132, 180
vocabulary. *See* language
voice, ix, xi, xiv, 12, 23, 63, 150, 160–162, 176–178
    of Plato, 64
    power of, 4, 26, 72
    of silence, 173, 181, 183
    See also under Jesus; John

W

washing (of disciples' feet by Jesus), xi,1, 54, 58, 79, 86, 123, 129–131, 141, 165–166, 174
water, xi, xiii, 123–134
Williams, William Carlos (1883–1963), 73, 190
wind, 31–32
wine, xiii, 14, 16, 18–20, 43, 54, 66–67, 74–75, 80, 83, 86, 99, 123–125, 128–129, 132
women, 54, 69, 70, 73, 90, 126, 131, 133, 135–144, 146. *See also* Martha; Mary; Samaritan
word, 51, 59, 62, 143
    as action, 26, 31, 45, 72, 75, 116
    of Caiaphas, 89, 95
    as flesh, 7, 9, 20, 66, 72–73, 111, 120, 122, 173, 185
    of God (Father's), 107, 113, 140, 143

word – continued
   of Jesus, 1, 5, 11, 14, 20–22, 26–29,
      32, 34, 38–39, 42–44, 53, 55–56,
      59, 61, 71, 75, 77, 82, 96, 102,
      104, 106, 111, 114–117, 120,
      122, 131–132, 140–141, 143,
      152, 157–158, 163, 169, 171–
      173, 178, 182–183
   of John, xi–xiv, 1, 9, 25–26, 38, 40,
      46, 62, 71–73, 99, 105, 129, 156,
      173–175, 181–184, 190
   meaning of (emptied, cryptic,
      interpreted), 3, 110–112, 114,
      117–118, 122, 137, 181
   of Nicodemus, 36
   the one word, 9, 41, 59, 71, 73,
      189–190
   at play, 38, 68, 115–116
   power of, 25–26, 29–31, 45, 55–56,
      71–74, 102, 104, 109, 136,
      143, 155, 173, 175, 177–178,
      181–182
   of the prophets, 59, 65, 72–74, 96,
      99, 176
   redefinition of, 9, 18, 53, 68, 115
   of the Sibyl of Cumae, 164
   and silence, 173, 175
   swerve from, 21–22
   the Word, ix, xiv, 1, 5, 7, 9, 25, 29,
      45, 56, 59, 67, 70–73, 75, 79, 111,
      119–120, 122, 125, 130, 143,
      157, 169, 173, 182–185
   See also language; naming and
      renaming
worship, xi–xii, xiv, 97, 140, 147, 154,
   165, 183
Wright, Charles, 31
writer. *See under* John

Z

Zagajewski, Adam, 188

www.ingramcontent.com/pod-product-compliance
Lightning Source LLC
Chambersburg PA
CBHW070304230426

43664CB00014B/2634